The BURDENS of PROGRESS

$\frac{1900}{1929}$

RICHARD M. ABRAMS
University of California, Berkeley

Carl N. Degler, Editor
American History Series

Scott, Foresman and Company   Glenview, Illinois

Dallas, Texas   Oakland, N.J.   Palo Alto, Ca.   Tucker, Ga.   London, England

For

MARCIA ASH ABRAMS

always

more than just

my wife

Cover Credit: Brown Brothers

Library of Congress Cataloging in Publication Data

Abrams, Richard M
   The burdens of progress, 1900-1929.

   (Scott, Foresman American history series)
   Includes biliographical references and index.
   1. United States—History—1901—1953. I. Title.
II. Series.
E741.A54   973.91   77-10900
ISBN 0-673-05778-X

1 2 3 4 5 6 7 8 –BPS– 82 81 80 79 78 77

FOREWORD

This book is one in a series that encompasses the history of the United States from the early days of the Republic to the present. The individual volumes cover specific chronological periods and may be used either separately or in combination. Both this book and the series as a whole are intended to be different from the material covered in the usual survey text.

Customarily a textbook is largely filled with a chronological account of the "essential" facts of the past. Facts and chronology are, it is true, the building stones of historical knowledge, and familiarity with both is essential, but they do not provide the structure of the past by themselves. Rather it is the framework of an era that students must grasp if they are to retain and make sense out of the myriad facts that any book—text or other—throws in their path. By framework, however, we are not suggesting a skeleton or outline, but the unity or essential thrust of the period—in short, its meaning.

Emphasis falls throughout upon explanation of the past. Why did events turn out as they did? What significance did these developments have for subsequent American history? What importance do they have for the present? How does the American experience compare with that of other countries in similar circumstances? How and why did American attitudes and values alter during the period in question?

The organization and some of the less important facts that are to be found in more conventional textbooks are absent from these pages. It is the conviction of the author and the editor of the series that understanding the relationship among events is more important than just memorizing customarily agreed-upon facts. Therefore, some facts have been omitted simply because they do not contribute to an understanding of the structure of the period.

This book has been written for American college students; that is, readers who have some acquaintance with the history of the United States. While the usual effort has been made to clarify and define obscure or unfamiliar terms and persons, a certain basic familiarity with the subject has been taken for granted. No students who have passed successfully through an American high school need worry about their ability to comprehend what appears within these covers, but it is hoped that their understanding of the direction and the causes behind the movements of American history will be enhanced by reading this book.

Carl N. Degler

PREFACE

The nation was born in revolution. Its people have coveted change. Its heroes have been reformers, its philosophers and its historians have glorified progress. To the typical American on the eve of the twentieth century it appeared a unique country, a land of promise where one person's gain was another person's opportunity, and the inevitable was not just death and taxes but improvement and growth. Such optimism overshadowed thoughts about the cost of change or about the value of tradition.

It is not that historians have been unmindful of the many human casualties to malice and circumstance in the course of the country's development. Indeed, as is appropriate for a reform-conscious nation, its historiography has celebrated the victims of greedy politicos, financial moguls, militarists, patriots, bigots, and racists. But there is another class of losers for whom the literature has offered little sympathy—people who watched whole categories of virtues with which they identified their personal standards of integrity and excellence grow outmoded as Progress swept them by.

This is not a book about such losers. It is, however, a book designed to tell the story of America's entry into the twentieth century with some special appreciation for the fact that there were losers, and for the fact that it is not as easy as we once may have thought to make a moral choice between the winners and losers, and between what was gained and what was given up. It is especially important that we appreciate these things because the generations under scrutiny here were among the first to come self-consciously upon the need to make such choices. That they did not meet the challenge either very eagerly or very well is no just cause for faulting them much. Historians have often made sport of their failures and follies, as they came to be seen by the end of the twenties, but where were the models for dealing with the problem? Millenia of human societies had faced the mysteries of their universe comforted by the certainties their lack of knowledge provided. The modern mind, nourished by the new sciences, glimpsed knowledge and perceived that there are no certainties besides change and no truths except those perceived by changing sensibilities. They who never doubted the maxim that one cannot build a house on shifting sands confronted the necessity of doing so.

My interpretation of what happened in America during the first quarter of this century is presented in six chapters. Though none is chronologically bound, there is a naturally historical progression through the first five chapters. Both the first and last chapters offer overviews of the culture. Chapter 1 concentrates on the state of the society as the new century emerged, but it anticipates much of what was to develop over the next decade or so. In particular it sets up the problem that by 1915 had become unavoidable, namely, how to justify the uses of power since the value system of the past had deteriorated. The breakdown of the marketplace as a mechanism that might fairly and efficiently allocate social rewards and resources made it necessary to consider who should have the power to change what to what and for whose benefit. Contemporaries never firmly grasped the issue throughout their struggles for reform, the story of which is set forth in chapters 2 and 3. Chapter 4 analyzes America's on-again, off-again enthusiasm for engagement in international politics over the entire period, although it begins with President Wilson's decision to intervene in the World War. This literary strategy is dictated by the logical momentum of the previous chapter and by the war's crucial importance for the period, maybe for the century. Chapter 5 picks up the postwar domestic scene, carrying the story to the Smith-Hoover campaign of 1928. I have little to say about the Crash and the Depression, nor do I say much directly about their origins for the reason that I believe it would be tendentious to do so. People in the 1920s did not know there was going to be a Crash, so their behavior and thoughts could not have been influenced by such expectation. The final chapter surveys the cultural turmoil retrospectively—and inconclusively. I have left it inconclusive because it is not clear to me that, nearly half a century later, we have found more satisfying answers than the generations we study here did.

Carl Degler of Stanford University has earned my thanks for both his patience and his keen criticisms of the entire manuscript. I could not hope to write with his ease and clarity, but his books long ago became models for my own work. David Potter read early versions of some of the chapters, and it will be my enduring regret that I did not finish in time to have the full benefit of his wisdom before he died. Gunther Barth, my friend and colleague, has my gratitude for letting me pick his brain on numerous occasions. So too do my students on whom I have perennially tried out the ideas presented here. Douglas Mitchell offered valuable encouragement and commentary as I neared completion of the book. Bonnie Smothers has made almost delightful the usually onerous task of turning manuscript into book; her always cheery and expert management of the chore immeasurably lightened the burdens of progress toward publication, and I am grateful to her for it. Finally, as always, there is Marcia, my wife and best friend, and my children, Laura, Rob, and Jennie, who make it all worthwhile.

Richard M. Abrams
Berkeley, California

CONTENTS

MAPS, CHARTS, AND GRAPHS

CHAPTER ONE

IN
THE PRESENCE
OF REVOLUTION

THERE WAS SOMETHING especially fresh, ebullient, expectant about life in America during the Progressive era. Contemporaries exchanged congratulations on how exciting it was to be alive; and those who had reached their majority before the outbreak of World War I reflected in later years on what seemed to be the uniqueness of their experience. One of them, social reformer John Haynes Holmes, recalled thirty years later: "Those of you who did not live in that period before 1914, or who are not old enough to remember it, cannot imagine the security we enjoyed and the serenity we felt in that old world." "Life," rhapsodized William Randolph Hearst, "was not 'one damn thing after another' then. It was one adventure after another." It was, remarked the poet Edgar Lee Masters, "a happy day which had promised to be happier."

A Climate of Progress

Morals, technology, science, and even business seemed to be marching in step toward a grand new world. Emerging from a terrible four-year-long depression that ended in 1897, Americans embarked upon a decade-long boom featuring buoyant prices, apparently full employment, an astonishing reorganization of the country's industrial system through massive corporate consolidations, and wondrous inventions— machines that could photograph a person's insides, others that could reproduce live action photographically, still others that realized humanity's ancient dream of flight, and a remarkable little box that could transmit voice clear across the ocean without cables or wires. All this helped inspire a new outlook on life's possibilities, a new optimism about enlarging the human experience, a hopefulness that the human animal had entered a new stage of evolution wherein nature would be tamed to end want, disease, even warfare. In fact, few things reveal so clearly the cheery confidence of the period as the inclination to believe that modern technology might even guarantee world peace. "War will become so destructive," John Jacob Astor told the New York *World* in 1903, "that it will probably bring its own end."

Few at the time doubted that moral progress was assured. "You have never lived in the period before the last war when we all believed it," Henry Stimson reflected in the 1920s. "Why it looked as if we only had to mop up a few minor parts of the world." Throughout the globe, the forces of progressive change appeared in the ascendant. Monarchy and the power of hereditary aristocracy seemed in retreat before demands that government be more responsive to popular needs. The unsuccessful revolution in Russia in 1905 portended more upheavals to come in the imminent future for that bastion of retrograde autocracy. Popular suffrage was spreading through Scandinavia and the Low Countries and in some South American nations as well. In 1911, the British stripped the House of Lords of nearly all legislative power, unencumbering the power of the House of Commons. That same year, revolutions put an end to the old order in Mexico and in China; and although the United States eyed the Mexicans warily because of concern over the security of American-owned properties south of the

New York Street Scene. *General Motors Photographic Section* border, Congress lost little time in extending formal recognition to the new Chinese government and congratulations to the "people of China on their assumption of the powers, duties and responsibilities of self-government."

Looking Outward. To most of the more progressive thinkers of the age, the American responsibility for the world's progress seemed beyond question. With a bravado that was only slightly excessive for his time, Indiana congressman—later a progressive Senator and prize-winning biographer—Albert Beveridge exclaimed in 1899: "God . . . has made us the master organizers of the world to establish a system where chaos reigns. . . . He has marked the American people as His chosen nation to finally lead in the regeneration of the world. This is the divine mission of America, and it holds for us all the profit, all the glory, all the happiness possible to men. We are the trustees of the world's progress, guardians of the righteous peace." Some of this may be attributable to an orator's license. But similar hyperbole may be found in private letters about the same time. For example, Lyman Abbott, renowned Christian layman and progressive publicist, wrote in reference to the prospect of annexing the Philippines: "We don't want more territory, but God doesn't permit a choice." Somewhat more pragmatically, though scarcely less righteously, Theodore Roosevelt told audiences shortly before he became president: "A nation's first duty is within its own borders. . . . [But] it is not thereby absolved from facing its duties in the world as a whole; and if it refuses to do so, it merely forfeits its right to struggle for a place among the peoples that shape the destiny of mankind." He felt confident, however, that Americans would "face the future high of heart and confident of soul, eager to do the great work of a great world power."

These were heady times. A pervasive, exhilarating optimism in the land lent an air of heedlessness to what Americans did and said. Woodrow Wilson, writing in 1907 when he was still president of Princeton University, asserted America's responsibility "to impart to the peoples . . . driven out upon the road of change, so far as we have opportunity or can make it, our own principles of self-help," to "teach . . . order and self-control in the midst of change" and any doors closed to America, he said, must be "battered down, even if the sovereignty of unwilling nations be outraged in the process!" Perhaps never since the Puritans' "errand into the wilderness" in the seventeenth century had Americans believed so profoundly in their mission to spread the virtues of civilization—of *their* civilization—to backward places.

The Ebullient Society. Indeed, the United States at the turn of the century in a broad way was probably the most successful society up to that time. Americans generally reveled exuberantly in their ascendancy. It was not an altogether misplaced exuberance. Americans' assessment of their achievements would bear test whether one applied simply the standards of western civilization or criteria such as any other major society may have used to measure its success. What nation in the world's history had ever offered its members so many options in styles of life or of livelihood, so many comforts and luxuries as commonplace possessions, or so much orderly opportunity for individuals to rise from mean circumstance to coveted status and affluence? And what society of comparable size had ever provided so high a standard of living for so

New York City's Woolworth Building, designed by Cass Gilbert and completed in 1913, remained the tallest building in the world for almost twenty years. It was a monument to steel; some critics said a "cathedral to commerce." *The New York Historical Society*

broad a segment of its inhabitants? Material achievements may represent only a part of any society's success story, but especially in the nineteenth century they were no small part. The unparalleled stream of foreign immigrants primarily in quest of better living circumstances in the United States would testify to that. For fully half a century after 1880, a steady 15 percent of the American population were foreign born. The arrival of more than twelve million immigrants between 1880 and 1910 accounted for over a third of the nation's population growth in that period.

When the chief statistician for the Bureau of the Census observed in 1901 that the material wealth of the nation had reached dimensions "greater than all the people in the Western Continent had been able to make from the discovery of Columbus to the breaking out of the Civil War," Episcopal Bishop William Lawrence of Massachusetts hastened to reassure Americans "that neither history, experience, nor the Bible necessarily sustains the common distrust of the effect of material wealth on morality." On the contrary, he observed, the struggle for bare existence developed intense self-centeredness and callousness. "Through the increase of wealth," on the other hand, "man has extended his interests, his vision, and his opportunities." "Material prosperity has come apace," Lawrence concluded, "and on the whole it uplifts." More than a dozen years later, the editors of *Collier's* appeared to confirm Lawrence's optimism: "Fifty years from now," they wrote at the start of 1914, "the future historian will say that the ten-years ending about January 1, 1914 was the period of the greatest ethical advance made by this nation in any decade."

To be sure, riches, comforts, opportunity, and equal status under the law were never as ample or complete as America's spokesmen claimed or its immigrants hoped. Robert Hunter, a contemporary settlement worker and social publicist, showed in his pioneering book, *Poverty* (1901), for example, that at least ten million Americans, or about 14 percent of the population, were living in chronic poverty at the turn of the century. Most of America's nine million black people, 85 percent of whom still lived in the rural South, suffered the humiliations of varying degrees of poverty and of racial discrimination in schools, public facilities, job opportunities, and the courts. Worse than that, they had become subjected to almost casual daily brutalities by whites who often flaunted their crimes with impunity. Lynchings of black people—to mention only the most conspicuous of the crimes—occurred at the rate of almost one hundred per year for most of the Progressive era. Americans belonging to smaller racial groups, such as the Chinese and Japanese (about 120,000 in 1900), and the American Indians (about 250,000) suffered similar indignities and dangers in the states where they were clustered, in California, the Southwest, and the north-central plains states. Hostility directed by many in the white Protestant majority toward various ethnic and religious groups, such as Jews, Italians, and Irish Catholics, also inflicted a variety of injuries on both the victims and the American ideal of equality: advertisements for jobs, hotels, and resorts often specifically barred persons with such backgrounds, while the professions uniformly made entry especially difficult. Women experienced the familiar restraints imposed on the female role by all traditionalist societies: they were made legally subordinate to their husbands in many matters, were denied the vote, were virtually excluded from all the professions except teaching, social work, and nursing and were expected to avoid business careers.

Of course, mutual hostilities among racial, ethnic, and religious groups were scarcely unique to America; nor did American women suffer more from oppressive discrimination than did women anywhere else in the world. In fact, it was partly the universality of such behavior that enabled Americans to maintain their principled dedication to equality while practicing more or less obliviously what, to modern sensibilities, constituted outrages to human decency. Similarly, although as Hunter pointed out, ten million Americans lived in poverty, probably a substantial proportion of them had only recently arrived from the Old World, having fled deprivation at least as appalling as anything social reformers were to observe in America. In sum, for a greater proportion of individuals who ever shared the rewards and burdens of a single large society, wealth, conveniences, attractive life chances, and equal standing before the law were altogether more available and complete in America than history had yet recorded anywhere. That there was still much oppression in a country of such pretensions may well suggest failure. But it was as much a mark of their progress that Americans looked upon the poor in their midst with sympathy and a determination to remedy the suffering.

America in 1900 still lacked a refined culture, especially by European standards. American fine arts, science, and educational institutions still had more to learn from Europe than the reverse. In the meanwhile there was an alternative standard by which many cultural leaders were measuring American success: The immensely bold and vigorous energy with which American culture, for all its apparent vulgarity, contributed to the emancipation of human potentiality.

Economic activity had provided the readiest outlets for such energies, but American society offered much toward emancipating the mind as well. James Bryce, the contemporary British observer of American life, who often derided Americans' preoccupation with commercial affairs, had noted in 1881 how in America "the average of knowledge is higher, the habit of reading and thinking more generally diffused than in any other country." That condition owed much to public policy which subsidized the development of intelligence as did none of the reputedly more cultured countries of the world. There were 6000 free public schools in the U.S. in 1900; within 15 years there would be twice that number, accommodating more than 15 million students at a cost of about $12 per student per year. There were more than 5400 free libraries in 1900 with more than 1000 books each. And with overall literacy of about 90 percent, it is not astonishing that by 1910 the country could support 2600 daily newspapers with a circulation of more than 24 million. Even Henry James, the novelist who found it more comfortable to reside in England most of his life and whose expatriation supposedly struck a rebuke to American culture, argued that America's "magnificent moral vigor" stood as a vital counterpart to European refinement; despite their commercialism and other anticultural proclivities, Americans at least were capable of what James called "individual life" which by comparison European society tended to smother in the nursery. These were cultural virtues none could belittle.

America in International Perspective. Europe still dominated the world's political and economic affairs. Russia was sovereign over almost half the Asian continent and governed also over a variety of European peoples, including Poles, Ukrainians, Lithuanians, Finns, and Georgians. The Hapsburg dynasty of Austria-Hungary ruled over a central European empire that included Czechs, Moravians, Bosnians, Croats, Slovenes, and Slovakians while also holding provinces populated chiefly by Italians and Poles. The French republic claimed hegemony over half of Africa plus parts of Asia and South America, and numerous islands in the Pacific, the Indian Ocean, and the Caribbean. Germany, hastening to catch up, had established footholds in three parts of Africa and on several island groups in the Pacific. The Ottoman Turks held tenuously to territories that ranged from the Adriatic Sea to the Persian Gulf and the Red Sea, subjecting Slavs, Greeks, Arabs, Kurds, and Armenians to the rule of the Sultan. Meanwhile, the British could continue to boast that the sun never set on their empire. The British, French, Germans, and Dutch also served as the world's bankers. Even in Latin America the Europeans held the major share of foreign investments, while their stakes in the United States itself were nearly triple the total amount of capital Americans had sent to enterprises overseas.

But America's burgeoning power was already the subject of self-congratulation, and of worldwide concern. Even before 1900 the great magnitude of American industry and agriculture, and the growth of U.S. exports, had caused European commentators to express anxieties over "the American invasion." By 1913 American trade accounted for 11 percent of the world's commerce, and would soon amount to more than the share of any other nation, including Great Britain. Although America had once been a prime market for European manufactures, by the first decade of the new century finished and processed goods made up the major part of U.S. exports, passing in value that accounted for by agricultural products. Meanwhile, American investments abroad would grow from under $1 billion in 1900 to more than $3 billion by 1914, $7 billion by 1919, and $17 billion by 1930. Although the United States would remain a "debtor nation" until after the outbreak of the First World War, this was principally because of carrying charges for exports on foreign-owned ships and because of American tourists' payments in Europe. Not counting those items, the balance of payments in foreign trade and investment had turned positive for the United States some years before the new century dawned.

Americans were supremely aware of their new potential. Although European scorn for Americans' preoccupation with business matters caused Europe to discount the role that the U.S. might ever play in world statecraft, America's devotion to economic enterprise was exactly what energized the country's emerging international power. By the end of the nineteenth century, the U.S. was already on the verge of bursting out onto the world scene. America's tragicomic triumph over Spain to "Free Cuba"—annexing the Philippines, Guam, and Puerto Rico in the process—was not the only notice given that the United States expected henceforth to be counted in on world treasure. In Samoa, five thousand miles from its nearest shore, the U.S. by 1889 had staked its own claim beside that of Germany and Britain. Hawaii, only fifteen hundred miles closer, became a U.S. territory in 1898. The unilateral declaration of an "Open Door" in China (1899) warned Europe, Russia, and Japan that American commerce was not to be shut out of Chinese markets. In Venezuela's border crisis with British Guiana (1895), the United States had sharply threatened Britain against further encroachments in the New World. In the Hay-Pauncefote Treaty of 1901, again at Britain's expense, the United States asserted its paramount prerogatives in the matter of building and operating a canal across the Central American isthmus. And in its dispute with Canada over the Alaskan boundary, the Americans extorted from Britain a settlement (1903) that denied every Canadian claim.

During the first fifteen years of the new century, the United States turned the Caribbean into a veritable American sea. For helping the Panamanians gain their independence from Colombia in 1903, the U.S. exacted a perpetual lease of a ten-mile-wide band of territory across the Central American isthmus. The Panama Canal itself was begun in 1904 and opened ten years later. Meanwhile, the great importance of the canal for U.S. economic and strategic interests dictated a policy designed to secure the entire region from foreign—mainly European—influences. In pursuit of those purposes, the State Department worked to liquidate British, French, and German loans to the

GROSS NATIONAL PRODUCT, PER CAPITA AND TOTAL

in Constant (1929) Dollars

	Total (Billion)	Per Capita (Dollars)	Implicit Price Index*
1930	95.1	772	96
1929	104.4	857	100
1928	98.5	817	100
1927	97.3	817	99
1926	96.4	821	101
1925	90.5	781	101
1924	88.4	775	99
1923	85.8	776	100
1922	75.8	689	98
1921	71.6	660	103
1920	73.3	688	121
1919	74.2	710	106
Averages			
1917-21	71.9	683	105
1912-16	62.5	632	64
1907-11	55.0	608	57
1902-16	46.8	569	52
1897-1901	37.1	496	47

*1929 = 100

SOURCE: *Historical Statistics of the United States: Colonial Times to 1957.*

weak and often corrupt governments in the area, and to replace them with American loans. To preclude foreign military intervention and to restore political stability to the badly organized and faction-ridden Latin republics in the region, marines were despatched at various times during the period to Cuba, Haiti, Nicaragua, and the Dominican Republic. Each such commitment drew the U.S. further into the maelstrom of international politics, but at the time it seemed merely one of the responsibilities that a powerful democratic country had to assume.

The Home Scene. While America's stake in international affairs grew, most Americans remained preoccupied with the cheerier features of the domestic scene. Between 1895 and 1914, the real Gross National Product of the country almost doubled, with production rising at an average annual rate of 3.1 percent. That was 50 percent faster than the population growth, indicating a substantial per capita increase that was all the more meaningful because the production of capital goods declined relative to that of consumer goods, especially durables such as household equipment and automobiles. In other words, after more than a half-century, during which as much as a quarter of the nation's work went toward capital formation (the building of production, communications, and transportation facilities and the accumulation of savings for further investment), Americans began to reap some of the benefits of their labor. They began

COST OF LIVING AND REAL WAGES, 1890-1930

Years	Retail Commodity Prices	Nominal Wages	Real Wages
1890	108	92	90
1900*	100	100	100
1910	113	120	116
1920	272	307	113
1930	227	305	134

*1900 = 100

to enjoy the increased availability of goods for their convenience, health, and pleasure. Significantly, in 1904, meatpacking passed steel to become the leading industry in the country, and by 1915 its product value was nearly twice that of steel.

With the doubling of the urban consumer market between 1890 and 1910, railroad construction underwent a second boom. To meet the growing urban needs for food, fuel, and construction materials, railroads doubled their tracks to provide for two-way traffic throughout the national network; they enlarged their freight cars to increase capacity; they rebuilt the carriages with steel to keep the heavier cars from pulling apart; and they reconstructed the roadbeds to accommodate the new loads.

This reconstruction effort facilitated a virtual revolution in life-styles throughout the country. Eating habits changed as refrigerator railroad cars, introduced originally in the 1880s by the great Chicago meatpackers, began to carry into the eastern population centers fruits and vegetables grown nearly all year long in Florida and California. Previously one could only enjoy fresh produce seasonally. A glimpse at grocery shelves told the story that more food was being prepared in factories and canneries, and less in home kitchens. Huge cold storage facilities cropping up around urban market centers further encouraged this development. Mail order companies, which expanded rapidly after the inauguration of rural free delivery in 1896, offered the latest equipment, plumbing fixtures, and "Parisian" styles to ordinary people in even the most remote communities; and the Parcels Post Act of 1912, by substituting low-cost mail deliveries for privately run express services, further reduced the distance between Main Street and Fifth Avenue. Meanwhile, between 1895 and 1914 the average work week for industrial labor declined from sixty to fifty-five hours, in the case of skilled labor in the building trades from fifty hours to about forty-five hours—still a long way from the modern eight-hour day and five-day week, but already evoking commentary on the growing availability of leisure. And more varied ways of making use of leisure time were appearing, inspiring new industries and stimulating new technology.

The Second Transportation Revolution. Modern machines made Americans more mobile than ever before. Not even the advent of railroads and the great "transportation revolution" of the early nineteenth century had afforded such freedom of movement. The turn of the century was the heyday of bicycling. It had become a major industry in the 1890s, training many a machinist who would later make feasible the newborn motorcar and aircraft industries. Techniques had to be perfected for fashioning automotive transmissions, chain drives, pneumatic tires, and wheel rims that would hold a tire even when caught in the rutted tracks of the street railways. Orville and Wilbur Wright developed the skills they needed for constructing the first successful aircraft in the bicycle shops of Dayton, Ohio, while Harvey Firestone began the Firestone Tire & Rubber Co. in Akron in 1900, specializing in solid rubber for carriage wheels and pneumatics for bicycles. Even women's dress styles yielded to the two-wheeled form of recreation and travel. The "Good Roads Movement" originated with cycling enthusiasts, and the American economy gained a boost from increasing public expenditures on macadam, asphalt, and concrete pavements not only in town but on roads leading into the country and extending between neighboring communities.

Of course the big push for paved roads awaited the maturing of the automobile industry, which among all the new elements to appear on the scene was to have the most important single influence on twentieth-century life. As late as 1906 the motorcar was regarded as a public menace and a social irritant. Woodrow Wilson, as president of Princeton at the time, joined other critics in complaining that "nothing has spread socialistic feeling in this country more than the use of the automobile." Motorcars, he told a southern audience, "are a picture of arrogance of wealth, with all its independence and carelessness." They were too fast, dangerous, noisy, and odiferous, and they frightened horses. But in 1913, Wilson became the first president of the United States to ride in a motorcar to his inauguration. Perhaps he believed the occasion demanded the class distinction that the vehicle had once suggested to him. On the other hand, by then Henry Ford, who had created the Model-T only in 1908, had already sold almost half a million of that machine. The simply built, low-cost "tin lizzy" was fast on its way to becoming a great democratizer. Until Ford's success with the Model-T, most auto manufacturers still designed their machines for the small high-priced market. By the eve of World War I, there were 1.5 million passenger cars registered in the U.S., which probably understates the actual number of autos in service; by 1920 there were more than eight million. As a relatively inexpensive means of frequent, rapid, and *private* transportation, the automobile added a special dimension to the meaning of personal liberty. Figuratively and literally, it enlarged the horizons of ordinary, workaday people. It offered to thousands of individuals and their families a sense of personal power, privacy, and dignity.

The advent of the automobile also provided the greatest single stimulant to economic growth since the railroads. The industry pioneered in the moving assembly line and in mass production of machine-made interchangeable parts. By 1919 auto manufacturing had become the third largest industry in the country behind meatpacking and steel; and by 1925 it had reached the top rank. Apart from inspiring the construction of more than 100,000 miles of paved roads between 1904 and 1914—nearly doubling the existing surfaced system—the automobile demanded enormous supplies of iron, steel, rubber, glass, and leather, to say nothing of gasoline and lubricating oils. Furthermore, it opened up a multitude of new, consumer-oriented industries, such as tourism, transient hotels for families, low-cost mountain and seaside resorts, quick-order roadside restaurants, and of course the ubiquitous service stations and repair shops. (By 1915, gas stations were already such an eyesore that the *National Petroleum News* offered prizes for the best designs, "quality of housekeeping," and floral decorations.)

The Impact of Electricity. Probably nothing symbolized "modern times" more dramatically than electricity. In the 1880s, William Stanley, Nicola Tesla, George Westinghouse, and Thomas Edison had solved the problems of generating large amounts of low-cost power, transmitting electricity over long distances, and developing practical alternating current motors and incandescent light bulbs. The new century marked the coming of age of the dynamo. So rapid were improvements that, repeatedly, costly new generators would become obsolete within a couple of years. Between 1902 and 1919, Americans increased consumption of electrical power ten times—from 2.5 billion kilowatt hours to 25.4 billion. By 1912 more than 16 percent of the still predominantly rural nation lived in households served by electricity; by 1929 the figure reached 70 percent. In 1919, 32 percent of all industrial machinery in the United States was powered by electricity, and by 1929, 80 percent—up from only 2 percent in 1901. Economists generally agree that investment in utilities, lighting, machinery, and appliances outweighed even the outlays for the automobile and automobile-related industries in generating the thirty-year-long prosperity following the slough of the late nineteenth century.

On the other hand, the "revolution" in housework supposedly wrought by electrical power during the first quarter of the century has often been exaggerated. Westinghouse did introduce the electric iron in 1906, but it was a rare household that possessed anything more elaborate than an electric fan, in addition to an iron. The first vacuum cleaner was not introduced until 1917, and the great mail order houses like Sears, which carried just about everything that might reasonably attract a sizable market, did not offer their first refrigerator until 1932. Still, there is little doubt of the large role played by electrical power—clean, quiet, efficient—in the exuberance so widely shared in prewar America that wondrous improvements in the human condition lay just ahead.

Entertainment in the Age of Technology. Meanwhile, entertainment became "big business," and following the example of manufacturing and merchandising, it organized on a national scale. Radio, invented in England by the Italian-born Guglielmo Marconi in 1898 and perfected to transmit voice by Nebraskan Lee de Forest in 1908, had to await the 1920s before it became a national pastime. But vaudeville was at its peak in the prewar era. Originating in Boston in the 1880s on the inspiration of Benjamin Franklin Keith, the light-hearted entertainment offered by comics, dancers, acrobats, singers, and sometimes light-opera troupes spread rapidly across the country. By 1911 when Keith died, the United Booking Office which he had founded with F. F. Proctor six years earlier had become the central clearinghouse for engaging theatrical perform-

Movies were the nation's first national mass medium. By 1910 millions were sharing common thrills, humor, and pathos at the nickelodeon where live pianist accompanied the action on the silent screen with appropriate sound effects. *The Bettman Archive*

ers throughout the country. The huge dimensions of the industry is further suggested by the 10,000-member National Vaudeville Artists Association, established in 1916 to balance the organized power of the theater owners.

The Association would grow to 16,000 members by 1929, but in the meantime, the advent of motion pictures had signalled the decline of vaudeville even before the World War. Show bills began including short films as early as 1901; by 1913, "full length" features were being produced in sufficient quantities to justify the operation of theaters designed entirely for "the movies." The first successful presentation of a full story-line on film was Edwin S. Porter's "The Great Train Robbery," an 8-minute reel in 1903 that benefited especially from outdoor settings and imaginative camera angles. Thus freed from the rigidities of theater settings, the movies quickly became popular entertainment. Nickelodeons and store shows appeared in almost every neighborhood of every town. They became the poor man's theater, attracting the masses of recently arrived European immigrants who had no need to know the language since, in the absence of sound, it was the action that carried the story anyway. For all their brevity, the films of the prewar era offered a "realism" not available in either literature or the theater. They concentrated on scenes or incidents from ordinary life, which was natural considering the predominantly low-income audiences that frequented the movie houses. Subject matter was typically sensational, baudy, comic, poignant, or maudlin. Increasingly, the filmmakers exploited amorous and even prurient themes that were easily projected through the medium. As Arthur Knight has observed in his history, *The Liveliest Art* (1957), "The 'kiss' may have been harmless enough in the theater, but seen full closeup it suddenly became so much more 'real.' " *Traffic in Souls* and *The Inside of the White Slave Traffic,* both released in 1913 in response to the current wave of interest in the evils of prostitution, inevitably—probably deliberately—appealed to sentiments somewhat less exalted than those avowed in the advertisements. *Souls* grossed more than $450,000, plainly establishing the box office value of erotic subjects. By 1915, Theda Bara—born Theodosia Goodman, a tailor's daughter in Cincinnati— had become the industry's first "sex goddess" following her role as a "vamp" in *A Fool There Was.*

The greatest advances in motion pictures came through the work of D. W. Griffith, who clearly saw the film as a medium for art as well as entertainment. He perfected the fade out, the flash back, the camera angle, and the zoom-in closeup. His outstanding innovation was the extravaganza, inaugurated with the twelve-reel, nearly three-hour long *The Birth of a Nation,* which was released early in 1915. Based upon Thomas Dixon's novel, *The Clansman* (1906), the film depicted a dramatic confrontation between the vigilante Ku Klux Klan and maniacal Negroes who ostensibly came to power after the Civil War. The stereotyped and degrading presentation of the Freedman during the Reconstruction period reflected prevailing racial views throughout the country in the new century. Huge enthusiastic crowds queued up to see the picture. In a few cities, showings triggered mob scenes and race riots. After a private preview showing in the White House, President Wilson marvelled at the film's technique—"like writing history in lightening," he exclaimed, adding that "unfortunately" the story of how the Klan had to rescue the South was "all too true."

Although ample scholarship exists covering the intellectual and social influences of various literary works, there is little of use for assessing what must have been the enormous impact of motion pictures. Not only did the development of the film industry present millions of people with cheap entertainment and a chance for amusement and escape, it unquestionably revolutionized common expectations of what life has to offer, to say nothing of altering conventional standards of propriety, decorum, modesty, and morality. Across the continent, Americans found themselves identifying with the same heroes and heroines projected onto the magic screen. The "star" came into being in 1912 with Adolph Zukor's import from England of the four-reel *Queen Elizabeth,* featuring Sarah Bernhardt in the title role; and by 1920, Mary Pickford, Douglas Fairbanks, Lillian Gish, and Charlie Chaplin were household names. Sumptuous life-styles depicted on the screen inevitably evoked popular efforts at emulation, even when film plots purportedly held up high living for criticism. It would be too much to attribute entirely to the movies the decline of Victorian restraints on personal and social behavior, but there seems little reason to doubt that the industry greatly helped to accelerate it.

Although the "sexual revolution" is usually associated with the 1920s, popularized as it was by F. Scott Fitzgerald's novels and faddish journalism in the popular magazines, actually there was considerable discussion about sexual insurgency in the prewar years. Discussion itself signified a revolt of sizable dimensions. As Mark Sullivan observed in his chronicle, *Our Times* (1925), "once sex as a subject of conversation became permissible, it became, naturally, general, to the considerable embarrassment of persons aged thirty or more, who could recall when the word 'leg' was questionable, and the word 'sex,' for example, was not questionable at all, but strictly forbidden." In what degree the "revolution" extended beyond talk to behavior remains a matter for guessing, especially since it is not clear that sexual practices in the nineteenth century were quite as constricted as official ideology about it suggested. But there are some signs of significant changes. Around 1910, for example, the appearance in newsprint for the first time of warnings against venereal diseases indicated not even so much a melting of frigid verbotens on the subject of sex as a recognition that illicit "love" was increasingly practiced by classes other than the depraved and the damned. The Mann Act of 1910, which purported to outlaw the transportation of women across state lines for "immoral purposes," was given such language as to suggest attention to some more common transgression than the allegedly widespread kidnaping of young girls into prostitution. Surveys taken in the 1920s indicate that especially upper- and middle-class women born after 1890 were twice as likely to have engaged in premarital sex as those born before. Unembarrassed sexual enjoyment was beginning a return to western civilization.

Given the "double standard," it was the scope of behavior permitted to women that lay in question. As the appointed guardians of "culture" and the children, women were charged with maintaining standards. Traditionally that had meant among many other things dutiful marital continence and premarital abstinence. Unless carefully controlled, it was commonly believed, a man's virile nature would necessarily impel him to commit sins of the flesh. Such transgressions were forgivable in the male of the species when engaged in with unregenerate or fallen women. But since a "decent woman" was not supposed to harbor such impulses, a single slip was all it took to prove a woman depraved. Changes in sexual mores, therefore, came to be measured by the changes in women's behavior that became acceptable.

But what was referred to as "the sexual revolution" during the Progressive era usually had little to do with sex, and much to do with women's altered place in society. And this was far more a function of economic changes than of social outlooks, though the one necessarily modified the other. Economic growth and industrialization had reduced the importance of agriculture. Whereas more than 50 percent of the nation's workforce in 1880 had labored on farms, by 1901 it was down to 38 percent; by 1920, less than 25 percent. Industry drew both women and men from European and American farms into American cities, and an increasing proportion of married women entered the industrial and mercantile workforce, primarily for economic reasons. Between

1900 and 1910 the percentage of married women "gainfully employed" rose from 5.6 to 10.7. The period corresponded to the greatest influx of immigrants in the country's history, a significant point when placed against the fact that as late as 1930 three of every five women employed were black or foreign born. Plainly most women worked because they were poor, not because of any revolution in sexual attitudes.

Yet in an important sense it is misleading to stress the increasing propensity of women to enter industry; it may be more appropriate to regard women confined to household chores in the urban setting as having *withdrawn* from the nation's workforce, especially if they had come to the city from the farm. A farmwife typically is fully employed in productive enterprise, even if labor statistics do not usually acknowledge her contributions to the GNP. In this respect, the underutilization of women's labor potential in urban society suggests the remarkable efficiency of modern industrialism in producing enough to sustain so large an underemployed population. To be sure, urban women's absence from the wage-earning and salaried workforce reflected social biases that limited women's job options chiefly to factory labor or domestic service. Except for teaching, the professions and managerial positions were virtually closed to all but the most determined individual. Even by 1910, in spite of the clerical and sales jobs created by modern corporate business and department store merchandising, almost 70 percent of all women employed in nonfarm occupations were doing factory or domestic labor. If more prestigious jobs had been available, more women would have sought employment for reasons other than sheer need.

All the same it would probably be a mistake to assume that most women then resisted or lamented their confinement to housewife and motherhood responsibilities. For every college-educated Carol Kennicott, of Sinclair Lewis' *Main Street* (1920), who suffered agonies of ambivalence over her uselessness and the emptiness of her leisure time—after having married a physician for the security, status, and love he offered her—there were *scores* of women who would have had it no other way. The fact that American women in the early part of the century were increasingly becoming underemployed urban housewives probably added more to the sense of contentment, freedom, and high expectations that was generally characteristic of prewar America than it did to the undercurrent of malaise and insurgency which found expression in feminist movements and in literature.

To the extent that newly appearing patterns of behavior did excite the prewar generation, rising expectations played a crucial role. Because urban employment and social activities tended to draw women outside the confines of the nuclear family, some women—especially from the upper and middle classes—naturally began to advance claims not merely for equality in pay and job opportunities, but for the chance to enjoy the fullest advantages of being "free, white, and twenty-one," as the contemporary expression put it. Conventions that stood as obstacles to such enjoyment became targets for attack.

And the attack began some years before the war. The emergence of the flapper in the 1920s was no sudden phenomenon born of postwar malaise. Her older sisters were merely overshadowed in the 1910s by political crusades, national and international, and by the force of convention which dictated that the uninhibited female represented an errant and (therefore?) a passing aberration. As early as 1908, cigarette smoking by women in public had become common enough to inspire New York City to ban it: Gotham's guardians correctly perceived that the act suggested contempt for conventional proprieties, and therefore a threat to the social order that supported them. Ragtime—known as "coon music," a contemptuous reference to the style invented by Negro bands in New Orleans during the 1890s—became "in" with the young sets of white society some time before 1910; and the "bunny hug" arrived shortly afterward. Irving Berlin's career-launching success with "Alexander's Ragtime Band" in 1911 marked the arrival of syncopated rhythms to respectability, which of course virtually

A lady's stockinged calf attracted more than casual male attention at the turn of the century, but a new urban ethic of personal freedom inspired new clothes styles and soon made such sights commonplace. *Photoworld*

erased the whole point to ragtime's popularity. As Zelda (Mrs. F. Scott) Fitzgerald remarked some years later, the flapper was a girl who did "not want to be respectable because respectable girls aren't attractive. . . . She was conscious that the things she did were the things she had always wanted to do." Zelda might have added that the things she had always wanted to do were things society had usually prohibited.

That included a variety of gestures designed to suggest sexual frivolity without in fact committing anyone to anything. Facial cosmetics, worn in Victorian times exclusively by whores and actresses, were gradually becoming essential to many among the young who aspired to the chic set. Women's clothes began to shrink and to ascend upward from the instep. The "rainy daisy"—a skirt designed to hang just above the ankles to keep out of puddles—had caught many a wandering eye when it was introduced in 1901. By 1910, even on dry days a quick eye might glimpse the slender beginnings of a stockinged calf, without interference from protective petticoats. More than that, the simpler, snug fit of the new styles left less to the imagination as to the corporeal realities underneath, a shocking turn of affairs for those who liked their titillation in subtler forms. While some sorrowed for bygone morals, others foresaw economic disaster: the president of the New York Cotton Exchange in 1912 lamented that clinging dresses and their "accompanying lack of undergarments" had eliminated "at least twelve yards of finished goods for each adult female inhabitant." The sheath dress had arrived in 1908, leading *Life* to quip in doggerel: "We don't wish to insinuate / That they weren't real before. / But where, oh, where are the hips that we / Don't notice any more?" More ominously, a leading social club protested that the sheath was "but one step backward toward the fig leaf." An uncanny prophecy! Within a little more than a decade the sheath, evolving into the chemise dress, would recede far up les femmes' nether limbs; and there appeared, hipless, bustless, and bobbed-haired, the New Woman, flappily seeking the fantasized sensations of Eve in the Garden just after the serpentine seduction. But that development awaited the postwar era.

The Burdens of Progress

In an important sense, these were only surface indices of change. More profound currents were powerfully at work undermining the supports of the old order. Few people were as yet aware of advances in European science that would render obsolete the very framework of conventional life, the very standards by which most people usually measured truth, morality, art, excellence, good taste, or simple "common sense." Indeed, as British scientist Alfred North Whitehead remarked around 1915, "The situation in the world today is that scientific theory is outrunning common sense." Sigmund Freud's *The Interpretation of Dreams* (1901) and *Three Essays on Sexuality* (1905) struck at the roots of human rationality, arguing that the conscious intellect lay subject to the power of subtle urges, drives, and instincts basically sexual in nature. In five lectures at Clark University (Worcester, Mass.) in 1909 Freud introduced psychoanalysis to America, where he was to enjoy his greatest influence. By 1913 Floyd Dell, a young writer, was noting that Freudian jargon abounded in the intellectual salons of New York; word-association parlor games and amateur dream interpretations had become a popular pastime; and Sherwood Anderson, then a budding novelist, complained: "It was a time when it was well for a man to be somewhat guarded in the remarks he made, in what he did with his hands." Meanwhile, Max Planck's Quantum Theory of Energy (1899), Neils Bohr's model of an atom (1901), and Albert Einstein's Special Theory of Relativity (1905) were about to upset the conventional model of the universe more than Charles Darwin's Theory of Natural Selection had done only a few generations before.

The Shattering of "Natural Laws." It had been assumed up through the nineteenth century that human events fit into some divinely constructed Harmony. It had been understood that it was the task of intelligence to ascertain the nature of that Harmony and to devise social institutions that encouraged conformity to it. Darwinism had shattered the nineteenth-century's religiously based explanation for the human predicament. But the evolutionary theory of the origins of species at least still offered a rational scheme for comprehending the Laws of Nature and the Harmony of the Universe. It was, as Henry Adams called it, a secular, nondenominational "substitute for religion." It had provided a modern, scientific rationale for the orderly, automatic progress of human society—encompassing change within a context of stability, and a promise of progressive advance that required no political meddling.

But the twentieth century would be informed by a new understanding which suggested that whatever order the world enjoyed was not produced by God or the forces of Nature but that created by human society for its own convenience. If Nature possessed an encompassing Unity, it was probably beyond human ability to comprehend. The best that humanity might accomplish would be to *impose* conceptual order onto the infinite observable occurrences of life. Physicists had already begun to explore a microcosm of phenomena that behaved according to mathematical laws of probability rather than to rules of definitive causal relationships. Eventually, these inquiries would lead to Werner Heisenberg's Uncertainty Principle (1925), according to which the very act of observing a phenomenon causes the subject of the observation to change. Although Heisenberg's work concerned the highly abstruse world of atomic physics, it tended to confirm already troubling questions about what it is we perceive when we engage in the act of observing. It raised further doubt about the possibility of unchanging or universal laws, and offered another reason to doubt the efficacy of reason. Although few Americans even among the country's scientists would begin to grasp the New Physics before the 1930s, an "uncertainty principle" was already abroad in America by the end of the century's first decade. "Moral confusion," wrote George Santayana in his *Winds of Doctrine* (1913), "is not limited to the world at large, always the scene of profound conflicts, but . . . has penetrated to the mind and heart of the average individual."

The new task for intelligence would require self-conscious choices among a multitude of social preferences, economic interests, political institutions, even contrasting systems of logic and of faith. For none of these choices could anyone claim permanent, providential, natural, innate, or presupposed virtues. The task was made all the more formidable by the knowledge that if there was indeed no Natural Unity to existence, then there existed no objectively perfect order toward which humanity might progress. The perception grew slowly, unwillingly in the American consciousness, and as it grew it shattered the confidence that had been building throughout western civilization for almost two centuries.

The main story of the Progressive era is that of the efforts to shore up that confidence, to restore the sense if not the fact of unity, to reaffirm a consensus on the central values and moral objectives of American society in the midst of the dramatic transformation of life then taking place. The efforts were born of the spirit of exuberance that marked the nation's mood at the turn of the century. For the most part it was an "age of reform" that fed not on real deprivation and distress, but rather on expectations aroused by achievements already won, and on an optimism that the traditional rules or conventions of social behavior could be revitalized to govern the future as they had the past.

The Challenge of Change. It is one of the burdens of progress that distress invariably accompanies innovation. Uncertainties raise tensions. The benefits of the new order are distributed unevenly through the society. Old advantages are lost to some, while others gain. The discomfiture of change, even for the better, in the short run evokes grievances and gripes, and a nostalgic sense of loss. It may even produce degrees of paranoia growing from the fact that people are forced to make choices among new sets of options. Perhaps "worst" of all, progress brings with it new expectations of what is yet possible. As the nineteenth-century French political philosopher Alexis de Tocqueville once observed, as the conditions of a society begin to improve, the disadvantages suffered stoically for generations become steadily less tolerable. In America at the turn of the century the civilization that had demonstrated how much could be achieved found itself without alibis for ideals unfulfilled.

The great insurgent interest in social justice that characterized prewar American politics grew from new sensitivities to poverty, inequity, and oppression, based, however, on old definitions of righteousness and humanity. It was one of the grosser ironies of the Progressive era that the political leadership never fully reckoned with the implications of the changes they were witnessing. Most sensed the radical nature of contemporary developments. "We stand in the presence of a revolution," Woodrow Wilson declared truly enough as he prepared to assume the presidency with a progressive mandate; "whereby"—he continued—"America will insist upon recovering in practice those ideals which she has always professed." Wilson's approach to the burdens he would soon take on foretold of progressivism's denouement. The notion of a revolution to recapture the past epitomized the limits of the progressive imagination; it betrayed the inability of contemporary leaders to appreciate just how profoundly progress had challenged the relevance of received conventions and ideals.

The Advent of the Twentieth Century

All eras are "transitional" in the sense that they provide passage for the preceding era into the succeeding one. But the character of the changes with which Americans had to cope in the first quarter of the century sets that era apart from most. By about the midpoint of the period the four main features of modern America that mark off the twentieth century from the nineteenth had begun to take on distinct form. They were: comprehensive federal regulation of the economy, urbanization, social pluralism fashioned chiefly from ethnocentric assertiveness, and the emerging of international leadership (which we have already touched on). In each case, the traditional guidelines for social policy failed. The inadequacy of conventional definitions of justice and traditional life-styles for solving modern problems left Americans keenly uncomfortable, frustrated, sometimes rebellious, and on the lookout for villains. A period that began in high spirits was destined to conclude in rancor and demoralization.

The Rise of the Regulatory State. Throughout most of the nineteenth century American law had progressively encouraged the emancipation of private power from public control. The rationale of this progress rested largely on an assumption that the welfare of the nation could be best achieved when each individual interest was free to maximize its own gains, and that justice was best served by leaving to the impersonal mechanism of the marketplace the allocation of material and social rewards. For this reason American law was generally shaped to encourage voluntaristic economic and social arrangements among private interests. Private contract, voluntary association, and incorporation, rather than action by the state, had increasingly set the terms on which individuals related to one another and to their society. "The history of liberty," Woodrow Wilson wrote, "is a history of the limitation of governmental power, not the increase of it." By the last quarter of the nineteenth century some commentators were even suggesting (in a way reminiscent of Marxists) that the state might eventually "wither away" as private forms progressively supplanted it.

By the 1880s, however, industrialism, urbanization, and the concomitant specialization of industry and labor had already brought about an interdependence of human beings which seriously eroded the structural preconditions of such nineteenth-century optimism. The justice of marketplace policymaking lay in the presumed voluntary character of private arrangements. This presumption lost its practical force once it became clear that, first, financial concentration had placed small groups of individuals in commanding market positions, and that, second, most individual farmers, workers, or businessmen no longer had a real option of withdrawing from an unfavorable market. Clearly, the marketplace could not be depended on for the equitable distribution of social benefits.

But there is always a lag between the erosion of circumstances supporting a particular political or social style and the appearance of a new mode responsive to the altered condition. The first clear and observable responses to what nineteenth-century industrialism had wrought did not emerge until the new century had aged at least a dozen years. At first Americans believed that nothing ailed the free market economy except illegitimate business behavior, and that all it required to set things right was for government to enforce the standing rules of the game. Few realized that government would soon become, of necessity, deeply engaged in rewriting the rules.

For example, the Sherman Antitrust Act of 1890, while superficially acknowledging that the marketplace had suffered injury, in fact only reaffirmed the classical assumption that except for deliberate conspiracies among competitors the market would perform perfectly. Because the act did not reckon with the real cost savings of large-scale integrated firms or with the voluntary disappearance of competing firms by means of mergers, it is scarcely surprising (though ironic) that the greatest consolidation movement the country had ever experienced would take place during the fifteen years immediately after the act was passed! It was not until 1914, with the Clayton Antitrust Act and the establishment of the Federal Trade Commission, that Americans officially acknowledged that some, *once legitimate,* business practices had to be constrained in the interest of a "fair market." The efforts thus to use government to resolve problems once assigned to private negotiations place the arrival of twentieth-century economic policy around 1914.

The Emergence of an Urban Nation. The economist Maurice Adelman has written: "If I had to choose a single statistical table which told the most about the history of the United States, it would be undoubtedly the one which showed that in 1820 roughly three quarters of the labor force were in agriculture and another one eighth in 'manufacturing and independent hand trades.' Something like 75 to 80 percent of the labor force were independent entrepreneurs." By 1956, Adelman observed, the figures had become reversed; at that date, 86 percent of the labor force were salaried or wage-earning employees, and scarcely 8 percent of the workforce were regularly engaged in farmwork.

By 1900 farming already accounted for only 38 percent of the workforce, only 35 percent of the population lived on farms, and although 60 percent of the population still lived in communities of less than 4000, nearly one third of the American population was competing for food, shelter, and services in 52 metropolitan areas of more than 100,000 people each. In the 1900-1920 period population growth in the metropolitan areas rose from two times to three times the growth of population in nonmetropolitan areas. By 1920 almost half the population (46 million people) lived in 94 metropolitan areas of more than 100,000 people each.

Americans generally recognized that in many ways the city represented a triumph of civilization—an efficient organization of human resources for the development of a rich and a progressive culture. In the most immediate, practical sense, it offered jobs, relatively high wages, opportunities for upward mobility, alluring forms of entertainment and recreation, and attractive choices among styles of life. These things obviously counted for more than the qualities of life that country living offered.

Yet most social commentators at the turn of the century anguished over the city-ward progress of the population. First, and perhaps most of all, it signalled the decline of that class of citizens commonly regarded as the "backbone" of democratic self-government. "Where men could meet face to face," lamented one civic reformer in 1903, ". . . the best men have always come to the top. All over the countryside [one could find] honest, reliable, capable men. . . . When we come into the cities, the worthless man finds opportunity." The nation was becoming increasingly populated by "dependent" blue-collar wage earners and salaried white-collar "organization men" —people who did not own their own land or their own tools, did not raise any portion of their own food, did not engage directly in producing the materials of life's daily

POPULATION GROWTH OF U.S., 1890-1930

(in millions)

	1880	1890	1900	1910	1920	1930
Urban (over 2500)	14.1	22.1	30.2	42.0	54.2	69.0
over 250,000	4.4	6.9	10.9	15.5	20.9	28.8
25,000-250,000	4.2	7.1	8.8	13.0	16.9	20.5
5000-25,000	3.9	5.8	7.5	9.8	12.0	15.0
Rural (under 2500)	36.0	40.8	45.8	50.0	51.6	53.8
Total	50.1	62.9	76.0	92.0	105.7	123.1
Percent Increase		25.3	20.8	21.0	14.9	16.5

SOURCE: *Historical Statistics of the United States: Colonial Times to 1957.*

necessities. Urban life seemed typically joyless, harried, uncreative, and perilous—a monumental casualty of progress. "Thoughtful people," wrote Chicago city planners Daniel H. Burnham and Edward H. Bennett in 1909, "are appalled at the results of progress; at the waste . . .; at the toll of lives taken by disease . . .; and at the frequent outbreaks against law and order which result from narrow pleasureless lives."

Much of the trouble had more to do with the pace of urban growth than with city life itself. The rapidity and the dimensions of it had caused shocking waste, exploitation, and an ominous deterioration of formal political processes. The very difficulty of providing adequate services for so large a mass of people meant that many essentials of living would be in perpetual short supply, and thousands of individuals would be forced into one-sided bargains to obtain minimal material comforts. Living conditions for great numbers of city dwellers thus approached a wretchedness worse than anything Americans had perceived about rural poverty.

Even the well-to-do could be made to suffer by those who gained control of the vital services—water, fuel, power, transportation, refuse disposal. The city seemed to create remarkable opportunities for monopolistic advantage. Moreover, while scarcity offered the chances for great private wealth, access to such opportunities came increasingly to lie in governmental hands. The grant of franchises, licenses, rights-of-way, construction permits and variances all issued from statehouses and courthouses. This meant that political decisions came to affect private fortunes more often and more vitally than common experience could recall. The implications contrasted conspicuously with what had prevailed in the nineteenth century. Then, the nation's most innovative talents typically had been able to ignore politics because entrepreneurial careers offered the readiest chances for self-fulfillment, and because political decisions had had relatively small effect on such careers.

These facts suggest some features about urban life that were more threatening than the congestion, corruption, and chaos usually emphasized by social critics. Those were the constraints implicit in the intricate degree of mutual dependence which characterized city life. "The city," remarked Fred C. Howe in 1915, "has destroyed individualism." Specialization and the demise of self-sufficiency necessarily bound individuals to the schemes and frailties of others. The city presented a multitude of levers for both subtle and direct control of human beings by human beings. Government loomed large in daily expectations and apprehensions. The options for individualistic living seemed strikingly reduced in the urban environment, while men of "character" found little encouragement.

For Howe, an advanced progressive thinker, those facts implied the need to devise social forms to supersede the individualistic political economy that had served the agrarian nineteenth century so well. But for most contemporary observers, the city's assault on traditional modes of individualism signalled the need to minimize or dilute the urban experience. Most urban reformers of the day appeared to yearn for a way to produce—as British town-planning pioneer Ebenezer Howard put it—"the spontaneous movement of the people from our crowded cities to the bosom of our kindly mother earth, at once the source of life, of happiness, of wealth, and of power." Even American Socialist party leader Eugene V. Debs declared in 1903: "Regeneration will only come with depopulation—when Socialism has relieved the congestion and released the people and they spread out over the country and live close to the grass."

The Progressive era witnessed a variety of good government crusades that did much to reduce graft, boodling, and inefficiency in city management by 1915, but municipal reform campaigns rarely showed awareness that the urban environment required distinctly *new* government services—such as publicly financed programs for the homeless, the helpless, and the unemployed. The Settlement House movement which began late in the 1880s, it must be noted, was a private effort *in lieu of* a public policy. Except for the fact that the settlement workers' activities enjoyed "legitimate" status in the society's value system, the social services they performed did not often differ fundamentally from the corrupt, or at least the irregular, activities of the political ward bosses. Both were forms of philanthropy, in the settlement house workers' case with an unusual degree of self-sacrifice thrown in. For this reason the arrival of the twentieth century in social welfare probably cannot be dated earlier than the ascendancy of reform leaders like Robert Wagner and Alfred E. Smith on the New York political scene, after 1915. It was only then that government began to take over from private philanthropy the task of providing urgent social services.

The Rise of Pluralism. A spreading acknowledgment of how inadequately the received norms served modern life touched upon Americans' very image of themselves as a nation. What was "an American"? What were "Americanism" and "Americanization"? The United States has always been a polyglot, multiracial, and multireligious nation. Different groups of Americans have always held contrasting views of the good life and the good society. Such differences often became expressed in political conflict and sometimes in social violence. The running controversy of the late nineteenth century over the right of Catholics to give their children an exclusively Catholic education, perhaps even at public expense, offers one example. The vigilante activities of the Ku Klux Klan, resurgent after 1915, to enforce prohibition laws and racial and religious "purity" offer further evidence.

All the same, in broad perspective social behavior in the early twentieth century shows clear deference patterns, a fact which simplifies the problem. That is to say that most blacks, Catholics, Jews, immigrants, as well as members of the white Protestant majority appear to have regarded the manners and mores of white Protestants of Anglo-Saxon heritage and middle-class status as standards against which one implicitly measured one's own Americanism. White, Anglo-Saxon Protestants, or "Wasps," as they have come to be called (usually pejoratively), represented the chief cultural or ethnic group. Other groups, at least until they successfully adopted the overt social traits of the "Wasps," functioned in but often self-consciously were not of American society. Cultural and political leadership thus typically fell to those who still bore strong traces of the colonial Protestant heritage.

There was beyond this fact a functioning, broadly founded consensus on certain beliefs that were so basic they are often overlooked. It included a belief in God and in an afterlife; a recognition of sin, original and continuing, and therefore an underlying conviction about man's inherent imperfection; a faith in the harmony of the Universe, and in the inevitable and ultimate reward of virtue and the punishment of sin; a belief that each individual bore the responsibility for his own redemption or perfection in the sight of God; and an acceptance of definite though not entirely knowable limits to human efforts toward the constraint of evil in the world. To be sure these were not peculiarly American traits; moreover, Americans were probably more optimistic about human perfectibility than Europeans were. But the habit of contrasting Americans with Europeans on this score has sometimes obscured the limits of the contrast.

It must be understood, further, that contemporaries—not merely in the United States but throughout the world—habitually divided human beings into innumerable *races,* each of which had some identifiable instincts that were unique to it. Such traits were not explicitly fixed as genetic and for that reason unchangeable, but insofar as they were theoretically traceable through the blood, for all practical purposes of intellectual discourse and social policy, it amounted to the same thing. Indeed, Americans typically used the word *blood* to account for different character traits of members of different classes as well as for people of different ethnicity. These assumptions may appear to tarnish the American commitment to egalitarianism. But it is important to understand properly just what Americans at the time believed that commitment entailed. The meaning of the egalitarian creed at the turn of the century was not that just anyone could gain high status, but that no one of good blood and breeding would be denied the opportunity to rise from low status because of the accident of low birth alone. It never implied that all persons, whatever their talents or background, should be regarded or treated socially as equals. It did imply equal treatment by the law, but even that had its problems with respect to women, children, aliens, naturalized citizens, and different racial groups. If there were "inherent" inequalities among those groups, the "equal protection of the law" guaranteed by the Constitution required that the law be applied with intelligent, discriminating adjustments to those inequalities.

The concept of race was especially fuzzy. Contemporaries used the word recklessly, as often to describe nationality and religious affinity as to denote physiognomy. Furthermore, not every assertion of racial superiority or inferiority signified racism in the modern sense. For example, Theodore Roosevelt often referred to "the interests of the white race," and justified the exclusion of Orientals from the United States as necessary because their "presence would be ruinous to the white race." But as Roosevelt's discerning and critical biographer, Howard K. Beale, remarked, he did not regard racial traits to be permanently or genetically determined but rather a matter of geography and environment. Moreover, he possessed no element of contempt for an individual who had attained qualities superior to those stereotypically attributed to other members of his racial group. "Insofar as he feared the Japanese," Beale wrote, it was "for the same reasons he feared Germans and Russians—because they were an economically powerful, militarily effective power." He reminded his "Aryan" blood-fellows that the Greeks and Romans never believed that "the white-skinned, blue-eyed and red or yellow-haired barbarian of the North . . . from whom you and I in large part derive our blood . . . should ever become a part of the civilized world. . . . The racial difference seemed too great." Roosevelt's condescension toward the so-called inferior races of his day originated in the apparent weaknesses of the nations where they predominated; that is, he reacted to the weakness, not to the race *per se*. As he put it, if some such nation should ever become strong enough to be treated seriously as an independent power, "it will almost necessarily mean that this nation has itself become civilized in the process; and we shall then simply be dealing with another civilized nation of non-aryan blood . . . without any thought of their being ethnically distinct."

These points are essential for understanding the chief premises of American thought at the turn of the century. Without them, many of the central phenomena of the day must appear ludicrous, incongruous, malicious, or hypocritical when actually they may have arisen from both goodwill and the most advanced intelligence available.

In fact, at the start of the twentieth century, the most informed views on the subject judged as impractical the existence of diverse ethnic commitments within the same democratic society. "Our democratic theories and forms of government," wrote the progressive social scientist, John R. Commons, in 1912, "were fashioned by but one of the many races and peoples which have come within their practical operations, and that race, the so-called Anglo-Saxon, developed them out of its own insular experience unhampered by inroads of alien stock." Like his contemporaries, Commons had no clear idea of what particular traits were racially or genetically fixed, but also like nearly all his generation he was convinced that, at best, different concentrations of talents resided within each distinct racial and ethnic group. In any event it was clear to Commons that the problem facing America was "how to unite into one people" an extraordinarily diverse collection of "races."

Before the end of the nineteenth century the issue had aroused widespread concern. The resurgence of chauvinism in the 1890s, the growth of patriotic societies, increased xenophobia, organized anti-Negro and anti-Catholic campaigns, and the emergence of modern anti-Semitism all proclaimed the seriousness of the issue. "The country isn't safe," said Harvard's A. Lawrence Lowell, "until all groups of foreigners have become so merged in the American people that they cannot be distinguished as a class, by opinion or sentiment on any subject, from the mass of the population."

Significantly, the sentiment found endorsement among ethnic and social leaders who sought the accommodation of their constituents to American society. *The Catholic World,* for example, contended that "unassimilated" groups were "like undigested food in the human stomach, painful and weakening to the body politic," and Archbishop John Ireland urged any immigrant who did not exult in the American way of life "in simple consistency [to] betake his foreign soul to foreign shores, and crouch in misery and subjection beneath tyranny's sceptre." Booker T. Washington urged nine million native-born Americans, who happened to be black and for whom segregation had become the American way of life, to forego racial militancy and seek material integration in the nation (at least in all things not "purely social") by applying themselves in the beneficent environment of the marketplace. "No race that has anything to contribute to the markets of the world," said Washington in 1895, "is long in any degree ostracized." The marketplace would be the great *solvent* for all fancied group differences.

It would be another twenty years after Washington's "Atlanta Compromise" address before it would become clear, even to most of the victims, that when put to Lowell's test of assimilation "Americanization" for members of some groups was patently impossible. There was no way some could cease to be "distinguished by opinion or sentiment on any subject from the mass of the population"; nor could American black people fail to be singled out for their physical traits. Nevertheless racial, religious, or ethnocentric assertiveness continued to draw rebuke until the era of World War I. At that point the Americanizationists overreached themselves in their attempts to coerce conformity and to isolate the "deviants."

The "One Hundred Per Cent Americanism" campaign that followed the outbreak of war in Europe evoked the inevitable ideological counterattack. In an important sense the twentieth century arrived when Horace Kallen in 1915, in his article "Democracy *Versus* the Melting-Pot," wrote, "The United States are in the process of becoming a federal state not merely as a union of geographical and administrative unities, but also as a cooperation of cultural diversities, as a federation or commonwealth of national cultures." Kallen was not only describing a condition of American life, or merely remarking on the increasingly apparent pluralist character of American life; he was also asserting the value of diversity for a democratic society. It is striking, moreover, how suddenly such assertions began appearing in various forms after 1914. "We must be the very best Puritan Anglo-Saxons we possibly can," New England scientist G. Stanley Hall told the Menorah Society in January 1915, "and you must be the best Jews possible, for out of these component elements American citizenship is made up." Louis D. Brandeis, who only a few years earlier had branded as "disloyal" all habits of thought that reflected special ethnic affinities, told a July 4th Boston crowd at

Faneuil Hall in 1915: "The new nationalism adopted by America proclaims that each race or people, like each individual, has the right and duty to develop, and that only through such differentiated development will high civilization be attained." Coincidentally, that same year, Booker T. Washington died; and the following year the "Black Messiah" Marcus Garvey arrived from the West Indies to launch his Black Nationalist movement in the United States.

The rebirth of the Ku Klux Klan in 1915, the subsequent efflorescence of sedition laws, the triumphs of the prohibitionists, the immigration restriction acts of 1915 and 1917, and the deportation of "undesirable" aliens in 1919 all suggest the tensions caused by the new awareness implicit in Horace Kallen's observation. The fact is, until Kallen (and later, more comprehensively, John Dewey) attempted to shape a theory of democracy based on a harmony of diverse cultural affinities, prevailing political theory had regarded it as inconceivable that a nation could remain united without the use of coercion unless it possessed a cohesive consensus on social values. For a country like the United States, which had placed self-interest at the core of its social mechanism and had delegated policymaking functions to dispersed centers of power, the role of consensus seemed even more crucial than in more authoritarian and ethnically homogeneous nations.

Self-Interest and Social Justice

Traditional American thought had been founded in the assumption that the self-interest motive would function within the implicit constraints of broadly accepted moral principles—that whatever constellations of power might arise from the free-wheeling competition of interests, they would remain limited or bound by a general consensus on the meaning of Justice and Virtue. To this extent, although Americans at the turn of the century lived in a society committed politically and economically to liberal principles, the dominant social and moral attitude of most people remained absolutist. Although Americans usually have conceded that people might disagree over a proper definition of the common good, through at least the first decade of this century they still typically expressed confidence that there was such a thing as a good common to all that was knowable and generally known to educated and "right-thinking" individuals. At the same time they insisted that any interests which could not be reconciled with the common interest must be illegitimate, and implied that such interests deserved to be suppressed.

To put it more graphically, it had been assumed—and with some validity at the time —that men readily understood what was meant by words such as "common interest," "character," "right," "responsibility," "fairness," "common sense," and "equality." "We are neither for the rich man as such nor for the poor man as such. We are for the *upright* man, rich or poor," declared Theodore Roosevelt, many times and in many different ways. For a few contemporaries, but especially for later generations, this appeared merely fatuous. "It took twenty years," wrote Alfred Kazin in 1942, "for the critical intelligence in America to mull over that and realize that he had said nothing at all." Yet Kazin was wrong; Roosevelt had said something meaningful to the generation he addressed. That audience understood the unspoken premises underlying Roosevelt's words; and although the influence of that generation in the society at large had already begun to recede, it still possessed the power to evoke the standards built on those premises as the basis for resolving social conflicts.

What Kazin correctly observed was that within twenty years such words would *no longer* mean anything of significance; the new generations coming of age even in Roosevelt's own time would lack the comprehension and life objectives that had once given such words meaning. As Frederick Hoffman noted in his literary study, *The Twenties* (1949), "Faith in the older generation, not unmixed with criticism of its enormities, persisted through [to 1915]; but when the war had ended, this generation discovered that it had lost most of its influence."

Without that comprehension and the commonly held convictions on which it was based, the principle of self-interest as a social instrument would lose its chief link to social justice. When divergent interests self-consciously realized they could not agree on what constituted a *common* interest or a *fair* accommodation or a *rightful* exercise of authority, only force would remain as the decisive instrument for policymaking. Unless the members of a society can respond willingly to some overarching interest that they hold in common, law comes to be viewed merely as the institutionalization of the dominant interest's preferences. Only coercion then remains to keep the society from disintegrating.

Until the end of the nineteenth century the very openness of American society the relatively easy availability of opportunities for wealth, status, and mobility—had kept the fact of fundamental differences from appearing to threaten vital interests. The twentieth century would have to deal with a different perception. The fact of pluralism was not new in America. The central role it seemed to be taking in shaping the nation's character was. As industrialized America filled out its continental limits, attracted more and more people of divergent cultural backgrounds, penetrated parochial enclaves of ignorance and vested interests, and produced an abundance of material goods controlled increasingly by consolidations of economic power, it spawned deep social conflicts that challenged the conventional meanings of Justice and Virtue. By 1915 the issue would be plainly joined.

SUGGESTED READINGS

Mark Sullivan's richly illustrated six-volume chronicle, *Our Times* (1926-34), still offers the most comprehensively entertaining introduction to the period. The political coverage is not keen, but the social commentary and anecdotes, and the photos, sheet music, cartoons, and advertisements quickly get the reader into the contemporary world as no other printed source can. The first three volumes, which are the best, were reprinted in paperback in 1968 and may still be found in bookshops. Lewis Atherton's

*Main Street on the Middle Border** (1954), Robert H. Walker's *Life in the Age of Enterprise, 1865-1900** (1967), and John W. Dodds' *Life in Twentieth-Century America** (1972) are more recent attempts (with uneven success) to present a flavor of "everyday life." Although published in 1920 and usually associated with the 1920s, Sinclair Lewis' novel, *Main Street**, actually affords a marvellously detailed glimpse of small town midwestern life during the years 1908 to 1918. Similarly, Robert S. and Helen M. Lynd's classic sociological study, *Middletown: A Study in Modern American Culture** (1929), contains wonderful coverage of daily life in the Progressive era as well as in the period it focuses on.

Henry Steele Commager's *The American Mind* (1950) offers a spritely survey of American views of the universe at the turn of the century. Alfred Kazin's *On Native Grounds** (1942; revised 1957) is the source of Kazin's commentary on TR and is a rewarding study of American intellectuals, especially in the literary world. Richard Hofstadter's *Social Darwinism in American Thought** (1955) discusses the Darwinist ingredient in the contemporary optimism regarding foreign affairs and the American "mission;" while the early chapters of his *The Age of Reform: From Bryan to FDR** (1955) analyses the moral presumptions of contemporary reformers. Walter LaFeber's *The New Empire** (1963), Howard K. Beale's *Theodore Roosevelt and the Rise of America To World Power** (1956), and the early chapters of Robert E. Osgood's *Ideals and Self-Interest in America's Foreign Relations** (1953) are especially good on America's international muscle-flexing at the turn of the century.

J. Willard Hurst's *Law and the Conditions of Freedom in the Nineteenth-Century United States** (1956) is a difficult but brilliant essay that reveals the social premises of the American legal structure and the role that the marketplace played in the traditional view of social justice. Samuel P. Hays' *The Response to Industrialism, 1877-1914** (1958) is a fine tour de force that also emphasizes the traditional American commitment to the marketplace as a chief arbiter of social advantages. Robert H. Bremner, *From the Depths: The Discovery of Poverty in the United States** (1956), and Paul T. Ringenbach, *Tramps and Reformers, 1873-1916* (1973), discuss the new sensitivities to the plight of the poor and are extremely valuable for understanding the impact of new perspectives on contemporary social activists. Thomas Kessner's *The Golden Door: Italian and Jewish Immigrant Mobility in New York City 1880-1915** (1977), using both quantitative and conventional techniques, is first-rate in establishing different mobility patterns for two immigrant groups and in reestablishing the validity of the view that America did provide abundant opportunity for upward class mobility. Robert Sklar's *Movie-Made America: A Social History of American Movies* (1975) is a provocative beginning toward an understanding of the impact of the motion picture industry on American culture. William L. O'Neill, *Divorce in the Progressive Era** (1967), and David M. Kennedy, *Birth Control in America: The Career of Margaret Sanger** (1970), afford extensive material on the changing roles of women and emergent sexual attitudes in the early twentieth century. Although rather wordy, the following biographies contain much valuable information on the effect of new technology on modern life:

---

*Available in a paperback edition.

Edison: A Biography* (1959) by Matthew Josephson, *Ford: The Times, the Man, the Company* (1954) by Allen Nevins and Frank E. Hill, and *Ford: Expansion and Challenge, 1915-33* (1957) Nevins and Hill. But see also The President's Research Committee on Social Trends, *Recent Social Trends in the United States* (1933).

Thomas C. Cochran's *The Inner Revolution** (1964) and his *Social Change in America: The Twentieth Century** (1971) contain extraordinarily perceptive essays on the nature of change, focusing mostly on the early twentieth century. John Higham's *Strangers in the Land** (1955) remains the classic introduction to the nativist response to immigration, but it contains also an excellent chapter on the racial assumptions of Americans, dovetailing nicely with Hofstadter on Social Darwinism. There is a need for a cogent historical synthesis on the importance of ethnic and racial diversity in American life, comparable, say, to Thomas Cochran's treatment of business, as in his *Business in American Life** (1972) and Hays' approach to the industrial impact in his *Response to Industrialism*. Racial, religious, and ethnic consciousness have often had more potent influence on political decisions in twentieth-century America than has economic self-interest or class consciousness. It is easy to find accounts of the economic interests at stake in the shaping of policy on foreign affairs, government regulation of business, civil rights, and even education. There is a large literature on the economic causes of American expansionism, World War I, the progressive movement, public school education, and the indifferent success of trade unionism. But there is virtually no sustained treatment of the ethnic, religious, and racial dimensions of these phenomena. Milton M. Gordon's *Assimilation in American Life** (1964) is an especially good analysis of the strength with which ethnic identification and sensitivities have survived all formal or outward appearances of assimilation, but the book is not designed to reveal the way persisting ethnic affinities among the American people have determined various cultural, economic, and political outcomes.

PROGRESSIVISM: THE SOBER SECOND THOUGHT

AFTER 1900, Americans self-consciously turned to the task of reconciling the nation's remarkable material progress with its faltering liberal institutions and social norms. At his first inaugural, in 1913, Woodrow Wilson observed: "Our life contains every great thing, and contains it in rich abundance. But the evil has come with the good. . . . We have squandered a great part of what we might have used. . . . We have not hitherto stopped thoughtfully enough to count the human cost. . . . There has been something crude and heartless and unfeeling in our haste to succeed and be great. . . . We have come now to the sober second thought."

The Progressive Rationale

Progress was the new century's chief problem, and the most important efforts to deal with it were more conservative than innovative. "If I did not believe," said Wilson in 1912, "that to be a progressive was to preserve the essentials of our institutions, I for one could not be a progressive." "The crux of my appeal," declared Theodore Roosevelt in 1911, "[is that] I wish to save the very wealthy men of this country and their advocates and upholders from the ruin that they would bring upon themselves if they were permitted to have their way. . . . It is because I am against the doctrines . . . of the Socialists; . . . it is because I wish to secure for our children and our grand-children and for their children's children the same freedom of opportunity, the same peace and order and justice that we have had in the past."

The effort took shape against two kinds of challenges. The first arose from the country's industrial and demographic metamorphosis. The country had become more thickly populated and more urban; it had come to possess vast numbers of conspic-uously diverse ethnic groups; and in the quest for efficiency, its business system had taken on a corporative or "collectivized" character that ran counter to its individualistic rationale. The second threat came from groups that demanded some radical institu-tional and normative changes. Wage earners, organized in unions, claimed a place in the policymaking councils of government and industry; ethnic minorities whose traits or affinities set them apart from presumed standards of "Americanism" urged acceptance, some formal recognition of "legitimacy," for their special social preferences; farmers demanded that government use its sovereign powers specifically to deny the decisions of the marketplace on behalf of a social system based on agriculture; socialists led a frontal assault on the nation's liberal and religious commitments.

The main reform campaigns of the early twentieth century focused on how to maintain, in the face of these challenges, the values and moral assumptions that lay at the center of conventional thought. As Henry F. May has put it in his *The End of American Innocence* (1959), it was an era in which "people wanted to make a number of sharp changes because they were so confident in the basic rightness of things as they were." They wanted to preserve the fruits of industrial progress while halting the erosion of human dignity that seemed to have accompanied it. They wished to mitigate the harsher cruelties of life for those who remained beyond the boundaries of society's

The cast of the musical play "Irene" selling Christmas seals (1919). In the new century actresses threw off Victorian opprobrium and became prestige-bearing models as entertainment and theater became big business. *The Bettmann Archive*

privileges and its rewards. They worked for these things partly because of a conventional humanitarianism that lay deep in the country's heritage, but also because of a fear that unless the nation gave special attention to the underprivileged, they might jeopardize by violence or other radical action the entire structure of conventional values.

In fact, in the 1890s, for a great many of those who would later become leaders of the progressive movement, social violence seemed the most immediate threat to the system they sought to preserve. Fear over economic and political instability peaked during those disorderly years. "The time has come," declared Lyman Abbott in 1894, "when forebearance has ceased to be a virtue. There must be some shooting, men must be killed, and then there will be an end of this defiance of the law and destruction of property. . . . The soldiers [at Pullman] must use their guns. They must shoot to kill." "I speak with the greatest soberness," said Theodore Roosevelt in 1896, "when I say that the sentiment now animating a large proportion of our people can only be suppressed, as the Commune in Paris was suppressed, by taking ten or a dozen of their leaders out, standing them against a wall, and shooting them dead. I believe it will come to that."

With the return of prosperity after 1897, the attention of these same people turned toward removing or modifying the conditions that underlay the violence they saw threatening the social order. They searched for a peaceful, legal substitute for Gatling guns and bayonets, and, moreover, a more morally perfect society. Toward those ends they would as occasion demanded make common cause with any interests, even those they feared the most among the deprived elements, as long as it did not seriously compromise their commitment to their own special view of civilization.

To put it briefly and yet more specifically, a large body of men and women entered into reform activities at the end of the nineteenth century to transform their view of civilization into a general program for social action. Mostly these were young men and women, in their thirties or early forties, mostly college educated, financially secure, and predominantly "Establishment types"—overwhelmingly Protestant, especially of the Calvinist sort, native born, and of British ancestry. They came, moreover, from outside the South, where urban merchants, shippers, and small manufacturers were disproportionately conspicuous in the reform movements—they came chiefly from the professions. Their actions, as Richard Hofstadter has put it in his *The Age of Reform* (1956), "were founded upon the indigenous Yankee-Protestant political tradition [which] assumed and demanded the constant disinterested activity of the citizen in public affairs, argued that political life ought to be run, to a greater degree than it was, in accordance with general principles and abstract laws apart from and superior to personal needs, and expressed a common feeling that government should be in good part an effort to moralize the lives of individuals while economic life should be intimately related to the stimulation and development of individual character."

The Sources of Progressive Reform

The most consistently important reform impulse, *among many impulses,* during the Progressive era grew directly from these sources. It is this reform thrust that we should properly call "the progressive movement." We must distinguish it from contemporary reform movements that were committed primarily to *other* considerations.

Legacy of Genteel Reform. The progressive movement drew much of its strength from a variety of earlier reform campaigns. There were, first of all, the old mugwumps* and civil service reformers, whose contribution was somewhat indirect. Committed to the principles of honesty, integrity, efficiency, and intelligence in government, these individuals had kept alive nonpecuniary standards of excellence at a time when the raw power of wealth and pork-barrel partisanship seemed to govern political behavior more than usually. Men such as Missouri's Carl Schurz, New York merchant-manufacturer E. A. Atkinson, Boston corporation lawyer Moorfield Storey, Harvard President Charles W. Eliot, *The Nation*'s Gladstonian editor E. L. Godkin, and President John Quincy Adams' grandson, Charles Francis Adams, Jr., had counted eminently among them. These men typically had stood for "sound money" (as opposed to the inflationary programs of the Greenbackers and "Free Silver" advocates), low tariffs, the professionalization of government service, economy, and nonpartisan municipal politics. They had also been highly suspicious of organized labor, and (as Eliot asserted on one occasion) tended to regard the strikebreaker as "a new type of American hero." After the turn of the century, the renowned reform administrations of Mayors Tom Johnson and Newton D. Baker of Cleveland, of Sam ("Golden Rule") Jones and Brand Whitlock of Toledo, and of Seth Low of New York tended to embody "mugwump principles."* So, too, did the city-manager and commission government plans developed first by Galveston, Dayton, and Des Moines and which spread across the country especially in the smaller cities and towns. Such plans removed the power to make administrative decisions from elected officials, such as the mayor and city council members, and placed that power in nonpartisan and technically "expert" hands. Efficiency and economy, and the infusion of "business principles" into politics, were to such reformers the benchmarks of good government.

The Social Gospel. The mugwumps and their progressive derivatives tended to assume that the ascendancy of good men was sufficient to produce good government and the good society. Although this remained a powerful premise among social critics, by 1900 reformers spoke more commonly of the power of the environment over morals. As the Episcopal Bishop William Lawrence remarked in 1901 (in an article usually cited as an example of clerical apologies for the wealthy), "grinding poverty does grind down." Accordingly, it behooved good Christians and devoted humanitarians to help make men "good" by creating an environment conducive to good living. In the 1880s and 1890s, "Social Christians"—from the socialistically inclined George Herron and W. D. P. Bliss to the more conservative William S. Rainsford of New York's fashionable St. George's Episcopal Church—joined with pioneers of the new profession of settlement house and social workers in an active commitment to social reform. As the Progressive era opened, the Social Gospel began to spread beyond organized

---

* "Mugwumps" was the belittling term applied by loyal Republicans in 1884 to those reform-conscious Republicans who refused to support the presidential candidacy of GOP nominee James G. Blaine. It was an Indian word meaning "leader." Euro-Americans used it derisively for someone who mistakenly thought himself a leader.

religion. Investigations of labor and living conditions by reformers such as Florence Kelley of Chicago, Robert Woods of Boston, Robert Hunter of Chicago and New York, and Paul U. Kellogg, the director of the "Pittsburgh Survey"* of industrial life, argued forcefully that poverty and depravity were produced by oppressive conditions, by mal-functioning social and political institutions, rather than by an absence of individual will or determination. With the aid of a bold, new style of journalism that came to be known as "muckraking," the social workers and the Social Gospel helped tear away the ignorance that had shielded Americans in their complacent assumption that worthy people need never fear deprivation in the land of opportunity. All the same, such progressives never doubted the standards by which they measured the degradation of the poor; to understand the causes of the subcivilized behavior of the nation's poor did not make such living styles more acceptable. The objective, as Robert Woods asserted, was to *civilize* the alien and the indigent—to introduce and hold them to Anglo-American standards.

The Prohibitionists. The temperance movement contributed much, although indirectly, to the progressive insurgency. Not all prohibitionists were progressives, and probably fewer progressives were prohibitionists (at least till after 1914), but tem-perance shared with the progressive movement many leaders, many common objectives, and, more important, most of the same enemies. Women's interest in the movement had a pragmatic bent. Especially because their designated roles made them dependent on men and the family, women often became the enduring victims of the physical and financial costs of drinking.

In its pristine form, early in the nineteenth century, the opposition to alcohol represented little more than a religiously based puritanical enmity to contaminating the body and mind with unnatural spirits. It would later take on a more optimistic character, envisioning a comprehensive reformation of American society. But it is clear that status anxieties, increasingly of a nativistic sort, formed the more important qualities of the movement some time before the century closed. Although the saloon was as American as apple pie, many guardians of the culture came to associate whisky, wine, and beer with "foreign" influences—or, more generally, with any subgroups whose social behavior seemingly threatened the received norms of deference and prestige. As Joseph Gusfield has observed in his study, *Symbolic Crusade* (1965), the movement had its assimilationist phases, which at least expressed sympathetic concern for the morals, manners, and means of the poorer urban classes; more commonly by the end of the century, it assumed a coercive character, whereby it strove singlemind-edly toward eliminating so-called alien life-styles. The fact that the American beer industry was dominated by companies with German names would contribute substan-tially to the successful climax of the movement during the era of the First World War.

All the same, in its most positive context, the temperance movement linked easily with civic reform and good government movements. It was hoped that the elimination

---

* The Pittsburgh Survey was sponsored by the Russell Sage Foundation. Inspired by earlier urban research done by many of the leading settlement houses, the Foundation sought to study one city exhaustively. The Survey was a cooperative project that produced six widely read volumes between 1909 and 1914. Its success was internationally renowned and emulated.

Suffragist used time-honored appeals to equity and to slogans that predated the Revolution. But eventually what proved most persuasive: that native-born women, such as this well-to-do picket (c. 1905), should count for as much in politics as uneducated foreign-born men. *The Bettmann Archive*

of drink would enhance workers' productivity, increase their expendable income, and improve their marital lives; it would reduce disease and squalor, and undermine the baleful influence of the saloons in politics. Since the "liquor interests"—always vulnerable to tax, inspection, zoning, and licensing laws—had worked strenuously to maintain defensive alliances with the established political organizations at city halls and statehouses throughout the country, they early counted among the principal targets of every reform group that had to contend with "the bosses," with corruption, or with political obstructionism and boodling generally.

The Woman's Movement. In similar fashion, the woman suffragists served as a phalanx within the progressive movement. On first glimpse, suffragism must appear to have been profoundly anticonventional, and therefore at odds with the main thrust of the progressive movement. Implicitly it was. To the extent that it would serve as prelude to women's claims to equality in employment, in education, and to the right to participate in life as intelligent beings with all the human sensibilities claimed by men, suffragism challenged the male-oriented premises of much contemporary social behavior. Feminism, in this larger form, seemed to threaten the family structure as well. For this reason, many progressives, including leading figures such as Wilson,

Roosevelt, and Brandeis, would staunchly oppose woman suffrage, almost until it became realized in the Nineteenth Amendment; even "The Great Commoner," William Jennings Bryan, would not declare for it until 1914.

On the other hand, by the twentieth century suffragism had a force and a bent quite distinct from the more general phenomenon of feminism. Nothing worked so well for the suffragists as the argument that women had long served as caretakers of American culture and moral values; and that therefore nothing would more effectively preserve the society's standards than women actively engaged in social and political affairs. By the turn of the century suffragist leaders, such as Susan B. Anthony, Elizabeth Cady Stanton, and Carrie Chapman Catt, were pressing for the franchise *not* on the grounds that all human beings were equal and deserved equal political rights, but that the nation was, as Mrs. Catt put it, "menaced with great danger." "That danger," she said, "lies in the votes possessed by males in the slums of the cities, and the ignorant foreign vote which is sought . . . by each party, to make political success." The suffragists pointed out that native-born women outnumbered foreign-born men and women combined, and that therefore the franchise would strengthen "native" political power. (Florence Kelley, whose interest in reform far transcended the suffragist movement, was in a minority among suffragist leaders in protesting: "I have rarely heard a ringing suffrage speech," she said, "which did not refer to the 'ignorant and degraded' men or the 'ignorant immigrants' as our masters. This is habitually spoken with more or less bitterness.")

Significantly, the suffrage movement by 1900 was led chiefly by women of wealth, wives of men in the professions, or (rarer) women who had achieved professional standing on their own. They were overwhelmingly Protestant, well-educated, and of old American stock. They were, in other words, exactly of the same background as the typical male progressive. Except in parts of the South, where the anticonventional feminist implications of suffragism evidently outweighed its potential for preserving traditional institutions, the temperance and suffrage movements were usually closely joined. Eventually, especially after the Triangle Building fire of 1911 in New York City that killed more than a hundred women factory workers, the suffragists would increasingly appeal for working-class support by arguing that the franchise would hasten passage of factory inspection and labor legislation for women and children.

Conservation. The conservation movement offers a special example of the progressive impulse to "reform if ye would preserve." The surge of interest in making wise use of the nation's rich heritage of natural resources accompanied the anxieties raised by the supposed closing of the frontier. The ebbing of "the era of free land" seemed to foretell the end of the easy affluence that many social analysts held responsible for the nation's openhanded, liberal qualities. As Herbert Croly wrote, in his influential *The Promise of American Life* (1909):

> The American democracy . . . has promised to Americans a substantial satisfaction of their economic needs; and it has made that promise an essential part of the American national idea. . . . The promise was made on the strength of what was believed to be an inexhaustible store of natural opportunities;

The Sierra Club, whose founding purpose was "to explore, enjoy, and render accessible the mountain regions of the Pacific Coast," assemble for their annual picnic in a Sequoia grove in 1903. Preservation of wilderness was the Progressive era's most unequivocal achievement. *Courtesy of the Sierra Club*

and it will have to be kept even when those natural resources are no longer to be had. . . . If it is not kept, the American commonwealth will no longer continue to be a democracy.

Conservation stood for a broad constellation of values that some historians have dubbed "the gospel of efficiency." It included the era's optimistic view of the power of reason, and of the ease with which science could be applied to social and economic problems. A generation that had grown suddenly aware of the limits to its resources, and worried that the depletion of its natural wealth would create dangerous social tensions, looked to modern technology, intelligence, and organization to produce alternative sources of affluence, an alternative "safety valve."

Spearheaded before 1900 by engineers, geologists, agronomists, and naturalists, the conservation movement gained support from farmers and businessmen who feared the monopolization of land, timber, and minerals by "the trusts"; from civic reformers worried about the future adequacy of water supplies as well as recreational retreats for the swelling cities; from utilities interests and a new breed of regional planners concerned with efficient utilization of waterpower and flood control sites; from agrarian reformers concerned about soil depletion; and from aesthetes disturbed by the despoiling of nature's treasures. Many reformers extended the principle to human resources. In industry and commerce, F. B. Gilbreth, H. L. Gantt, and Frederick W. Taylor developed systems of "scientific management," which subjected muscles and machinery to precise time-and-motion prescriptions. Meanwhile, many labor bills, particularly child labor measures, gained support from nationalists, such as Senators Albert Beveridge and William E. Borah, who used conservationist arguments on behalf of safeguarding America's future manpower.

The Populist Link. The contribution of the Populists* to the progressive movement is a little complex. It is possible to say, as many historians have said, that a large part of the Populist program was enacted during the Progressive era. The two movements did coincide in a general way in their advocacy of expanding popular participation in governmental processes, increasing federal regulation, and restraining "the trusts." The Populists stimulated interest in political devices for outflanking the power of entrenched party organizations, devices such as the initiative and referendum (I & R), direct primary elections for the nomination of party candidates, popular election and recall of certain judgeships, recall elections to remove public officials suspected of corruption or malfeasance in office, and direct election of U.S. senators. Reformers during the Progressive era continued to have an interest in circumventing incumbent power with similar devices. The Populists also stimulated an interest in a more adequate banking system, though it must be pointed out that until the Populist ghost had been safely laid to rest, the chief response to the stimulus consisted in the retrogressive Gold Standard Act of 1900. Perhaps the most important contribution lay in the Populists' disruption of party regularity, an especially important achievement in the case of the GOP which for too long had enjoyed exaggerated popular loyalty to a politics of vanity, spoils, and partisan boosterism. By dramatizing the plight of one special interest group, distressed staple-crop farmers, the Populists did much to orient politics to serious social and economic problems; although, again, the most immediate effect was to turn the Democratic party, which had cosponsored Bryan for president in 1896, into a decided minority party for the next generation.

Having said all this about how populism foreshadowed progressivism, we must also note that it is hard to name a half-dozen important progressives who had supported the Populists in the 1890s; indeed, most progressives fought them vigorously. It is possible to say, further, that there would almost certainly have been a progressive movement had there been no Populists at all, and it would probably have taken much the same form. The Populist upheaval did indeed raise anxieties that inspired many to seek ways of removing the chief grievances on which radicals fed; but the settlement workers, labor legislators, muckrakers, suffragettes, antisaloon zealots, dissenting intellectuals, and municipal reformers who formed the mainsprings of progressivism did not wait upon populism for their ideas or their commitment. We will treat this more fully later.

Crosscurrents of Political Thought

The progressive ethos transcended all the thrusts that gave it political consequence. Moreover, it built up a momentum of change that carried American society beyond its

* In the 1890s, a number of farm associations organized to promote legislation to help farmers combat unfair railroad practices, high interest rates, limited access to credit, and low farm prices. Finding the existing party system unresponsive, they organized The People's party, and nominated candidates for the presidency in 1892, 1896, and 1900. The word "Populist" derived from the name of the party.

traditionalist moorings. Progressives generally sensed the first point; most became aware of the second only belatedly, and because they feared the drift away from traditionalism, in the '20s and '30s a significant majority of them would turn against reform. But meanwhile, publicists, intellectuals, and politicians sharply articulated the unease that flowed through a broad cross section of the society, the growing discontentment with "things as they are."

Walter Weyl, one of the more iconoclastic social critics, expressed the unease in his book *The New Democracy,* which some have called "the bible of progressivism." "America today," he wrote—it was published in 1912—"is in a somber, soul-questioning mood. We are in a period of clamor, of bewilderment, of an almost tremulous unrest. We are hastily revising all our social conceptions. We are hastily testing all our political ideals." To be sure, most Americans were not "hastily revising" anything very much at all, but they—a great many of them—were *examining* their conceptions and ideals, and in a still-absolutistic social climate it amounted to much the same thing. Many indeed found themselves, in Weyl's words, "profoundly disenchanted with the fruits of a century of independence,"—dismayed by the discovery that the American promise remained so largely unfulfilled even when the means for its realization seemed in hand.

It was not (to continue with Weyl's commentary) that we had failed to achieve wealth and power; it was not that our political institutions had grown less democratic, that our patriotism was less profound, or that our hope for equality was less earnest. With all our riches, we inflicted infinite cruelties upon our workmen, our women, and "the anaemic children of the poor," while the "hosts of unemployed men, whose sullen tramp ominously echoes through the streets of our relentless cities," portended "the sharpening of an irreconcilable class conflict" that would put the final punctuation to the American dream.

As if these were not sufficient reasons for reform, Weyl concluded his survey of the problem with a familiar reference to America's world mission: "Our evils," he remarked, "if uncorrected, must grow with the country's growth. . . . In the lifetime of babes already born, the United States may be a Titanic commonwealth bestriding the world. . . . It may be the greatest single factor, for good or evil, in the destinies of the world. . . . It is because in America we are about to play the game of life with such unprecedentedly enormous stakes that we are at last taking thought of the fearful chance of ill skill or ill luck."

How to Reorganize Society. There was general agreement among the leaders of American thought that the nation could not afford to develop further without some deliberate direction by intelligent will. The "tremulous unrest" of which Weyl wrote reflected in large part the great stir of minds contemplating the projected new order. Two great issues confronted them. *One,* how should the resources of the society be reorganized to serve the new needs? *Second,* what role should the state assume in promoting The Good Society?

Any attempt to summarize the proposals for direction that came out of the Progressive era must inevitably oversimplify. With that as a warning, it is possible to say that contemporary thought on how the state should restructure the society's resources tended to fall into two very general categories: (1) that of the centralists, whose principal idea is summed up in the title of Wisconsin University President Charles R. Van Hise's book, *Concentration and Control* (1912); and (2) that of the decentralists, whose principal spokesmen, Richard T. Ely and Louis D. Brandeis, continued to emphasize the hazards of great power in the hands of too few. Nearly all agreed that the state must step in to regulate the economy.

The centralists generally argued that the marketplace should give way to government or government-supervised agencies staffed by scientists, technicians, and other experts who would bring rationality and efficiency to the process of allocating the rewards that American society had to offer. Impressed by the industrialists' triumph over scarcity, the centralists sought to "rationalize" the economy, so as to eliminate the waste inherent in competition; so that affluence might be distributed more effectively; so that the distressing pockets of misery and discontent might disappear; so that the nation might regain a sense of common purpose. Probably most of them had been ardent imperialists in the 1890s, and tended to focus on the dual objectives of a vigorous foreign policy and domestic unity. Indeed, many would find universal military training an ideal instrument for such purposes. Universal military training, said Raymond Robins, Progressive party national chairman in 1916, "will do more in one generation to break down class and sectional prejudice, to develop disciplined, vigorous, and efficient citizenship, and to unify the diverse groups of our national life in a vital Americanism than all the other forces combined." To such progressives, large-scale, integrated, corporate enterprise represented not so much a menace as an example of modern, scientific recruitment of power. The energy it harnessed, if guided by a social interest, had an unlimited potential for good, at home and abroad. The centralist approach was considerably more popular among intellectuals, and among certain financial groups, than among politicians. Theodore Roosevelt was its most conspicuous political exponent.

The decentralists, on the other hand, showed a commitment to a definition of progress more in keeping with the historic liberal concern for individualism; they saw history moving away from controlled order; and therefore they tended to regard the impact of consolidated, collectivizing associations, whether corporations, unions, or government bureaucracies, as a setback to the advance of liberal enlightenment. Concentrated corporate power especially distressed them. They relied heavily on business competition to insure a dispersion of power, a responsible use of power, and institutional incentives for economic efficiency. Most of all, they regarded competition as essential to maintain private enterprise itself (in contrast to the "public" nature of corporate enterprise) which, as they saw it, constituted the nation's chief character-building institution. The task of government, they argued, was to forcibly reopen the marketplace, restore competition, prevent conditions that destroyed competition, secure "a free and fair field." They would "regulate competition" so they would not have to "regulate trusts." This approach was favored by clearly the greater number of progressives, including William Jennings Bryan and Robert M. LaFollette, but Woodrow Wilson was its most eloquent political exponent.

The Responsibilities of the State. Contemporary thought on what responsibilities the state should assume on behalf of The Good Society can be said to have fallen into three categories—moralist, neutralist, and pragmatist. The three attitudes were not entirely exclusive, that is, the same individuals often held different measures of all three. And there was no evident correspondence to the centralist-decentralist dichotomy. Probably most progressives believed, as Hofstadter pointed out, that "government should be in good part an effort to moralize the lives of individuals." "We regard the state," said Richard T. Ely, "as an educational and ethical agency whose positive aid is an indispensible condition of human progress"; the idea of the neutral state spun out of Spencerian theory, he argued, "is unsafe in politics and unsound in morals." The neutralists argued that social conflicts were best resolved in the marketplace where natural laws, wiser and more even-handed than human laws, prevailed. For the moralists, neutrality implied the absurdity that an enlightened people might not use their collective power embodied in democratic government to force a righteous and not merely a competitive solution to social problems. But the most vigorous new currents of thought pointed toward a conception of the state that was neither neutral nor moral.

This may be called the secular, or pragmatic, view. Oliver Wendell Holmes, Jr., in *The Common Law* (1881), and Lester Ward, in *Dynamic Sociology* (1883), had early suggested that a society's legal and moral structures had less to do with fixed or natural laws than with the ethical and material preferences of the society's dominant groups; whatever interests held the power advantage tended to incorporate its preferences into moral and legal codes. Although Holmes and Ward exerted little influence in the nineteenth century, after 1900 secularist and pragmatist currents of thought gained great strength.

Building on the "Reform Darwinism" of Ward, on the pragmatism of American philosophers Charles Peirce and William James, and also perhaps on the work of Karl Marx, a number of scholars in different disciplines approached the common conclusion that all values are relative, that they derive from particular sociological and historical environments, and that what was "true" or "sound principle" for one society or one generation might have little validity for another. American economist Thorstein Veblen pointed out, especially in *The Theory of Business Enterprise* (1901), that the "Natural Law" of the free market, unimpaired by political intervention, may once have worked well to stimulate productive enterprise and improve the economic well-being of the whole nation. But modern technology and corporate business organization had altered the environment in which the fair distribution of rewards for honest effort and the material prosperity of the nation could be left to Providence and the marketplace. What was "fair" and "in the national interest" were ultimately political matters, to be settled by political processes. Political scientists J. Allen Smith, Frank Goodnow, and Arthur Bentley and historian Charles A. Beard, especially in his iconoclastic *An Economic Interpretation of the Constitution* (1913), drew attention to the economic biases of the Founding Fathers. The Constitution, they suggested, was not a neutral or value-free structure of laws inspired by Providence, but gave special advantages to merchants and property holders. This was not to impugn the motives or honesty of the

Founders, but only to argue that different classes in modern America might legitimately demand changes in the basic structure of laws. The work of Roscoe Pound in legal scholarship and especially of John Dewey in philosophy, education, and psychology also shifted the focus in the search for Truth from the unchanging heavens and hereafter to the evolving needs of human beings. The test of ethics, of moral standards, of laws must be how well they serve human purposes.

Altogether, these scholars argued that there are few fixed points of law, few "ultimate" goals or values, few moral anchors which a society can logically attach to any social policy. They suggested that right and justice are a function of power modified only by sympathetic good judgment; and that therefore the only test of a "legitimate" social policy is that it accurately reflect the society's *de facto* interests. It remained for politicians—aided by the findings of the political scientists, the economists, and the social philosophers—to discover what those interests were.

The moralist and pragmatist approaches to the role of the state in The Good Society plainly clashed on a very serious point. If "morality" ultimately is derivative of power rather than of some fixed law, natural or divine, the effort of a state to "moralize the lives of individuals" must be potentially tyrannical. It is one thing to lose to a majority on a matter of social policy; it is another to be forced by a mere majority's law to adopt the majority's values and life-style.

But like so many conflicts of view and interest within the progressive movement, this one would not emerge prominently until well into the second decade of the century. Partly this was because even the pragmatists, for the time at least, tended to share the particular moral assumptions of the moralists; and if they argued, as some of them did, that The Good Society did not need a consensus on "ultimate values and goals," this meant, as Henry F. May has remarked, only that "in most cases . . . they believed so deeply in a consensus on these matters that they could not imagine a serious challenge."

Meanwhile, what served most immediately to unify the progressive intellectuals was the obstinate power of a political, economic, and intellectual old guard which (1) had vital political or economic interests at stake that were threatened by specific reforms; (2) denied that existing conditions could be improved on without threatening more vital conditions of a just social order; or (3) acknowledged the need for reform but, for reasons of temperament or fecklessness, usually found faults in each reform proposal as it came forth. Old Guard cynics such as Joseph G. Cannon, Republican Speaker of the House for eight crucial years until he was ousted by progressives in 1910, defined the motives of reformers as one-third ignorance and two-thirds villainy. More intelligent conservatives, such as Nelson Aldrich, the millionaire Republican leader of the Senate for more than twelve years, more candidly represented incumbent political and economic interests that were the very targets of many particular reform proposals. Both the Cannons and the Aldriches enjoyed powerful support from old-line intellectuals, especially economists but also most church leaders. Such intellectuals, committed to intricately structured theories about the nature of Nature, continued to designate the state as incomparably the greatest menace to individual liberty or, alternatively, they argued in favor of a kind of iron law of injustice according to which the sum total of social iniquity could not be reduced, but injustices merely redistributed.

The crucial importance of the progressive intellectuals and publicists lay in the work they did in battering down the obstructionist wall of ancient ideas. For all their differences among themselves, they provided a unifying rationale for the diverse and even conflicting interests that had in common a desire to redress the balance of advantage in various sectors of American life. The lowest common denominator of progressive political activism consisted in the self-interest of diversely discontented groups. The rhetoric of reform invented by the intellectuals and publicists of the day took the edge off the special pleading, giving the cause of reform a practical basis for concerted action against the Old Guard. The rhetoric undoubtedly blurred real lines of cleavage among the reformers, but this was not significant as long as the reform cause remained outside the main councils of power.

Non-Progressive Reform Movements

The progressive movement can be distinguished from other contemporary reform movements partly by the particular social order it defined as "normative," but also by its definition of what forces threatened that order. Five contemporary thrusts, which in a broad sense constituted reform movements in their own right, counted among the antagonists of the progressive movement.

The Corporate Reform Movement. This needs little elaboration, except that it is not customary to refer to the ascendancy of business corporations as a reform movement. It is quite common, however, to call the development "the corporation revolution," which, as we noted earlier, is not an inappropriate way of describing the conversion of a system of private proprietary enterprise to a system of predominating giant corporate consolidations. To put it briefly, the corporate reorganization of American business (a) challenged the traditional relationship of ownership and control of private property; (b) threatened the proprietary, small-business character of the American social structure, jeopardizing (as one contemporary put it) "the rights of the common man in business"; (c) caused a redefinition of "business efficiency" from maximal *production* per unit input to maximal *profits;* (d) displayed an outstanding capacity for overbearing and socially irresponsible uses of power; and finally (e) sanctioned novel business practices that constantly strained the limits of both conventionality and legality. For all these reasons, the corporate reform movement clashed with the progressive movement.

The Socialist Reform Movement. In some respects, the socialist reform movement deserves to be placed as the premier target of progressive reform. For, as already suggested, a great many of those who became activated in the cause of reform did so out of fear that unless something was done to restrain the corporations, to relieve social misery, to counter the provocative irresponsibility of the rich, then the variously discontented might well turn to socialism. "The only way to meet the socialistic and restless spirit of the times," said Louis Brandeis in 1906, "is to meet and remove each individual case of injustice."

On the other hand, we must deal with the fact that many historians have treated socialism and progressivism as parts of the same phenomenon. They argue that both movements reflected a common protest sentiment, and they point to the fact that progressivism and socialism peaked during approximately the same years. The contention has its virtues, but its weaknesses are more compelling. The socialist strength arose primarily from disenchantment with the conventional institutions of private profit, commercial competition, and property ownership, and in considerable measure with the society's religious institutions as well. The main body of reformers in the era, on the contrary, strove to preserve those institutions. In the interest of clarity and precision, therefore, it should be more useful to emphasize the distinctions between the socialists and the progressives.

Socialism, of course, meant a lot of different things both to those who called themselves socialists and to those apprehensive of it, a breadth of meaning that partly explains the historiographical confusion. The concept had deep traditional roots in America, usually associated with various utopian or cooperative community schemes of middle-class, intellectual, and sometimes clerical origins. During the 1890s, Edward Bellamy's utopian novel, *Looking Backward* (1888), introduced socialism to a remarkable number of the "respectable classes." Some socialist workingmen's organizations, mostly led by German immigrants, also had roots before the Civil War. After that war, the national trade union movement, led by William Sylvis, linked its cause to the Marxist International. In 1892, under the leadership of Daniel De Leon, the twenty-year-old Socialist Labor party fielded the first Marxist presidential candidate.

The main socialist thrust, however, came from the Socialist Party of America (SPA), organized in 1901. The SPA represented a broad coalition of non-Marxists, ideological revolutionaries, and Marxist-avowing trade unionists. Many of them had broken away from the difficult and dogmatic De Leon. Although Eugene V. Debs was titular leader, the party's most powerful figures were Victor Berger, leader of Milwaukee's brewery and typographical workers, Max Hayes, of the International Typographical Union, and Morris Hillquit, organizer of New York's needleworkers. The SPA managed to embrace, at least for a time, active syndicalists such as Bill Haywood of the Western Federation of Miners, with whom Debs joined in organizing the industrial Workers of the World (IWW) in 1905, as well as Christian Socialists whose dedication to Christianity was only one point of major conflict between them and the Marxists.

For most of the Christian Socialists, for some social workers (e.g., Florence Kelley), and for several literary radicals, too (e.g., William Dean Howells), "socialism" was a highly intellectualized and sentimental thing that consisted mainly in their inability to accept capitalism—because, as Social Gospel leader Walter Rauschenbusch put it, "Competitive commerce exalts selfishness to the dignity of a moral principle." In their practical proposals they differed little from what most contemporaries were content to call progressivism, except perhaps for their greater readiness to find in public ownership the solutions to specific social problems—such as inadequate housing or the high costs of social services.

Of the many elements in the spectrum between the Christian Socialists and Hay-

Charismatic "Big Bill" Haywood, right, poses with Elizabeth Gurley Flynn and other IWW leaders (c. 1910). Wobblies appealed to mining camp, occasional, and itinerant workers with few stakes in organized society. By 1912 gains in eastern factory towns shook conservatives. *Brown Brothers*

wood's militant syndicalists (who were expelled in 1912 for refusing to mute their endorsement of violence and sabotage), three SPA groups deserve attention. One was comprised of diverse associations of East European immigrants, such as the Finnish miners of the Minnesota iron district, and the many Jewish, Russian, and Lettish workers and intellectuals of Chicago and the big eastern cities. For these people, Marxism was largely an intellectual group heritage and an ethnic bond as well as a political ideology. The ethnic ingredients in their socialism seriously limited their influence with the community at large, and even with their own children, but it had great intellectual vigor. Another element consisted of the militant-sounding "Marxists" from the agrarian regions, most of whom came to Marxism by way of Populism. These farm-country radicals were capable of the most strident pronouncements of revolution and class struggle. But their revolutionary program for their own constituency, chiefly low income farmers, amounted to little more than (the antisocialistic) Henry George's prescriptions for a confiscatory tax on tenant-operated land rent plus national subsidies for the maintenance of private family-farm ownership. In Progressive era elections, the SPA received some of its greatest proportionate support from the tenant farm areas of the Midwest and Southwest, especially Oklahoma.

It was the trade unionists, though, who provided the SPA with its most constant source of strength. Usually referred to as on the "right wing" of the socialist movement, men like Victor Berger and Max Hayes sought a socialist society—by which they meant primarily a society in which operatives controlled the industries in which they worked—through both the electoral process and the centralized unionization of workers along industrial lines. They had little enthusiasm for radicals such as Bill Haywood, leader of the IWW, who rejected available political institutions and whose challenges to the American Federation of Labor (AFL) committed the offense of "dual unionism." The Hayes-Berger-Hillquit forces sought rather to take control of the AFL and to deflect it from the avowedly nonpolitical, accommodationist policy set in the 1890s by Samuel Gompers and Adolph Strasser. Although their AFL strategy failed, the trade unionists helped elect more than a thousand public officials during the Progressive era, including two congressmen (Meyer London from New York City and Berger), and scores of legislators (especially in Wisconsin). They were most successful in small factory towns and the western mountain mining communities, but they also elected mayors in such sizable places as Minneapolis, Duluth, Schenectady, N.Y., Berkeley, Milwaukee, and Dayton, Ohio.

Debs was the perfect spokesman for the SPA coalition. A nonconforming, gregarious, hard-drinking "Hoosier" from Terre Haute, Indiana, who, as a leader of the Brotherhood of Railway Firemen, had once put strikes in the category of "mob recklessness," Debs was almost literally driven to socialism after the Pullman Strike (1894) by the truculence of railroad industry employers and by the immaculate obtuseness of the second Cleveland administration; together those stalwart representatives of American capitalism confirmed, for Debs' experience, Marx's chief arguments about what could be expected from "the ruling classes." Debs learned to regard the state as the armed servant of the capitalist class, and he came to speak bitterly of the irreconcilable clash of interests between the classes. Yet it was not Debs whom Rauschenbusch had in mind when he complained that too many socialists emphasized only narrow class interests. For usually Debs employed the homespun imagery of "justice and brotherhood for all" that was more commensurate with the traditionalist wellsprings of so much of the American socialist movement. This feature of Debs' approach helps explain the almost affectionate regard he enjoyed among thousands of nonsocialists who sometimes voted for him. He took about 6 percent of the popular vote for president in 1912 and 3 percent in 1920 when he ran while in federal prison for his antiwar activities.

All the same, to recapitulate, socialism represented a movement deemed inimical to the objectives of those in the mainstream of contemporary American reform. For some progressives the Marxist assault upon religion was sufficient reason for their hostility. Moreover, no matter how earnestly even the non-Marxist socialists may have emphasized their concern for human dignity, progressive reformers feared that their willingness to subordinate the prerogatives of private property and of individualistic options to some more or less comprehensive social program constituted a serious threat to the very conventional standards of justice and of excellence to which the progressives had devoted themselves.

The Labor Union Movement. It is important to emphasize *unionism* here, because clearly most progressives favored labor *legislation* and worked earnestly to improve industrial relations by a variety of methods, including profit sharing and stock-option schemes for wage earners. On the whole, progressives shared the popular suspicions of unionism, whether the unions were of the socialist variety or of Samuel Gompers' AFL. This is perhaps hard to understand, especially considering (from the post-New Deal perspective) the AFL's remarkable conservatism. Once a socialist himself, Gompers early gave up on social reform and confined his efforts to the simple demand for "more." "Each 'ism,' " he said, "has stood as an evanescent . . . dream of poor humanity groping blindly in the dark for its idea, and it has caused many a heart-wrench to relegate . . . movements which do not move, to the dead ashes of blasted hopes and promises." For the benefit of socialists who believed they knew the answers, "The way out of the wage system," he remarked on another occasion, "is through higher wages." Gompers and his cohorts went to pains to demonstrate their affinity for capitalism. John Mitchell, head of the United Mine Workers, averred he had no interest in "ownership of industry by the people, or that they may own stock in any industry, or that they may share in the profits of industry"; he argued that to him " 'democracy in industry' [means only] the freedom of working men to belong to their unions, the right of workmen to sell their labor collectively. . . . There is no attempt to control the business end of industry."

Yet the very idea that workers should combine to "sell their labor" evoked images of "conspiracy" and illegal restraint of trade, especially for a society that (like Mitchell) implicitly regarded labor as a commodity. And despite Mitchell's protestations that unions were not seeking "to control the business end of industry," collective bargaining clearly implied wage earners' participation in the policy making councils of industry and government on matters ranging from wage bills and labor recruitment to plant construction and foreign competition. Unions, moreover, implied a number of social changes that progressives found repugnant: (1) class schism—the disruption of the ostensible community of interest between an employer and his employees, and the virtual institutionalization of the conflicts between them; (2) policymaking by coercion—against employers' and property owners' prerogatives, and against the supposed rights of individual employees; (3) the substitution of force for merit in hiring and promoting; (4) replacement of the work ethic with an emphasis on security and leisure values; and (5) the loss of the option by both employers and employees to bargain as individuals, to escape from collectivized terms of employment.

To some degree the contemporary aversion to unionism reflected the very weakness of the labor movement. Between 1897 and 1903, the number of workers in unions increased three times. This may suggest why some employers became alarmed, except that even at the end of that period of growth only about two million workers were in unions, or less than 7 percent of the nonagricultural workforce. Then a concerted employers effort, spearheaded by the NAM plus the floodtide of un-unionized immigrants, would bring that figure down to 5.5 percent by 1910. Less than 20 percent of even skilled operatives were unionized as of 1910. Except for a somewhat artificial "boom" during the World War, the figures would remain about the same through the 1920s. Such a small segment of the working population could still be looked upon as a pain-

Unannounced cuts in weekly pay, after Massachusetts reduced the workweek to 54 hours, triggered the Lawrence Strike (January 1912). When police killed a woman striker, 3 strike leaders were arrested for murder. Such scintillating arrogance eventually built sympathy for unions. But not yet. *Brown Brothers*

ful nuisance; its claims for recognition as a legitimate American institution alongside business corporations, political parties, the public school, and the church understandably suggested to a great many people simple impudence.

Most progressive reformers expressed their forward-looking social attitudes by merely accepting unions as a sort of necessary evil, even though they sometimes asserted their views in more affirmative ways. Many regarded unions as one vital source of countervailing power against the great corporations. Indeed, organized labor would provide substantial support for progressive candidates even where reciprocal enthusiasm was absent. Some found unions potentially useful for purposes of maintaining industrial peace—better to deal with relatively educated union leaders than to have to endure the anarchic reflexes of the ignorant mass of unskilled and often foreign-speaking workers. Many bankers and even some industrial leaders shared this view. The National Civic Federation, with Mark Hanna as president and Samuel Gompers as vice-president, had at its inception in 1901 the rationale of reducing work stoppages by fostering the mutual business interests of the corporations and the unions. Hanna's death in 1904 and, perhaps more important, organized employers' campaigns to break unionism would eliminate that idea for at least the duration of the era. Even where some progressives endorsed collective bargaining as a preferable alternative to labor legislation, the argument usually had a distinct paternalistic odor: "The improvement of the conditions of wage earners," asserted one New York group, "should, where possible, be secured by the action of the wage earners themselves . . . because . . . such associated activity develops both the moral and the intellectual nature of those who take part in it. . . ."

By and large, progressive reformers favored legislation that could make union activism unnecessary. They fought for factory and mine safety laws, workmen's compensation and employers' liability laws, child labor legislation, and even maximum-hours and minimum-wage laws. Most of these gains could have been exacted from employers by powerful independent unions. Significantly, Gompers strenuously opposed most labor legislation, especially maximum-hours and minimum-wage laws. It is equally noteworthy that only rarely could progressives be found supporting legislation *to facilitate union organization.* Usually they opposed measures to protect peaceful picketing against local court injunctions, to limit the use of court injunctions against strikes generally,* to exempt unions from the antitrust laws, to give unions legal power to fine members who failed to pay their dues, or to require jury trial of union leaders charged in equity proceedings with violating antistrike injunctions.

The progressives, to sum it up, could see the virtue of unionized labor as a potential ally against the corporations and also as a basis for a more orderly and reliable labor force, but they feared that unions (like corporate capitalism and socialism) would reduce individualistic options for both wage earners and especially for small employers, and moreover constituted a demand for partnership in the decision-making processes of the political economy by a class that had been traditionally excluded from such a role. As George Mowry has remarked of the California progressives, it was one thing "to be benevolent to the underdog as individual"; it was quite another to have to confront labor "as a competing social class."

Agrarian Radicalism. A fourth reform movement with which progressivism differed can be described as agrarian radicalism, or populism as it would have been called in the 1890s. The aspects of populism which anticipated progressivism have already been discussed. The present concern is with marking their differences. Class distinctions are vital here. Both agrarian radicals and agrarian reformers (or progressives) sought to recapture for local agricultural interests the control of politics that commercial and financial interests—particularly out-of-state or extraregional interests—had gained in the

---

* American courts have the power to stop or enjoin a practice that, in a court's judgment, will cause irreparable damage or injury before normal legal proceedings can run their course to determine whether or not the practice is legal. Beginning in the 1890s, judges who were sympathetic to employers frequently issued peremptory injunctions against picketers and strike leaders, with the effect of permanently breaking strikes. Violation of injunctions is punishable by contempt of court proceedings which the issuing judge himself conducts without the need of a jury. The Clayton Act of 1914 provided for trial by jury for labor leaders charged with such violations during labor disputes.

course of the nineteenth-century revolution. But "agricultural interests" encompasses both the larger, more prosperous farm-owning elements along with their merchant allies, and the poorer subsistence, tenant, and sharecropping farm operatives. In general it may be said that the radicals directed their appeal to the latter groups, to the "wool hat brigades" and "rednecks"—as suggested by some of their graphic nicknames ("Alfalfa Bill" Murray, "Cyclone" Davis, "Sockless Jerry" Simpson, "Pitchfork Ben" Tillman). It can be instructive to note the distinction between even William Jennings Bryan, the radically oriented Democrat who was not a Populist but who accepted the People's party nomination in 1896 and, on the other hand, Robert La Follette, the anti-Populist, progressive governor and senator from Wisconsin. Whereas Bryan stressed evangelical imagery and fundamentalist morality, sought support with attacks upon the nation's great cities, and would finally gain notoriety in the 1920s for his assault upon modern scientific thought, La Follette stressed liberal education, made systematic use of university-trained and -centered experts, and generally sought solutions to the problems of modern society through the advancement of scientific intelligence.

But the difference between agrarian reform and agrarian radicalism has political meaning, too. For one thing, the radicals spoke readily of state ownership of various industries that serviced the farm sector—e.g., railroads, storage warehouses, grain elevators, and credit facilities. In a sense this was not altogether as radical as it seemed, despite the socialist implications. Indeed, although many agrarian radicals drifted into the Socialist party after the demise of populism, as Theodore Draper has wisely observed in his study of the American Communist party: "The demand for government ownership and control that came out of the Populist tradition was not a step toward collectivism, socialism, or communism. It was a peculiar American device to defend the capitalism of the many against the capitalism of the few." In practical terms, their radicalism consisted in seeking low-cost farm services by having the state own and operate them, much the way the government-owned post office serviced mail-order companies such as Sears, Roebuck and Montgomery Ward.

By contrast, although agrarian reformers would also urge state support of the farm economy, they typically made their peace with the conventional business ethic. Usually, they stressed regulation rather than ownership, and they promoted various indirect aids to agriculture in the form of guarantees to private businesses that serviced the farm sectors: e.g., establishing rediscount banks to increase country bank liquidity and to reduce the risks in loans on crops and farmland. Such demands would be realized with passage of the Federal Rural Credits Act of 1916 and the Intermediate Credits Act of 1923, and the Agricultural Marketing Act of 1929. They placed considerable faith in education, and typically sought government subsidies for the purpose. The Smith-Lever Act of 1914 would establish an elaborate agricultural extension service, with the Federal Government underwriting the costs of county agents working in each state to improve farm efficiency. Copying from innovative industrial managements, they worked to strengthen the bargaining positions of farmers through better coordinated marketing of their crops and through purchase and rental pools for their implements and materials.

The leading reformers in agriculture had only contempt for the Populists and agrarian radicals. They included Seaman Knapp, the outstanding contemporary pioneer in "scientific agriculture" and in farm demonstration work, and Clarence Poe, editor of *The Progressive Farmer*. For Poe, the "Pitchfork Bens" and "Cyclone Davises" were just "rough, primeval, untrained men" who had nothing to contribute to farm progress. To progressives, in agriculture as in other areas, the radicals posed a threat on a par with the monopolists and the vested interests. An enumeration of active opponents of the Populists would list practically every leading progressive, including La Follette, Van Hise, Woodrow Wilson, Theodore Roosevelt, Louis Brandeis, George Norris, Albert Beveridge, Herbert Croly, Richard Ely, Thorstein Veblen, and William Allen White.

The Ethnic Movement. Finally in the category of nonprogressive reform there is what, for want of a better rubric, we should call the ethnic movement. This development embodied demands for specific social and political recognition of ethnic (or ex-national) affinities and affiliations. Its success would imply the legitimation of diverse cultural standards with respect to dress, decorum, religion, educational tastes, living styles, and language. Its immediate objectives frequently included explicit acknowledgement of an individual's ethnic identity in elections, in appointments to public office, judiciary posts, and school boards, in government contract allocations, and in civil service employment policies. In education, the "movement" had deep roots in the long-standing demands of American Catholics for public support of parochial schools, as well as in the insistence on the use of the German language by certain German-American communities especially in the Midwest.

In each respect, the ethnic movement clashed with the progressive movement. First of all, concessions to such demands implied acknowledgment of the fragmentation of American society and therefore the demise of the progressives' hope for unity on the conventional model. Second, it meant a retreat from official standards of integrity, honesty, and efficiency in government in favor of standards based on personal loyalty, partisanship, and sectarian provincialism. The two movements would collide head on during World War I when ethnic militancy grew in response to mounting assaults upon what Theodore Roosevelt and others dubbed "hyphenated Americanism."

As in the cases of the other nonprogressive movements, there were some progressives who showed a marked sympathy, even where their ultimate purposes diverged. Jane Addams was one of several settlement workers who evidenced an extraordinary understanding of distinctive ethnic traits and aspirations in her work with immigrants at Hull House. (Or, at least she discerned the utilitarian, clinical value of encouraging such traits.) In seeking to rehabilitate her often demoralized "clients," Addams discovered the effectiveness of interesting them in activities reminiscent of their native cultures. By reinforcing their link with their own past, such activities lent legitimacy to their native customs and strengthened their self-respect. Her experience had measurable influence on John Dewey, a fellow Chicagoan, in his development of a philosophy for social pluralism.

Yet, on the whole, at least until the tensions of the war era led many to reconsider

EUROPEAN IMMIGRATION TO THE UNITED STATES, 1870–1900

Figures are approximate

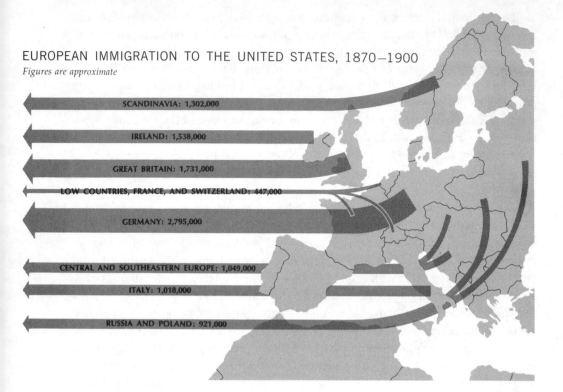

SCANDINAVIA: 1,302,000

IRELAND: 1,538,000

GREAT BRITAIN: 1,731,000

LOW COUNTRIES, FRANCE, AND SWITZERLAND: 447,000

GERMANY: 2,795,000

CENTRAL AND SOUTHEASTERN EUROPE: 1,049,000

ITALY: 1,018,000

RUSSIA AND POLAND: 921,000

EUROPEAN IMMIGRATION TO THE UNITED STATES, 1901–20

Figures are approximate

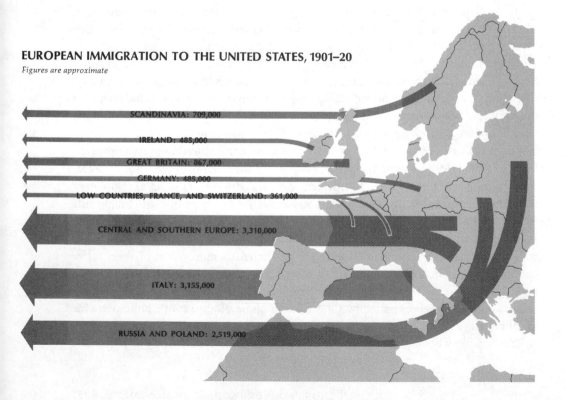

SCANDINAVIA: 709,000

IRELAND: 485,000

GREAT BRITAIN: 867,000

GERMANY: 485,000

LOW COUNTRIES, FRANCE, AND SWITZERLAND: 361,000

CENTRAL AND SOUTHERN EUROPE: 3,310,000

ITALY: 3,155,000

RUSSIA AND POLAND: 2,519,000

IMMIGRATION, 1888-1930

Year	Total Immigration (in thousands)	Total Immigration as Percentage of Population Increase in Preceding Decade	Net* Immigration (in thousands)	Net Immigration as Percentage of Population Increase in Preceding Decade	Percentage Males in Total Immigration
1881-90	5247	40.6	4481	35.1	61.1
1891-1900	3688	28.5	2536	19.2	62.3
1901-10	8795	55.0	5434	33.7	69.9
1911-20	5736	41.0	3589	26.3	63.5
1921-30	4107	24.0	3061	18.1	55.6

*Net Immigration = Total minus immigrants who left during census period.

their position, Addams' colleagues in the settlement house and Social Gospel movements emphasized reducing ethnic diversity in favor of Anglo-Americanization. Even so sympathetic a humanitarian as Louis Brandeis was asserting in 1905, "Habits of living or of thought which tend to keep alive differences of origin or to classify men according to their religious beliefs are inconsistent with the American ideal of brotherhood, and are disloyal"; Walter Weyl in 1912 urged restricting immigration to 100,000 or 200,000 of the most readily "assimilable" Europeans each year—or almost exactly what the National Origins Act of 1924 would prescribe; and in 1914, sociologist E. A. Ross (one of the rare progressives who had supported the Populists in 1896) published his book, *The Old World in the New,* in which he concluded that most Slavs, Italians, Jews, Greeks, Armenians, and Orientals were fundamentally unassimilable.

Summary of the Progressive Impulse

The progressive movement, then, consisted in a broad coalition of reform thrusts united by a common objective; namely, the maintenance or restoration of the conventional consensus on a particular view of the universe, a particular set of values, and a particular constellation of behavioral modes in the country's commerce, its business, its social relations, and its politics. Such a view, such values, such modes were challenged by (in random order) (1) the influx of diverse religious and ethnic elements into the nation's social and intellectual stream, (2) the overwhelming success and power of the corporate form of business organization, (3) the weakening of the work ethic that had been bound up in the old proprietary and craft enterprise system, and (4) the increasing centrality of a growing proportion of low-income, unskilled wage-earning classes in the nation's economic and social structure.

In a different sense, a challenge also lay in the discovery of the social sources of poverty and degradation—and in the threat of radicalism which it seemed to imply.

Ironically, the progressive ferment itself was to stimulate the emergence of a phil-osophical and scientific rationale for cultural diversity within a single social system. That rationale would produce the intellectual *coup de grâce* to the progressive view of civilization.

The progressive movement would try to save the old view, and the old values and modes, (a) by seeking to educate the immigrants and the poor so as to facilitate their acceptance of and absorption into the Anglo-American mode of life, or by excluding the "unassimilable" altogether; (b) by means of antitrust legislation, or, at the least, by imposing regulations upon corporate practices, in order to preserve a minimal base for small proprietary enterprise; (c) by legislative accommodations to the newly important wage-earning classes—accommodations that would provide some measure of wealth and income redistribution, on-the-job safety, occupational security, and the like—so as to forestall a forcible transfer of policymaking power away from the social and economic groups that had conventionally exercised that power; and, (d) by broadening the political selection process, through direct elections, nominations, and legislation, in order to reduce tensions caused unnecessarily by excessively narrow and parochial cliques of policymakers.

When the economic and political reforms proved inadequate to restore the consen-sus, failing to give the unprivileged an evident stake in it, progressive reform energies turned increasingly to using the force of the state to proscribe or restrict specifically disapproved modes of social behavior. Thus, the era would see the proliferation of restrictions on gaming, drinking, sabbatarian, and sexual habits. Ultimately, as social tensions reached critical dimensions during the war era, a major segment of the pro-gressive movement sought, by means of state and national "anarcho-syndicalist" and sedition laws, to constrict even political discourse itself. That was to fail, too.

But we are moving ahead of our story.

SUGGESTED READINGS

As one might expect, the literature on progressivism is vast. Harold U. Faulkner's classic *The Quest for Social Justice, 1898-1914** (1931) was the first successful syn-thesis of the period, still well worth reading for the economic and social emphasis. *The Era of Theodore Roosevelt, 1900-1912** (1958), George E. Mowry, and *Woodrow Wilson and the Progressive Era, 1910-17** (1954), Arthur S. Link, are more up-to-date scholarly surveys, but the Link book especially is too heavy on political matters. Richard Hofstadter's *The Age of Reform** (1955) is a more successful though contro-versial essay on the progressive ethos; it tries to explain why so many well-to-do men and women became interested in reform in a prosperous era. Hofstadter's hypothesis that "status anxiety" motivated many of the progressives has inspired many contrary studies. With David P. Thelen's "Social Tensions and the Origins of Progressivism," *Journal of American History*, v. 55, Sept. 1969, we may have come full cycle: Thelen

* Available in a paperback edition.

urges returning to the view that "no particular manner of man became a progressive" and that reformers were simply those who perceived faulty institutions and practices in need of correction.

On the many components of progressivism: Charles H. Hopkins' *The Rise of the Social Gospel in American Protestantism, 1865-1915* (1940), the classic survey of the subject, can be rewardingly supplemented by Clyde C. Griffen's "Rich Laymen and Early Social Christianity," *Church History,* v. 36, March 1967, which explains the relationship of radical clergy with their rich, high-society constituents. Roy Lubove's *The Progressives and the Slums* (1962) and *The Professional Altruist: The Emergence of Social Work as a Career, 1880-1930** (1965) and Allen F. Davis' *Spearheads for Reform: The Social Settlements and the Progressive Movement, 1890-1914** (1967) are excellent for the urban social-service workers in the progressive movement. Andrew F. Sinclair's *Era of Excess: A Social History of the Prohibition Movement** (1962) and Joseph R. Gusfield's *Symbolic Crusade: Status Politics and The American Temperance Movement** (1963), as well as Gusfield's shorter "Prohibition: The Impact of Political Utopianism," in John Braeman, et al, eds., *Change and Continuity in Twentieth-Century America: The 1920s* (1968), are the most cogent analyses of that complex movement. Both authors cover Progressive era as well as 1920s developments. Their hostile approach to Prohibition can be balanced by J. C. Burnham, "New Perspectives on the Prohibition 'Experiment' of the 1920s," *Journal of Social History,* v. 2, Fall 1968. Eleanor Flexner's *Century of Struggle** (1959) and Andrew F. Sinclair's *The Better Half* (1965) are good surveys of mostly the political elements of the women's rights movement, but Aileen S. Kraditor's *The Ideas of the Woman Suffrage Movement, 1890-1920** (1965) is especially stimulating. S. P. Hays, *Conservation and the Gospel of Efficiency** (1959), goes beyond the development of conservation policies to examine the policymaking process within the context of modern governmental institutions. On the general theme of "the gospel of efficiency," Samuel Haber's *Efficiency and Uplift: Scientific Management in the Progressive Era, 1890-1920** (1964) is a gem of intellectual history.

On the intellectual ferment: *The Crossroads of Liberalism: Croly, Weyl, Lippmann and the Progressive Era, 1900-1925** (1961), Charles Forcey, *Doubters and Dissenters* (1964), Frederick Jaher, *Men of Good Hope** (1951), Daniel Aaron, *Rendezvous with Destiny** (1952), Eric Goldman, and *The New Radicalism in America: The Intellectual as a Social Type** (1965), Christopher Lasch, are valuable studies of progressive theorists and personalities. Henry F. May's *The End of American Innocence** (1959) gets into the intellectual, literary, and artistic environment of the era with a sensitivity no other work approaches. Richard Hofstadter's *The Age of Reform** is nicely supplemented by the relevant chapters of his *Anti-Intellectualism in American Life** (1962) and *The Paranoid Style in American Politics and Other Essays** (1964), and by Otis L. Graham Jr., *An Encore for Reform: The Old Progressives and the New Deal** (1967), whose study of more than a hundred progressives who lived on into the New Deal era is unsurpassed for what it reveals about the character of progressivism.

On the nonprogressive reform movements of the era: *Trust and Corporation*

Problems (1929), Henry R. Seager and Charles A. Gulick, Jr., though old, is still excellent for the corporation revolution and the consolidation movement. In fact, just because it is old, it has more detail of relevance for the period under study here than newer, more comprehensive works such as G. Warren Nutter and Henry Adler Einhorn's *Enterprise Monopoly in the United States: 1899-1958* (1969). Hans B. Thorelli's *The Federal Antitrust Policy: Origination of an American Tradition* (1955) and the early chapters of William Lee Baldwin's *Antitrust and the Changing Corporation* (1961) analyse the social as well as the political and economic implications of the monopoly problem at the turn of the century. The most cogently presented accounts appear in article form, notably Alfred D. Chandler's "The Beginnings of 'Big Business' in American Industry," *Business History Review,* v. 33, Spring 1959, and his "The Large Industrial Corporation and the Making of the Modern American Economy," in *Institutions in Modern America* (1967), S. E. Ambrose, ed.

The socialist reform movement is surveyed clearly in David A. Shannon's *The Socialist Party of America* (1955). Ray Ginger's *The Bending Cross* (1949), reprinted in paperback as *Eugene V. Debs* (1964), is an exciting and thorough biography. Daniel Bell, *Marxian Socialism in the United States** (1952, 1967), and James Weinstein, *The Decline of Socialism in America, 1912-25* (1967), present contrasting views on the demise of the socialist movement. John H. M. Laslett and Seymour Martin Lipset, eds., *Failure of a Dream? Essays in the History of American Socialism** (1974) is an indispensable collection of articles, old and new, by scholars and active socialists, including direct challenges and responses to one another.

American Labor* (1960) by Henry Pelling, a British scholar, briefly but sharply surveys the subject, focusing on the uniqueness of the American experience to explain why trade unionism in America did so poorly and shunned radical politics, as compared with the unions in the European industrial countries. Like Pelling, Marc Karson, *American Labor Unions and Politics, 1900-1918** (1958), calls attention to ethnic diversity and to the peculiar antiintellectualism of American unionist leaders, but Karson is not altogether convincing in his argument that the predominantly Catholic leadership of the AFL foredoomed it to conservatism. Lloyd Ulman's swift institutional survey, "The Development of Trades and Labor Unions," in Seymour Harris, ed., *American Economic History* (1961), can be supplemented by his more detailed *The Rise of the National Trade Unions* (1955). Evidence of the estrangement between unionists and the progressives appears in at least three state studies: *The California Progressives** (1951), G. E. Mowry, *Labor and the Progressive Movement in New York State, 1897-1916* (1965), Irwin Yellowitz, and *Conservatism in a Progressive Era: Massachusetts Politics 1900-1912* (1964), R. M. Abrams. Michael Rogin, "Progressivism and the California Electorate," *Journal of American History,* v. 55, Sept. 1968, suggests a different view.

Hofstadter's *The Age of Reform* was the first book to make a point of the differences between Populist and progressive reformers, although his emphasis on the Populists' anti-Semitism and authoritarianism has been sharply challenged. Beyond this, the best way to understand the distinction between radical and progressive approaches to agrarian problems is through biographies. Some of the most relevant are: C. Vann Woodward's *Tom Watson: Agrarian Rebel** (1938), Francis B. Simkins' *Pitchfork Ben Tillman** (1944), David P. Thelen's *Robert La Follette and the Insurgent Spirit** (1975), Paul Glad's *The Trumpet Soundeth: William Jennings Bryan and His Democracy, 1896-1912** (1960), and Joseph C. Bailey's *Seaman A. Knapp: Schoolmaster of American Agriculture* (1945).

Progressive attitudes toward the unassimilated ethnic and racial groups are best revealed in the contemporaries' own writings, notably Robert Woods', ed., *Americans in Process: A Settlement Study* (1902), E. A. Ross' *The Old World in the New* (1914), John R. Commons' *Races and Immigrants in America* (1911), William Allen White's *The Old Order Changeth* (1912). Horace Kallen, *Culture and Democracy in the United States: Studies in the Group Psychology of the American Peoples* (1924), develops the point he made in his landmark "Democracy *Versus* the Melting Pot," published in *The Nation* in 1915. And Randolph S. Bourne's "Trans-National America" and "The Jews and Trans-National America," both written between 1915 and 1918, are reprinted in *The War and the Intellectuals: Collected Essays** edited by Carl Resek (1964).

CHAPTER THREE

THE POLITICS
OF REFORM

THE SPATE OF REFORM legislation after 1900 points to reformers' success in overcoming the nineteenth-century hesitancy to use government—particularly the federal government—for broad social and economic purposes. It illustrates, too, Americans' determination to restrain entrepreneurial options in favor of a somewhat revised conception of liberty and justice. The achievements, however, cannot be attributed altogether to the efforts of the progressive reformers, even where progressives provided the chief impetus or publicity. The practical alliances necessary for the achievement of each particular reform tended to vary considerably. Each reform had a different appeal to different progressive reformers. Moreover, each reform attracted support from among different, powerful, nonprogressive, and even nonreform groups— from businesses concerned with commercial advantages, politicians on the make, journalists seeking provocative stories. It is not too much to say that without the support of these powerful nonprogressive elements, practically no economic and few political reforms would have been achieved.

Undermining the Old Order

A confluence of forces helped erode the supports of the old order, tipping the balance in favor of reform. One was the increasing reasonableness of the agrarian and labor agitation in the light of the information that the Social Christians, the settlement workers, and the muckrakers were making available. A public appetite for scandal, whetted by publisher William Randolph Hearst and "his" Spanish War, found eager journalist providers—some earnest, like S. S. McClure, some only cheap exploiters of the method—but all equipped with the new, inexpensive printing techniques that could bring into every home an undeniable photographic record of conditions in slums, slaughterhouses, and saloons, conditions that rivaled war itself for grime and gore. Meanwhile, the dramatic reversal of the price curve in 1897 and a 40 percent increase in the cost of living over the next fifteen years helped predispose many middle-class and fixed-income groups to ponder questions of social iniquity.

To Restore Lost Advantages. In addition, alarm grew among many who would never drink of the progressive spirit that some of the monsters whose existence they had once attributed only to the intoxicated imaginations of "wild-eyed radicals" had indeed some reality. Industrial consolidations pressed smaller businessmen into corners, sometimes forcing them to sell outright, sometimes only constricting their profit margins or endangering their access to money, materials, and markets. Progressive reform in many states often found its expression in laws that purported to protect local business interests against the interstate "trusts." The Texas Railroad Commission, for example, contrived railroad rates to deflect Texan traffic from New Orleans in the interest of a prosperous Galveston or Beaumont; and many states taxed premiums of out-of-state ("foreign") insurance policies to minimize the outflow of savings. Mean-

"Uncle Joe" Cannon, Speaker of the House, 1903 to 1911, epitomized Old Guard obstructionism. Republican insurgents allied with Democrats to clip his powers in 1910. It was one of the many small and temporary triumphs of progressive reformers. *Library of Congress*

while the great railroad consolidations of the 1890s had the effect of depriving many a businessman of an independent railroad company that had once served him almost as its special client. By the Progressive era, the business efficiencies (or cuts in service, depending on one's viewpoint) had turned many hopeful market towns and jobbing centers into stagnant way-stations, upsetting the earnings expectations of many local shippers, bankers, and real estate developers. Midwestern shipper associations contributed substantially to the fight for railroad reform legislation, culminating in the Hepburn and Mann-Elkins Acts of 1906 and 1910.

To Preserve Threatened Advantages. At the same time, many long ascendant groups also sought government intervention. New England manufacturers, once dominant in textiles, for example, supported national child labor legislation to reduce labor cost advantages in the South where low-paid children made up a large portion of the labor force. Big railroads stirred restively against rebate extortion by big shippers such as Swift & Co. and Standard Oil. Eager to stabilize rate schedules, the railroads helped President Roosevelt, who was concerned chiefly to soothe the public's irritation over the dishonesty of rebating, to push through an antirebate measure, the Elkins Act, in 1903. Many corporations that operated in the national market, such as the big eastern life insurance companies, complained to Congress of discriminatory state legislation; they (unsuccessfully) fought beside many proregulation congressmen and President Taft for a national incorporation act. The National Association of Manufacturers (NAM), usually a dogged defender of "laissez-faire," lobbied in Washington for export subsidies. The organization strove unsuccessfully for direct grants to the privately owned merchant marine, and successfully for more and better trained consular officials to serve businessmen's needs in foreign ports.

The Meat Inspection Act of 1906, a landmark in progressive reform usually attributed to an outraged public's response to Upton Sinclair's depiction of the meat-packing industry in his novel, *The Jungle,* gained much of its impetus from European boycotts in the 1890s following allegations that U.S. meats were contaminated. In 1906 the big meat packers, fearful of the climate produced by Sinclair, generally opposed inspection, but by that time the National Board of Trade and even sections of the NAM had joined the campaign for effective federal inspection. Some historians contend that the 1906 act may have benefited commercial interests, export merchants, and even the big packers themselves (by imputing federal approval to the quality of their meat) more than it did the health of the nation.

To Head Off Radicalism. The origins of the less heralded Smith-Lever Agricultural Extension Act of 1914 may also be found in the efforts of well-established business interests. Manufacturers, railroad managements, bankers, and various trade associations hoped to stabilize the farm economy and also to obviate the economic sources of populist agitation. The Illinois Bankers Association, Wells Fargo, the Great Northern, Pennsylvania, and Rock Island Railroads, the Council of North American Grain Exchanges, and American Steel & Wire were among the interests that first financed agricultural experiment work and then sponsored the campaign for the 1914 act. Ostensibly designed to improve the productivity of marginal farmers, helping them meet the competition of modern bonanza farms and corporate agriculture, the act tended actually to aid the ascendant agricultural interests. The policies of the American Farm Bureau Federation, founded in 1919 out of state bureaus organized under the auspices of the act, would reflect the collaboration of the government extension agents with the wealthier merchants and farmers in each county. (See Chapter Five.)

Sometimes business interests sought the protection of regulatory agencies against popular demands for more radical measures. Consider the case of Samuel Insull, the English-born financier who would become notorious after the Great Crash of 1929 because of his disastrous pyramiding of midwestern utilities holding companies. In 1900 he was trying to persuade his colleagues in the National Electric Light Association that state regulation would protect the power companies from boodling city politicians and from the growing municipal ownership movement. (By 1906 there were 1250 municipally owned power plants, although mostly in small towns where limited profit opportunities deterred private investors from supplying local power needs.) Regulation of business served the purposes of reformers well in states such as Massachusetts where there was a secure tradition of skilled and honest civil service. In other states, reformers such as Robert La Follette in Wisconsin, Chicago's Charles Merriam or Seattle's J. Allen Smith tended to favor public ownership over regulatory commissions. The mere establishment of a public service commission thus did not always signify the success of progressive reform efforts.

To Promote "Business Efficiency" in Government. In the fight for modern, "clean" city government, business and progressive interests coincided especially well. Most good government associations and municipal leagues were financed by local merchant associations and boards of trade. On many occasions, these organizations provided the good government candidates against the local politicos. In order to circumvent the tightly marshalled ranks of the ward bosses, they often supported popular ("populist") government measures, such as direct primaries, recall of municipal officials, and the initiative and referendum, in coalition with social workers, church reform groups, and other disinterested civic organizations. But as Samuel P. Hays, James Weinstein, and other students of urban politics in the Progressive era have noted, both the intent and the effects of the good government campaigns had ambiguous meaning for urban democracy.

The "goo-goo's" (as their enemies called them) sought efficiency and economy above all in city government. That usually meant the sacrifice of various social services which "the bosses" performed, often illegally, for their low-income and immigrant constituents. It is a commonplace that "the bosses" held power by buying votes— either directly, or more often by providing jobs, legal aid (courthouse favors), pensions, and other extralegal services for their loyal clientele. But it would not be easy to demonstrate that this corruption conflicted with "the people's" interests; or at least with their more immediate interests. City government in the Progressive era provided few formal social services. When good government administrations scrutinized city contracts, the effect was often that hundreds of excess workers lost their jobs with no ready alternative livelihood available, no severance pay, no unemployment insurance to tide them over. When expenditures were trimmed and taxes cut, it usually meant diverting contract awards to low-paying nonunion employers, as well as reduction of work projects for the unemployed. When they introduced "honesty" at the courthouse, it resulted in many more slum youngsters or uninformed laborers going to jail for want of legal advice, access to bail money, or simply a friend in court ("character witnesses" and the like). Administrative economies cut off scores of old-timers and handicapped persons from sinecures that served them in lieu of welfare payments, pensions, or workmen's compensation. The bosses of course had a vested interest in maintaining their clients' poverty and dependence and they were far from evenhanded in dispensing favors. But as long as the progressives could offer no immediate substitute protection for the disadvantaged, the bosses could claim the willing support of most of their constituents.

When reformers took city government "out of politics" with nonpartisan municipal elections, city managers, and executive commissions, they removed some of the extraneous national and state issues from city politics. But they also removed the governmental process several steps further from the ordinary citizen whose ties to the process ran chiefly through the local party club. The commission government idea grew out of the view that the city is essentially a large corporation which is best run on business principles by a board of directors. The popularity of the view is suggestive of the continuing popularity of "business standards" throughout the Progressive era; more than four hundred cities, mostly the smaller cities of New England, the Midwest, and the Pacific Slope, adopted governing commissions by 1914. The view had many merits, including the elevation of technical experts to positions of responsible power. But it also had paternalistic qualities that contradicted the ostensibly democratic aims of the progressives' assault on "boss rule."

City reformers sometimes openly sought to reorganize the governing structure in order to reduce the power of the "ignorant," "alien," and "irresponsible" masses who provided the backbone of the bosses' power. Those pariahs understandably were concerned less with the efficient attainment of conventional administrative objectives (such as low taxes and balanced budgets), and more with shaping policies that might make government more suitable to their needs. For them, as well as for the political "interests" threatened with displacement, the "goo-goo's" remained only enemies. And sympathetic historians have often seen commission government largely as the effort of businessmen to protect their interests against taxes and boodlers.

This interpretation has merit, but it is also true that the Progressive era witnessed a streamlining of city government that was much overdue. Under pressure from reform-conscious business organizations, unwieldy city councils were reduced from sometimes more than a hundred councilmen to numbers more suitable for intelligent debate and policymaking. The business-minded reformers introduced cost accounting methods and established municipal budgets which permitted more careful handling of revenues and a modicum of advance municipal planning. Finally, the campaign against graft—though it could never be entirely successful—forced the restructuring of outdated legal codes and the creation of formal institutions (e.g., sealed bidding on city contracts) that helped make graft unnecessary for businessmen who understandably sought to circumvent obstructionist regulations.

Partisan Insurgency. In discussing the political force of essentially nonprogressive elements behind many progressive objectives, one must not overlook the power of personality and ambition. No reform movement has been without its political opportunists. Yet "opportunism" is probably too loaded an expression to use for a political leader's responsiveness to shifts of power or opinion in his constituency. Richard Lowitt, the biographer of George W. Norris, has noted, for example, how late the outstanding Nebraskan progressive discovered the reform cause. Norris began his career on the payroll of the Chicago, Burlington, & Quincy Railroad. The C. B. & Q. was one of the great independent railroads absorbed at the end of the nineteenth century by J. J. Hill and J. P. Morgan interests. For the new, larger rail network, the managers believed it uneconomical to maintain certain services in the sparsely populated districts of western Nebraska, where Norris came from. At the end of 1905, while Congress was deliberating on the Esch Townsend and Hepburn bills, Norris wrote to a former supporter explaining why he could no longer oppose federal regulation as he had in the past. "There seems to be a lack of desire to accommodate the local shippers. . . . It is surprising the people along that branch are as quiet as they are. There seems to be practically no way for passengers to travel, and very poor methods of handling freight." Constituents once fearful that regulation might frighten further railroad investment from their remote section now sought regulation in the hope of regaining services they had lost; Norris' shift reflected the change in his power base.

Intra-party insurgency marked the politics of the Progressive era, coming to a climax in the Republican-Progressive split in 1912. (See page 76ff.) Although it would contribute substantially to the reform cause, insurgency often had much more limited objectives. Factional tensions, especially in the GOP, had roots not only in the changing political needs of constituents, as in Norris' case, but also in the simple longevity of incumbent party leaders. Albert B. Cummins of Iowa, whom historians sometimes pair with La Follette among progressive paladins of the Midwest, offers a complicated example of mixed idealism and opportunism. "I started out in public life with the ambition to be Senator," he bluntly explained to a friend in 1908, as he prepared to renege on his agreement not to challenge aging incumbent William B. Allison; "I feel that this is the only opportunity that remains to me." Twice before 1900 Cummins had failed in his ambition, but in 1901 he won the governorship when Allison, the equal of any political man, arranged an accommodation with the party's restive "Young Turks." Boxed in politically by septuagenarian incumbents in an essentially one-party state, Cummins had to exploit issues that could give him popular leverage against the Old Guard's organizational power. Inevitably, he chose stances that gave expression to young Iowans' discontent over eastern domination of the party, eastern financial control over the state's transportation system, and eastern intervention in state politics. (One of the most influential Iowan political leaders, James Clarkson, for example, took up permanent residence in the East.) On the other hand, Cummins' coolness to direct primaries once he had become governor, together with the moderateness (one could almost say irrelevance) of his state program, may cast a shadow on the purity of his zeal for reform. For example, the renowned "Iowa Idea" which he advanced in 1901 consisted in little more than a call for tariff revision, a demand that had no relation to state issues but which gained attention because it struck a symbolic blow at national party solidarity on the protectionism issue.

In his *Autobiography,* William Allen White, the talented editor of the Emporia (Kansas) *Gazette,* candidly discusses the making of another midwestern firebrand. White had gained national acclaim in 1896 for his stinging rebuke to Kansas Populists in his editorial, "What's the Matter with Kansas?" He had sent the editorial to Mark Hanna, then managing McKinley's campaign against Bryan, and Hanna had had thousands of copies distributed to newspapers and campaigners throughout the nation. Until 1905, throughout TR's first administration and years after La Follette had revolutionized Wisconsin politics, after Hazen Pingree and William U'Ren had shaken complacency in Michigan and Oregon, and after James Hogg, Charles Aycock, Hoke Smith, and Braxton Bragg Comer had introduced progressive reform to the South, William Allen White continued to write editorials "defending the boss system as an institution which created the most responsible government." But suddenly, as White tells the story, he was converted.

> It came about with the election of Charles Curtis to the United States Senate. He was my sworn factional enemy. . . . So my indignation boiled quickly at the subserviency of Curtis [to the Kansas railroads] . . . . The railroads cleaned us up in short order. And along about that time . . . will be found my first reform editorial.

These examples do not exhaust the varieties of politicians in the service of reform. The point is that however they may have come to reform, such men provided the practical power that reform required. Politicians in search of issues to foster their careers were as indispensable to reform as the thousands of men and women whose ideals drove them to dedicated public service.

Theodore Roosevelt

The confluence of forces that have just been discussed helps to explain why the progressive movement emerged when it did. But no discussion could be complete without reckoning with the impact of Theodore Roosevelt. It is more than a textbook device to refer to the first decade of the century as "The Age of TR." Roosevelt did more than any individual to infuse reform with respectability and "manliness" (a matter of remarkable concern for that generation), to reestablish popular respect for the federal government as an effective instrument for the public weal, to bring a national focus to the diffuse reform energies at large, to call the nation's attention to the domestic and international implications of its industrial growth.

Theodore Roosevelt, probably as he most wished to be remembered: President of the United States of America, with a hand firmly placed upon the globe, symbolic of his bold leadership and international vision. *Culver Pictures*

Roosevelt's critics, contemporary and retrospective, have usually condemned him for being preoccupied with power, preeminently his own. His defenders have stressed his idealism. The two views, however, are not inconsistent. Roosevelt unquestionably coveted power, but it is also true that he did so on behalf of social reform and that his concern with reform long preceded its popularity.

The Early Years. Born into the New York City aristocracy in 1858, young "Teedie" or "Theo," as his three siblings called him, early had to concern himself with the question of "power." He was a fragile child who suffered gravely from "asmer" (as he spelled it) and myopia. He would eventually throw off the asthma, but his eyes would deteriorate until, by the time he entered the White House, he would be virtually blind in one eye. Small as well as frail, he often depended on his younger brother, Elliott, to do his fighting when bigger boys teased him. It is not altogether farfetched to see in his boyhood experience the origin of his concern with strength. "One prime reason for abhorring cowards," he would write in his book, *The Strenuous Life,* "is because every good boy should have it in him to thrash the objectionable boy as the need arises." One can find in that remark the essence of the Roosevelt foreign policy!

When Teedie was twelve, the elder Theodore Roosevelt—a large, strong, and intelligent man whom his son evidently revered—diverted his son's interests from books and insects to athletics. With barbell, chinning bar, and punching bag, the young Roosevelt worked to develop his physique. At the family estate on Sagamore Hill he learned to shoot and to ride. Though still small and wiry when he entered Harvard in 1876, he joined the boxing and wrestling teams. He was never very good at either, but he did earn a reputation for being able to "take it."

By the time he became president, TR had already become something of a model American hero with accomplishments for every taste. He had successfully entered politics in the depths of the Gilded Age and at virtually the lowest political level, as an assemblyman in New York State, by itself a deed of heroic proportions for "a young man of breeding" from the partisan jungle of New York City. He had written several books, including a widely used text on the Naval War of 1812. He had also ridden with cowpunchers in the Dakota Territory, busted broncos, flattened a (drunken) tough in a bar, led a posse to bring to justice a pair of desperados, matched shots with "wild" Indians in Wyoming, hunted bear, buffalo, and elk, and once actually brought down two deer with a single bullet. Meanwhile, he had been to Europe several times, had attended schools on the Continent, and moved in some of the highest circles of English social life. Back home, his political career took him from the sublime to the gritty: he served Presidents Harrison and Cleveland in the rarefied air of the U.S. Civil Service Commission; then he returned to Manhattan to become a Police Commissioner devoted to wiping out police graft, protection rackets, gambling rings, and prostitution. Finally, this astounding young man—who would be the youngest ever to become president— had actually led a cavalry charge (albeit without horses) in a real war. Not even Jackson or Grant had fulfilled a young man's daydreams of valor more perfectly.

Ascendancy to the Presidency. The New York governorship easily fell to the war hero in 1899. Once there, however, the position quickly became an all around nuisance: for Roosevelt, because New York state politics threatened to obstruct his by now well-formed ambitions for the presidency; for New York's GOP leaders, because TR's presence tended to disturb their well-formed arrangements of power and boodle. By an agreement with the "bosses" of Pennsylvania, New York's Tom Platt successfully promoted Roosevelt to the vice-presidency in 1900, despite the strenuous objections of President McKinley's political manager, Mark Hanna.

Hanna's fears were quickly realized. In the first week of September 1901, during a public reception at the Pan-American Exposition in Buffalo, President McKinley extended his hand in mechanical greeting to twenty-eight-year-old Leon Czolgosz whose carefully bandaged hand held a gun. Shot twice, McKinley lingered eight days.

The new president hastily reassured the country that he would continue the policies of his martyred predecessor. Roosevelt would in fact do no such thing; that is, if one interprets those policies to mean McKinley's sunny, somnolent approach to social problems. On the other hand, if one has in mind the political reformation which Hanna and McKinley purportedly accomplished, TR was more faithful to his promise. Roosevelt's style of politics accentuated the differences between him and McKinley, but in many ways it also obscured how closely his administration would fulfill the requirements already suggested by Hanna.

TR and the Corporations. Especially since Matthew Josephson's *The Politicos* (1935), historians have often observed that 1896 marked a new era in national party politics. In that year Hanna is supposed to have turned the Republican party from a private club to which businessmen paid tribute for economic favors into a public organization to serve businessmen's general needs. But there is little evidence that under McKinley federal policy responded more to what businessmen seemed to want than it had before. On the other hand, intentionally or otherwise, Roosevelt's administration approximated the Hanna ideal more closely.

The Dingley Tariff (1897) is supposed to be symbolic of "business control" of the GOP during the McKinley era. In fact, raising import barriers only continued former practices of giving political favors for those special interests that had the appropriate congressional connections; there is little evidence that it satisfied the most serious concerns of the country's business interests. By 1895, major industrial interests had already joined intellectuals inspired by historian Frederick Jackson Turner* in worrying about the "close of the frontier" and the relative decline of the domestic market; together with leading commercial and financial groups even the National Association of Manufacturers had begun urging withdrawal from protectionist tariff policies and government promotion of overseas market opportunities. On the day of his assassination, McKinley had responded to such concerns, if only to the point of calling for reciprocal trade agreements with individual countries, beginning with Cuba.

It was Roosevelt who won Cuban Reciprocity, after a hard battle against domestic tobacco, cane, and beet sugar growers. He also put through the Consular Reform Act to aid export interests in foreign ports. And in response to a decade of mounting pressure from trade associations, Roosevelt conferred with commercial leaders in 1903 to push through Congress the establishment of the Department of Commerce & Labor, for the purpose of gathering market data at home and abroad. (Labor would win separate cabinet status under Taft.)

Roosevelt's efforts to achieve amity in industrial relations by encouraging collective bargaining also adhered closely to Mark Hanna's initiative. By intervening in the Anthracite Coal Strike of 1902 on behalf of a settlement largely favorable to the workers, Roosevelt effectively broke the precedent of presidents who had sent troops to break strikes (Hayes in 1877; Harrison at Coeur d'Alene in 1892; Cleveland in Chicago in 1894). It is less well known that behind the scenes Hanna had engineered precisely the same settlement for the coal workers to avert a strike in 1900 and he was indeed the effective force in the 1902 intervention as well. Hanna had dramatized his view of the mutuality of labor and management interests by taking the presidency of the National Civic Federation, which Samuel Gompers served as vice-president. His own business interests and political power meanwhile had earned him the confidence of the business titans, including George W. Perkins. Perkins was vice-president of the New York Life Insurance Co., after 1900 a vice-president of J. P. Morgan & Co., and

* Turner's "The Significance of the Frontier in American History" originally appeared in *The Annual Report of the American Historical Association for the Year 1893* and has been reprinted in dozens of popular anthologies. It is one of the most influential essays in U.S. historiography.

the principal organizer of United States Steel, International Harvester, International Mercantile Marine, and other goliath consolidations. In 1912 he would become chairman of the Progressive party. During the Anthracite Strike, Hanna worked strenuously as goad and go-between for Perkins and the mine management on the one hand, and Gompers and John Mitchell of the United Mine Workers on the other. Until Hanna had his first success in bringing pressure from Morgan to bear upon the mine managers, Roosevelt feared to act at all. Yet such is the impact of style in politics that Roosevelt, with his ability to appeal directly for public support, emerged as the hero of the affair while Hanna, with his Gilded Age technique of behind-the-scenes manipulation, remained notorious as a "Boss" and "Standpatter."

Similarly, Roosevelt gained renown as a trustbuster, which ostensibly distinguished his policies from those of the McKinley administration. The contrast existed, but not in the fashion usually assumed. Roosevelt's approach to the trust issue in fact offered an accommodation to the trust organizers which McKinley apparently never considered. To be sure, McKinley did little for businessmen who sought broadscale antitrust action against monopolistic business practices. On the other hand, his administration did successfully conclude three antitrust prosecutions causing considerable discontent within the financial community. Twice in 1897, the Supreme Court had upheld federal prosecution of railroad rate pools *(Joint Traffic Association; Trans-Missouri Traffic Association);* more significantly, in the *Addyston Pipe & Steel Company* case (1899), the Court had unanimously approved use of the Sherman Act for the first time against a manufacturing company. The latter case raised widespread consternation about what kinds of commercial arrangements might be devised without incurring prosecution.

Antitrust Reviewed. Roosevelt, by contrast, urged reappraisal of the feasibility of antitrust law. In his annual messages to Congress, he repeatedly pointed out the impracticality of the *Traffic Association* decisions, noting that railroads could not conduct business without rate agreements. He pressed for amendments to the Interstate Commerce Act to protect shippers against extortionate rates while removing the need for antitrust prosecutions against rate pools; this, too, was part of the background of the Hepburn Act of 1906. Meanwhile, in 1903 Congress passed the Expedition Act to give court priority to antitrust cases, the more quickly to ascertain the law in the matter. Finally, at Roosevelt's insistence, Congress in 1903 established the Bureau of Corporations within the new Department of Commerce; the bureau served to create at least *liaison*—and some would see a veritable *entente*—between the corporate world and the federal government.

It is possible to give contrary interpretations of what TR intended for the bureau. Reform historians have treated it as a step toward reducing the unrestrained power of corporations, which it was, especially in its provisions for investigating and publicizing corporate practices. Radical-revisionist historians have argued that the bureau served as a sop to popular antitrust sentiment meanwhile legitimating extralegal commercial arrangements of which Roosevelt approved—which is almost as certainly true. The difficulty probably lies in a misapprehension of TR's objectives, for which his style is largely responsible. The Northern Securities case highlights the problem.

In 1902, a syndicate of railroad and financial interests, including Morgan, Rockefeller, E. H. Harriman, and J. J. Hill, organized the Northern Securities Company to merge the Northern Pacific, the Great Northern, and the C.B.&Q. Railroads. Roosevelt slapped them with an antitrust suit. The Northern Securities case, plus Roosevelt's equally successful prosecution of the "Meat Trust" and his dramatic assaults on Standard Oil, gave him his durable reputation as a "trustbuster," a sobriquet he found politically useful. Roosevelt's critics, eager to find him a fraud, have noted that in fact he began fewer antitrust proceedings in seven years than his more conservative and generally lethargic successor Taft did in four; this point among others, they suggest, argues that at least covertly Roosevelt was "a friend of the financial interests" and served them well.

The "trustbuster" title, however, belies not so much the facts as TR's intentions. Roosevelt was indeed not an opponent but an advocate of consolidations, and there was nothing covert about his position. His messages to Congress, his public addresses, and his private letters are replete with enthusiasm for the reorganization of commerce and industry in the interest of efficiency—even as he unfailingly tied such views to the need for public regulation. In large measure, this placed him on the same side as Morgan and other consolidationists. Yet his interests diverged sharply, and this is vital in understanding Roosevelt's impact.

Roosevelt favored consolidation primarily for reasons of national power. He had little genuine sympathy for business values. "I don't dislike [he wrote] but I certainly have no especial respect or admiration for and no trust in, the typical big moneyed men of my country." It must be remembered that he was of a class—wealthy, but "poor gentry" in comparison to the Morgans and Rockefellers—that had watched the nation's industrial upstarts take control of policymaking. Significantly, the standards he chose for measuring social and personal excellence differed drastically from those of the nation's moneyed elite. To wealth and business enterprise he contrasted manliness, service, and patriotism—perhaps the last most of all; he was above all a nationalist, a chauvinist, even a jingo. He had entered politics, he wrote, "to be one of the governing class," and to prove that he was not "too weak to hold my own in the rough and tumble." By the conventional standards he would have failed to measure up to the new men of power—much as reliance on class prerogatives and traditionalist scruples had emasculated the "genteel reform" efforts to stand off the *nouveaux riches* during his father's generation. By exalting different standards TR staked out a realistic claim to leadership.

In this light, the Northern Securities case was important *not* because it demonstrated TR's reactivation of the antitrust law, but because it established Roosevelt's determination to assert the power of government, under the aegis of patricians such as himself, over the self-arrogated autonomy of corporate power. And this is the significance of Roosevelt's anecdote about his indignation when (according to him) Morgan protested the indictment, pleading "Why couldn't your man [the attorney general] and my man just confer on the matter and fix it up between them?" Roosevelt's assertion of power in the face of billion-dollar corporations gains force especially if understood in the context of the tendency of business leaders to view government as a lesser suzerainty. His accomplishment must be measured also against the debilitating ineffectuality of eight successive presidents who preceded him, climaxed by Cleveland's ignominious supplication to Morgan in 1895 to save the nation's gold reserves and McKinley's open fecklessness on the war issue in 1898. Roosevelt himself noted during his campaign for reelection in 1904: "The Northern Securities suit is one of the great achievements of my administration. . . . [F]or through it we emphasized . . . that the most powerful men in the country were held to accountability before the law." That TR felt it necessary to make the point so dramatically suggests how poorly his predecessors had contained powerful men.

TR's Contribution. The simple respect that Roosevelt regained for the federal government counts among his most important contributions to the direction of social action over the next several decades. In recounting his achievements, one must not understate the singular importance of his ability to attract intelligent and talented people into government. Roosevelt was more daring, energetic, intelligent, and articulate than most of his predecessors and successors. He moved with startling verve, and he addressed the nation with unusual candor and pertinence. His style was contagious though not easily emulated. Like so many "to the manner born," he was anxious about power but relatively indifferent to the external symbols of status. He could drag dignitaries through the park on foot and horseback, receive diplomats in his bathrobe, and generally revel in eccentricities carefully suppressed or concealed by ambitious refugees from Canton, Ohio, (McKinley) or Plymouth Notch, Vermont (Coolidge). Such qualities encouraged the spirit of rebelliousness that reform required in an era still largely stifled by Victorian formalism and folderol. "I gave him up!" William James recalled to a friend shortly after Roosevelt stepped down from the presidency. "I gave him up," James wrote, because Roosevelt seemed incapable of anything besides "the ordinary street-level talk of fairness and courage, and down with mollycoddles. . . . At the same time I believe his influence on our life and on our people's feelings about public life has been of enormous value."

Taft: Conservative as Progressive

Political style—or rather the extraordinary want of it—would play a major role in the failure of TR's personally selected successor. As the massive, mustachioed, amiable, and able William Howard Taft took office in March 1909, no one could have anticipated the political disaster that lay ahead. Taft, like Roosevelt, came to the presidency one of the best-prepared men to hold the office. A graduate of Yale, he was learned in jurisprudence, had served in the federal judiciary, and had valuable administrative and overseas experience as the first U.S. High Commissioner of the Philippines. At the time of his election to the presidency, he was Roosevelt's secretary of war. The country had fully recovered from the slump of 1907. Taft had waged an intelligent campaign and had acquired a deserved reputation as a progressive. The latter he gained partly because the Old Guard had fought his nomination, but also because he advocated reform. His plurality over William Jennings Bryan, who had run his third and final losing campaign, was half the size of Roosevelt's in 1904, but then Roosevelt had run against a conservative nonentity, Alton B. Parker, an undistinguished New York judge who split his own party with impolitic remarks about those voters foolish enough to advocate free silver and easy-money. The more appropriate point is that Taft did many times better than McKinley had against Bryan in either 1896 or 1900; indeed, Taft won half a million more votes than McKinley had in his reelection in 1900, while Bryan gained only fifty thousand over his 1900 total. Upon his inauguration, many commentators noted the extraordinary goodwill that Taft enjoyed in the country.

A casual review of the reform achievements of the Taft administration would seemingly also belie Taft's reputation in popular history as a nemesis of progressivism. Taft genuinely attempted to enforce the antitrust laws. He seriously tried to reverse the momentum of ever higher tariff barriers, and he sought, in the progressive fashion, to "take the tariff out of politics" by establishing a Tariff Board that would use experts to ascertain true cost differentials between domestic- and foreign-produced goods. In completing long-stalemated negotiations for a reciprocal trade agreement with Canada and in getting the Senate to ratify the treaty (something TR failed to achieve with a Newfoundland Reciprocity Treaty), Taft not only struck a blow for lower duties but he came near cracking the preferential trade position that Great Britain enjoyed among the Commonwealth nations. He responded enthusiastically to demands, highlighted by the Populists more than a decade earlier, for a national income tax (the 16th Amendment would be ratified before he left office), and for the protection of small depositors against bank failures (banking interests lost their campaign against Taft's determined efforts for postal savings). He fought unsuccessfully for a national incorporation act to rationalize the disorderly legal requirements that confronted interstate businesses, but he achieved a national corporation tax against bitter Old Guard resistance. He appointed Julia Lathrop, Jane Addams' long-time associate at Hull House, as the first chief of the U.S. Children's Bureau, charged with broad authority to study and publicize all matters affecting minors in factories, farms, mines, schools, hospitals, courts, and their own homes. Finally, from the Mann-Elkins Act of 1910, the ICC for the first time gained power to restructure railroad rates.

Background to Failure. On their face, such achievements should have qualified Taft as a progressive reformer on a par with TR and Woodrow Wilson. Yet Taft suffered from handicaps, some of them circumstantial and some temperamental, that would forfeit him that place in history. Personally, he was unsuited for the presidency. Weighing over 350 pounds, he was generally disinclined to push himself. His inattention to details would cost him politically in the case of nearly every reform measure introduced during his administration. Above all, he hated politics and had not wanted to be president. But his wife was a president-maker and twice made him turn down offers of an appointment to the Supreme Court, possibly because a judicial career was her mother-in-law's preference for him. ("I do not want my son to be president," Taft's mother wrote in 1900. "A place on the Supreme Bench, where my boy would administer justice, is my ambition for him.") When Roosevelt appointed Taft secretary of war in 1903, his wife expressed her happiness: "This was much more pleasing than the offer of the Supreme Court appointment, because it was in line with the kind of work

President William Howard Taft, doing what he least liked doing—campaigning for votes. Taft's political career proved that neither ability nor a strong sense of right was enough to lead a complex society into the 20th century. *Brown Brothers*

I wanted my husband to do, the kind of career I wanted for him and expect him to have." When finally elected president in 1908, Taft lamented: "If I were now presiding in the Supreme Court . . . I should feel entirely at home, but [instead] . . . I feel just a bit like a fish out of water." He comforted himself with the thought that "as my wife is the politician . . . perhaps we can keep a stiff upper lip." Unhappily, Mrs. Taft took ill shortly before the inauguration and remained a virtual invalid for the duration of her husband's administration.

Taft's personal problems aside, a combination of political circumstances confounded his reform program. He inherited a powerful Old Guard congressional leadership whose old-fashioned notions about justice and law he tended, moreover, to share. He fell heir to a popular urge for "social justice" that had taken on a highly emotional character by the time he reached the White House. Finally, he was forced to confront an intra-party sectional conflict that he only imperfectly understood and increasingly aggravated during his administration.

The Quest for Social Justice. The issue of social justice was central to Taft's enigma; it deserves some attention. Justice implies order, for it is a concept based on the assumption that there is a way of ascertaining the balance of right and an equitable distribution of privilege and rewards without a resort to coercion in each case of conflicting interest. But every formula for order that a society embodies in its law necessarily favors one type of activity over another—necessarily restrains as it emancipates, necessarily disadvantages some to the advantage of others. To speak of a popular urge for social justice during the Progressive era is to suggest that major interests and influential individuals had ceased to regard the existing balance of right or distribution of privilege as an equitable one. One cannot extract from the various thrusts of the progressive movement a single new conception of justice; rather, each group seemed satisfied to define "equitable" according to its own interests. Yet altogether there was widespread agreement that the existing distribution of rewards was *inequitable.* And that was what much of the political wrangling was about.

Progressive Politics and the Tariff. The agitation over tariff reform symbolized the unfocused discontent. Reducing the tariff would not have significantly retarded the rising cost of living. But revisionism bespoke the resentment that many shared over government protection of interests that seemed manifestly capable of caring for themselves. Furthermore, over a period of time any particular tariff schedule can cost specific commercial interests some competitive disadvantages. By the time Taft became president, the Dingley Tariff was eleven years old, making it possibly the most aged tariff law in the nation's history. Roosevelt's unique success among modern presidents in avoiding revision during his administration meant that the pressure from groups suffering real or fancied injuries attributable to the tariff would reach inordinate levels even apart from the surge in the cost of living. As Roosevelt viewed it, there was "no moral matter" at stake in a redistribution of duties, but merely a contest for privileges among competing business interests; it was therefore only a question of "expediency," he said.

What Roosevelt failed to see—and Taft was scarcely more perceptive—was that in politics "justice" is a concept deriving directly from the competition for privilege. Within the Republican party, that contest had distinct sectional meaning. Western Republicans had always been uncomfortable under eastern leadership of the party. They had had to accept hard money policies when their constituency leaned toward easier money to stimulate their region's relatively undeveloped economy. The GOP's antisilver posture after 1896 had especially hurt many Westerners not only because it was another blow to easy money but also because silver mining was an important western resource. The eastern party leadership, moreover, had continued to stand behind the big railroads, because of eastern investments, long after railroads had lost favor in the Middle and Far West. To hold the party together in national contests, the leadership turned increasingly to the protectionist issue. Import tariffs had proved attractive to working-class voters who competed with low paid operatives abroad. And beginning with the McKinley Tariff of 1890, whose schedules freshman Congressman Robert La Follette had helped to write, agricultural products gained similar favor. After 1900, however, protectionism began to lose its magic as a party unifier. The Republican insurgents from the Middle and Far West did not repudiate protectionism, but as La Follette complained, the particular duties in effect offered agricultural interests too little. As the Westerners viewed it, social justice consisted in rectifying the shortage of benefits they received from government.

The two tariff measures that passed during Taft's presidency failed to meet that test. The first, the Payne-Aldrich Act of 1909, even contained increases in certain schedules, causing outrage and open rebellion among western Republicans in the Senate. In the angry and prolonged debates over the Old Guard's arrogant disregard for consumers' interests, the public generally missed the fact that in the roll calls on individual schedules, the insurgents supported the producer interests of their own constituencies about as loyally as did the conservative representatives of eastern industrialists. The point did not elude Taft, who charged the insurgents with hypocrisy, an accusation he emphasized when the same insurgents fought his laboriously negotiated reciprocity treaty with Canada. The treaty not only achieved an unprecedented advantage for American commerce with a member of the British Commonwealth system, it offered the possibility of a real break in the price curve by providing American consumers free access to Canadian foodstuffs. When the insurgents to a man voted against the treaty, Taft scored them as "tariff frauds." He thus won a point in logic, while demonstrating his obtuseness on the stakes at issue.

The western Republicans had never forsaken protectionism but only wanted a better break for agricultural interests. The treaty just compounded the imbalance perpetuated by the Dingley and Payne-Aldrich tariff acts. In return for free entry of U.S. manufactured goods into Canada—a gain for the largely eastern industrial complex that had been seeking new markets—Canadian farmers would be permitted to compete freely with American grain and potato growers. The treaty thus seemed to confirm the insurgents' charges about "Wall Street domination" of the Republican party.

Railroad Reform. The same issues emerged in the struggle over the Mann-Elkins railroad regulation reform bill. Once again, Taft neglected midwestern needs. The chief provision of the measure he asked Congress to pass simply established a court of commerce, designed to expedite review of ICC decisions. The new agency would, to be sure, offer relief to shippers who complained that by the time their petitions were ruled upon the business opportunities at stake had long since vanished. Midwesterners, though, had been complaining especially about the ICC's inability to end rate *discrimination.*

The Hepburn Act of 1906 had empowered the ICC to put a ceiling on rates, but the Commission could do nothing about special *low* rates that favored select shipping points. The favored points were usually cities with access to rival transportation, especially water routes, which meant interior cities like Salt Lake City, Des Moines, Wichita, and Sioux Falls lost distributing business to the big coastal, Great Lakes and Mississippi River ports even when the business was geographically closer to the interior points. The Hepburn Act so plainly failed midwestern purposes that the bill's original sponsor, William P. Hepburn of Iowa, had ultimately voted against it.

Taft's bill characteristically missed the point. A tedious wrangle over the Commerce Court occupied most of the debate. It was carried on in the familiar Progressive era dialogue concerning the need for powerful and decisive regulatory commissions ("progressive") versus the constitutional need for court review of decisions made by administrative agencies ("conservative"). The debate effectively diverted attention from the crucial feature of the act that emerged for Taft's signature in 1910.

This crucial feature was contained in an amendment introduced by Senator Joseph Dixon of South Dakota. Specifically, it superseded the clause in the Interstate Commerce Act which permitted railroads to charge lower rates for longer hauls even over the same routes if they could show competitive conditions required them. The Dixon clause left open the possibility for long-and-short-haul differentials, but in effect it empowered the ICC to suspend the entire rate structure and to place the burden upon the railroads to justify each differential.

Taft's signature, for the first time, gave the ICC effective rate-making powers, but this was lost in the symbolism of his defense of the Commerce Court against insurgents' efforts to reduce court review powers. The court review issue obscured the divided commercial interests of the insurgents while enabling them to remain united as "champions of regulation" against the administration on a matter of little importance; for if the Commerce Court did not review the Commission's findings then the Supreme Court would continue its own review. On the Dixon Amendment, however, the roll call reveals a different lineup: insurgents such as Wesley Jones of Washington, whose Seattle enjoyed favorable long-haul rates, opposed Dixon; standpatters such as Reed Smoot of Utah, whose Salt Lake City suffered from the rate advantages enjoyed by Seattle and San Francisco, voted for the amendment.

Social Justice and Conservation. The Ballinger-Pinchot controversy which exploded on Taft before the end of his first year in office revealed the full range of the president's haplessness. In a general way, Taft shared Roosevelt's enthusiasm for conservation, and he retained most of the conservationists from the previous administration, including Chief Forester Gifford Pinchot. Pinchot was one of the architects of the multiple-purpose resource development policy that had just got under way as TR's administration drew to a close. Pinchot's zealous style had served Roosevelt well—like Roosevelt, he would stretch the law to its outer limits, for example to set aside sections of the public domain without explicit congressional sanction. To Taft, however, he seemed "a radical and a crank." Taft retained him only because, to much of the public, Pinchot symbolized progressive conservation policies. Yet Taft needed a gesture of independence from his predecessor and political benefactor. So he replaced James Garfield, TR's distinguished secretary of the interior, with Richard Ballinger of Seattle, a former department subordinate who had left office precisely because of policy differences with Pinchot.

It seems likely that Taft never examined Ballinger's credentials very closely. He had been satisfied that Ballinger was acceptable to the "people" in the West, and that he had a "reasonable" view of government regulation of western resources. But, as George Mowry has put it, "What was reasonable to the 'people' in the West was often downright heresy to eastern conservationists. . . . In exploiting public wealth for private gain such 'people' in the West had been rather free and easy with their interpretation of government restrictions." It was characteristic of Taft that such a fine point escaped him.

Taft's appointment of Ballinger quickly proved disastrous. Moving with remarkable speed to reverse his predecessor's policies, Ballinger persuaded Taft that Roosevelt had acted illegally in withdrawing from use millions of acres of land and hundreds of waterpower sites pending a regulated utilization program. (The Supreme Court actually would subsequently uphold Roosevelt's, not Taft's, view of the law.) More calamitous for Taft, Ballinger hastily acted to validate certain claims to Alaskan coal fields, in which a Morgan-Guggenheim syndicate and associates of Ballinger himself had had longstanding interest. Ballinger's predecessor, Garfield, had found the claims tainted with fraud. When Ballinger removed Louis Glavis, the department's investigator of the claim, Glavis appealed to Pinchot, and the two of them appealed to the public through *Collier's Magazine.*

Loyal as ever to men he thought well of, emotionally repelled by the "muckraking" techniques of men like Glavis and Pinchot, and consequently heedless of the evidence presented, Taft fired first Glavis and then Pinchot for insubordination. He then proved no match for the withering assault that followed. The *coup de grâce* came when Louis Brandeis, acting as counsel for Glavis and *Collier's* during the congressional hearings on the affair, was able to show that the report on which Taft claimed to have based his exoneration of Ballinger had been predated and that Taft in fact had made his judgment essentially on an earlier account drafted in Ballinger's own office. Taft later found it necessary to force Ballinger from office. He then appointed Walter Fischer, a friend of Pinchot, to succeed him. He also regained from Congress authorization denied to Roosevelt to withdraw lands by executive order, and he ultimately withdrew more lands from the public domain than Roosevelt had. But it would all be lost in the shouting. Once more, Taft's failure to reckon with the specific interests at stake, plus his misplaced loyalties and clumsy personal style negated his most earnest intentions.

Republican Downfall. By mid-1910, less than eighteen months after it began, the Taft administration was in a shambles. It was an incongruous fact. The country continued to enjoy an almost unprecedented prosperity. Total output in manufacturing, fuel production, and metals mining had more than doubled over the decade just completed and was continuing to rise. Farmers in particular were in the midst of what they would later regard as their "Golden Age." Labor and certain salaried groups were not so well off, but the customary Republican constituency seemed to be thriving. Yet Republican unity was shattered, and Taft's government stood as a symbol for the unreconstructed Old Order.

In November, 1910, the Democrats swept the congressional elections; it was the first time in eighteen years that they would organize the House. (Most of the Senate was still elected by legislatures, the majority of which were GOP dominated.) Democrats also captured several normally Republican governorships, including those in New York, New Jersey, and Massachusetts. Shortly after the election, insurgent Republicans met to form the National Progressive Republican League. The league's chief purpose was to defeat Taft's renomination. Insurgents openly awaited a sign from Roosevelt that he might take up the standard, but until that time they gave their support to Wisconsin's Senator La Follette.

Taft's political behavior during the next ten months verged on the suicidal. In order to force Canadian reciprocity through the Senate, Taft faced down both the insurgents and the Old Guard in his party. Abandoning his previous concern for party solidarity, he forged an alliance with the Southern Democrats to turn the trick. Even as he exulted in his triumph, he confided to his wife that he supposed the treaty would remove him from "the consideration of practical politicians" for the nomination in 1912. He could hardly have irritated the insurgents any further. But now the Old Guard assailed him as well for breaching protectionist principles. The Democrats repaid his blandishments by tormenting him with "shotgun" tariff bills (so-called because they amended individual duty schedules) which he felt impelled to veto because they by-passed his newly created tariff board. And to complete the disaster, the Canadians would reward all his efforts by finally rejecting the treaty after Democratic House leader Champ Clark publicly suggested that approval of the treaty would ease Canada's inevitable absorption into the United States.

Taft's ultimate calamity arose from his antitrust activities. A strict legalist, Taft had less trouble than many of his contemporaries with the supposed ambiguities of the Sherman Act. "The decisions of the Supreme Court," he wrote to one business critic, "are easily interpreted and anyone can follow them if he is only willing to understand that . . . combinations to . . . suppress competition, to control prices, and to establish monopoly are unlawful so far as they affect interstate trade." "Wall Street is an ass," he fumed to intimates. The bankers, he complained, apparently believed government must apologize each time it prosecutes for law violations made in the name of high finance. When cautioned by GOP veterans that he was going too far, Taft bristled: "We are going to enforce that law or die in the attempt." By early 1911, many in the Old Guard began making plans for the funeral. A Roosevelt candidacy began to appear attractive in another quarter of the GOP.

TR's Return. Roosevelt, meanwhile, sought to stay out of the fight. He had gone to Africa in 1909 to hunt lions and also to free his successor from the irrepressible Roosevelt talent for publicity. He had resented a number of Taft's political actions, as well as several reported social snubs of Mrs. Roosevelt while he was abroad. The dismissal of Pinchot in 1910 just about convinced Roosevelt that his successor had betrayed the reform movement. Still, he remained aloof, fearing to test his popularity with an awkward comeback against his former friend and protégé.

Then, in October 1911, the Justice Department announced its intention of prosecuting United States Steel for antitrust violations. Its case had partly to do with U.S. Steel's acquisition of the Tennessee Coal & Iron Co. in 1907—to which Roosevelt as president had at least tacitly given his consent.

The case had its origins in the Panic of 1907. Rising prices had stimulated a spectacular expansion of world trade which in turn had stimulated an extraordinary worldwide demand for capital and credit. To exploit the situation, hundreds of "trust companies" sprang up in the United States to channel speculative funds into investment opportunities that the more conservative banks could not supply either because of the limits of their reserves or because the investments were too risky by conventional banking standards. Unlike banks, the trust companies had no reserve requirements— indeed, practically no requirements at all. When the inevitable happened, when trade slackened and creditors demanded payments, the strain was too great. The recession hit the U.S. especially hard because of the unprotected trust companies. The collapse

J. P. Morgan, Sr., shortly before his death in 1913, when he was the dominant figure in American corporate finance. Morgan's command of respect among large investors, on both sides of the Atlantic, enabled him to pioneer in modern investment banking and large-scale corporate consolidation. *The Bettmann Archive*

of the Knickerbocker Trust Company in October precipitated a run on other such companies, and on banks associated with them.

Some of the panic seems to have touched Roosevelt. Predictably, financial spokesmen had chosen to blame the president for the crisis, whining that he had "undermined business confidence" with his reform program. Roosevelt had fought back with denunciations of the "malefactors of great wealth." But meanwhile he moved, much as Cleveland had done a dozen years earlier, to solicit Morgan's aid in shoring up Wall Street. Morgan, it seems, was pleased to cooperate. He and the president together worked to move funds to weakened banks. Morgan also had an additional suggestion. The Trust Company of America (TCA) was one of the keys to the financial weakness. As it happened, the principal owners of the Tennessee Coal & Iron Co. (TCIC), located in Birmingham, Alabama, were heavily in debt to the TCA. Morgan and U.S. Steel's executives Henry Frick and E. H. Gary proposed that they buy the TCIC to free its owners to repay the TCA. But the Morgan group worried that Roosevelt might invoke the Sherman Antitrust Act.

Roosevelt apparently promised nothing but also managed to imply that Frick and Gary should go ahead. He was probably unaware of the advantages the Birmingham company's manufacturing, coal, and iron resources would bring to the giant steel corporation in its move toward domination of the industry. He was intent upon facilitating an end to the financial crisis. In August 1911, when he testified before a congressional committee investigating U.S. Steel, he belligerently defended his position. When, two months later, Attorney General George Wickersham announced the anti-trust suit, Roosevelt exploded. It seemed—and it would be hard to deny—that Taft was deliberately implying TR had been a dupe or co-conspirator in the case. On the day of the announcement of the suit, TR intimated to Republican insurgents that he would be available to run against Taft.

Taft would win renomination in spite of his blundering politics, his dislike of the presidency, and his despair of winning. ("I think I might as well give up so far as being a candidate is concerned," he told his wife. "There are so many people who don't like me.") For a time, Roosevelt seemed to have both the insurgents and a good share of the Old Guard behind him. The Old Guard soured on Taft because he seemed a sure loser, but also because of TR's spirited defense of business consolidations and his denunciation of antitrust zealots as "rural torys." Then, in February 1912, Roosevelt made a speech in support of popular recall of state judicial decisions that affected the constitutionality of legislative policies. Conservatives fled hysterically, charging him with "undermining the integrity of the judiciary." Meanwhile La Follette and many of his friends opposed Roosevelt because they had never trusted him and because his reentry into politics destroyed La Follette's candidacy.

So, Taft ran again. A major segment of the Republican insurgents and progressive reformers left the GOP to set up the Progressive party behind Roosevelt's independent candidacy. And the Democrats surprised almost everyone by nominating Woodrow Wilson, a new political personality who had attracted attention as a vigorous progressive governor of New Jersey.

Inaugurating the Era of Woodrow Wilson

No man ever gained national political leadership so soon after his entry into politics as did Woodrow Wilson. His rapid ascendancy is all the more remarkable because his careers as an attorney and as president of Princeton University had both fallen short of success. The Virginia-born, Georgia-raised son of a Presbyterian minister had had to abandon his law practice in Atlanta shortly after he had begun it in 1880. Then, after an outstanding twenty-five-year career as a teacher, historian, and political scientist, he had met two humiliating defeats as Princeton's president; the first, in his effort to abolish the cliquish undergraduate eating clubs, and the second, in 1910, when he failed to prevent the dean of the new Graduate School, who had support from power-ful alumni, from gaining autonomy within the university.

The Election of Wilson. Despite the defeats, James Smith, Jr., the powerful leader of the New Jersey Democrats, picked Wilson to head the state ticket in 1910. Insurgency was rife that year, and Smith hoped to head off the party's rebels with the nomination of an "independent." George Harvey, the conservative editor of *Harper's Weekly,* suggested Wilson to Smith. Actually, Harvey had been promoting Wilson's candidacy for several years as a conservative Democratic alternative to William Jennings

Bryan. And like other white Protestant young men of his day, Wilson had indeed harbored some presidential dreams.

Wilson became one of twenty-six Democrats elected to a state governorship in 1910. Within a year he won national attention by repudiating "the bosses," capturing control of the state Democratic party, bucking the utility corporations, and dramatically pushing through the legislature a series of remarkable measures. By early 1912, most popular indices suggested he was ahead of the field of potential candidates for the Democratic presidential nomination.

All the same, Wilson did not win the nomination easily. Party leaders resented the newcomer. Those from the Midwest and South, where the party had been strongest, suspected his "eastern" credentials, and noted moreover his long-standing hostility to Bryan, who had been the party's standard-bearer three times. Moreover, organization workers generally could not overlook Wilson's proven "unreliability" as a loyal party man. Consequently, when the Democratic National Convention opened in Baltimore, Missouri's Champ Clark, the long-tenured, hard-drinking, and otherwise undistinguished Speaker of the House, already held an apparent majority of commitments from the convention delegates. That would have been enough to give him the nomination today, but in 1912 party rules required a two-thirds majority.

The knowledge among the Democrats that because of TR's bolt from the Republican party they would be naming not merely a candidate but a president may have played a role in stopping Clark. But it was not until the 45th ballot that the bloc of delegates committed to Alabama's Oscar Underwood yielded to the Wilson supporters, and with that shift in votes, Clark's ranks capitulated. On the next ballot, eight days after the convention had begun, Wilson gained the nomination.

The election that November was virtually an anticlimax. Voter turnout was low. As expected, Theodore Roosevelt, running under the Progressive party label, split Republican voters down the middle. He and President Taft shared the Republican poll four million to three million, while Wilson got the votes of approximately six million Democrats, somewhat fewer than Bryan had carried in the 1908 campaign. The pluralities Wilson won in the states gave him the electoral votes of all but eight, making him president with an overwhelming margin in the electoral college but with only 42 percent of the popular vote.

Wilson's Mandate. Although all the major candidates avowed "progressive" programs, one may argue about the political inclinations of American voters in 1912. It is noteworthy that Taft's totals represented probably a solid phalanx of conservatives, and that, moreover, a large number of Republican conservatives declined to vote because Taft's defeat was foregone. TR, meanwhile, garnered a lot of votes among conservatives who were attracted by the magic of his name, or who also discounted Taft's chances and preferred Roosevelt to any Democrat. Much of Wilson's support came from among the most backward constituencies in the nation, including the Deep South and the big urban machines—such as New York's Tammany Hall—in the North. Nevertheless, Wilson self-consciously believed he brought with him to the White House a decided mandate for reform on behalf of social justice.

To a considerable degree, the mandate owed less to the clarity of Wilson's own thinking than to the mere logic of the political debate over the previous several years. As Wilson would remark in the early months of his presidency: "We are greatly favored by the circumstances of our time. We come at the end of a day of contest." It remained in doubt, however, toward what specific social objectives reform should be directed. The shibboleths of the movement for "social justice" would have to be analyzed to be acted upon.

The Altered Notions About Justice. In the course of the nineteenth century, American law, the American social order, and implicitly the American conception of justice had become structured so as to give the widest options to private power and so as generally to favor innovative over established and nonprogressive interests. The idea of progress as well as the idea of individual freedom had been built into the definition of justice, subordinating ideas of stability and social obligation. Contemporaries tended to view as "just" such measures that encouraged change and reduced constraints on individual behavior; they considered "unjust" measures that protected "vested interests" or imposed community responsibilities on private actions. Both progress and freedom, however, had been conventionally measured by material achievements; "liberty" usually had to do with an individual's access to job or entrepreneurial opportunities. As already noted, by 1912 it had become clear that the power bestowed upon private initiative had itself begun to threaten such access and to swing the balance of advantage in the society over to the side of certain established or "vested" interests. "The individual," Wilson remarked in 1912, "is caught in a great confused nexus of all sorts of complicated circumstances, and to let him alone is to leave him helpless as against the obstacles with which he has to contend."

Partly as a consequence of such new understanding, public sentiment had begun to stress stability and efficiency over individual spontaneity and competition, to emphasize group or community interests, and, increasingly, to favor a governmental definition of "The General Interest." The movement toward government regulatory action was one sign of this impulse. Implicitly, it marked a spreading acknowledgment that in the future the broader decisions concerning who should get what advantages must come from public policymaking agencies. "We are just upon the threshold of a time," said Wilson, "when the systematic life of this country will be sustained, or at least supplemented, at every point by governmental activity." Theodore Roosevelt in 1912 went so far as to argue: "Every man holds his property subject to the general right of the community to regulate its use to whatever degree the public welfare may require it." On another occasion that year he said: "We are for the liberty of the individual up to, and not beyond, the point where it becomes inconsistent with the welfare of the community." In an era that was sensitive about the customary prerogatives of private property, such statements had a radical ring suggestive of a policy designed to reduce the privileges of the already powerful in the interest of the commonweal.

But most progressives failed to notice that their definition of The General Interest usually excluded the specific concerns of many insurgent groups currently pressing claims upon the nation's resources. For such groups, Roosevelt's readiness to subordinate "the liberty of the individual" to "the welfare of the community" had plainly insidious implications; for in the current structure of the American consensus, those interests had yet to gain legitimacy. That is, within the existing definitions of the legitimate, no mere rearrangement of priorities could be of benefit to groups such as the ethnic minorities or the labor unions, or, for that matter, the black, the aged, or the chronic poor. In fact, it became evident soon enough that assertions of the superior claims of the community could be decidedly dangerous. The "One Hundred Per Cent Americanism" campaigns of the war era, the introduction of racial segregation into the federal civil service in 1913, the mass deportation of "undesirable" aliens in 1919 and 1920, and the union-busting practices of the second Wilson administration highlighted the menace to individual civil liberties presented by claims that the welfare of the society as a whole demanded prior attention.

It is most instructive on these points that AFL president Samuel Gompers would remain consistently suspicious of governmentally determined formulas for promoting The General Interest, whether in the shape of minimum wage laws or antitrust prosecutions. "This is absolutely the era of the association as contrasted with individual effort," Gompers agreed. "Labor and industry cannot be halted or turned back to conform to old conceptions and old customs." But unions, left out of the customary reckoning of The General Interest, Gompers argued, had to beware of what he called "paternalism." In other words, unionism represented one example—trade associations were another, professional associations, organized charities, farm cooperatives and bureaus were others—of the contemporary turn away from "individualism" toward group action and alignments. But unlike businessmen and churches and the professions and even the farmers, wage earners *could not expect* political action to promote modes of social and economic behavior essential to their well-being.

Few of the progressives who ascended to power on the strength of the prevailing insurgency ever quite understood what was at stake in the political struggles they would encounter. They would continue to behave as if the apparent nineteenth-century consensus on what constituted "The General Interest" had remained intact. They would go on assuming that an assertive posture on behalf of "The General Interest" would be government's only new obligation. Meanwhile, they would continue to suppose that special or group interests had no legitimate place in politics, even when, as Arthur Link and others have noted, "the work of special-interest groups or classes seeking greater political status and economic security" had become one of the most significant features of the era. It would not be until the New Deal that Americans generally would come, in Daniel Bell's words, "to *legitimate* the idea of *group* interests, and the claim of groups, as groups, rather than individuals, for government support." Meanwhile contemporaries such as President Wilson would insist: "The most fatal thing we can do in politics is to imagine that we belong to a special class, and that we have an interest which isn't the interest of the whole community."

Roosevelt, Taft, and Wilson typified the inability of their generation to understand the true nature of the interests in conflict. Theodore Roosevelt had disdained the tariff controversy because, as he saw it, it presented no "moral issue"—no question affecting Social Justice and The General Interest—but concerned "merely" the reshuffling of commercial advantages among competitive interests. He consequently overlooked growing segments of American society, especially in the Midwest, that had come to define The General Interest precisely in terms of redistributing commercial advantages. Roosevelt and Taft had both sought to evade dealing with the issue of long-and-short-haul railroad rate differentials on the grounds that it was "merely" a question of whether one group of economic interests (railroads and eastern industrial interests) gained advantages from their greater economic power or other groups (e.g., western and southern farmers and shippers) would gain advantages from greater numerical or political power. The two presidents thereby failed to see that large sections of the country had come to define The General Interest precisely in terms of the prevalence of "democratic power" over "economic power." Finally, when Woodrow Wilson, in opposing the eligibility of long-term agricultural loans for rediscount at the new Federal Reserve Banks, argued in 1913 that "The farmers, of course, ask and should be given no special privilege such as extending to them the credit of the Government itself," he revealed his failure to recognize exactly what agricultural interests were demanding.

Wilson's "New Freedom"

Wilson shaped his New Freedom program around the idea that government's chief problem was to revitalize the market system by neutralizing the "special interests." In his campaign against Taft and Roosevelt, he had promised to restore competition in business and "a free and fair field" generally. The legislation passed by the Sixty-third Congress (1913-15) reflected the intentions well. It will be useful to sketch some of that legislation, and to indicate how far short of Wilson's declared social purposes that program fell.

The Underwood-Simmons Tariff Act. In accord with their historic posture on the subject, the Democrats promptly leveled the protectionist walls the GOP had erected during the previous half-century. No longer would the government provide special advantages to some economic interests at the expense of others—that at least was the theory. In place of the import duties that had sustained federal revenues, moreover, the Underwood Tariff Act imposed the first (very modest) income tax under the authority of the newly ratified 16th Amendment.

The Federal Reserve Act. The country had been in critical need of banking and currency reform for a quarter of a century. If the Populists had not taken the lead in the cause during the 1890s, it might have come sooner; the general hysteria they inspired tended to handicap for at least a generation nearly every reform they proposed. The Bankers' Panic of 1903, on the other hand, failed to produce action at least partly because proposals for rationalizing the banking system came at a high point in the consolidation movement when even conservative interests had grown acutely apprehensive over the power of the eastern bankers. The Panic of 1907 evoked a more positive response, specifically in the passage in 1908 of the Aldrich-Vreeland Emergency Currency Act. That measure authorized nationally chartered banks to issue circulating notes (paper currency) backed by private industrial securities. It was the first time private assets were officially used to support the value of bank notes. The provision directly anticipated the technique that Congress would use in establishing the Federal Reserve System in 1913.

The Federal Reserve Act was unquestionably a major reform measure. Among other things, it established twelve regional banks that would issue currency based not only on national assets (gold, silver, government securities) but also on private assets represented by various commercial sales notes. The state thereby gave official recognition to the achievement of a high degree of voluntaristic order and responsibility in the conduct of business. It officially acknowledged that certain types of private "promises to pay" were adequately reliable representations of real value on which to base government-issued currency, i.e., common symbols of enduring value. In doing so, the government sharply reduced the archaic dependence on "precious metals," such as gold. (The "Gold Standard" would remain, of course, but as a kind of backup system for guaranteeing a stable minimum for currency values, to provide some limits to extension of credits by banks, and as a common standard for international exchange.) Furthermore, it placed in the hands of a national agency (the Federal Reserve Board) some power to moderate the business cycle through its ability to raise and lower rediscount rates and reserve requirements, and to engage in the selling and buying of government bonds in the open market.

Like the Underwood Tariff, the Federal Reserve Act promised a "free and fair field." By making commercial and certain agricultural paper (IOUs representing business transactions) exchangeable for Federal Reserve Notes at any of twelve Federal Reserve Banks, it permitted the supply of money to expand or contract as commercial activity increased or diminished. That made good sense, for money is supposed to facilitate the exchange of goods and services. Thus the act worked to remove the obstacle to "free enterprise" inherent in the previously prevailing currency system. That system was inflexibly tied to the gold supply and to the national debt and had given undue advantages to those with the readiest access to financial institutions.

But in a larger sense, the Federal Reserve Act attempted little more than a technical adjustment of the banking system. One will find in the act not a single provision that would help reduce the advantages big businesses have over small or new ones in getting credit—no clause that might serve to curb bankers' "favoritism" toward their biggest clients, no requirement that banks reserve a portion of their resources for small or new businesses, no suggestion that the federal government might underwrite small loans through some new agency or otherwise redirect the country's savings or capital to purposes dictated by long-term social preferences as opposed to short-term economic considerations. Nor will one find any mention of interlocking relationships between the major commercial banks and the major insurance companies and investment houses, though at one time Congress had shown an interest in banning interlocking directorates. It is perhaps not surprising that though the number of commercial banks would decline from 30,000 in 1919 to 25,000 in 1929, the banks' share of total net income from private production would rise from 2.2 percent to 4.6 percent in the same period.

These points are especially noteworthy because Wilson and the Democrats had stressed in the 1912 campaign the issue of the "Money Trust's" stranglehold on the nation's business. "The great monopoly in this country," Wilson had said, "is the money monopoly." Both the congressional investigation headed by Arsène Pujo of Louisiana and Wilson's close adviser, Louis Brandeis, in his book, *Other People's Money,* had emphasized the credit difficulties faced by businessmen seeking to enter an established field, or simply trying to expand existing operations in a field dominated by one or a few giants (which often had bankers on their boards). Pujo had specifically noted that mere readjustment of the monetary system would do little good. "Whether under a different currency system the resources in our banks would be greater or less," his report argued, "is comparatively immaterial if they continue to be controlled by a small group. . . ."

In sum, the Federal Reserve Act would improve the country's credit resources, but it did little or nothing to meet the conditions previously outlined by Pujo, Brandeis, or Wilson himself.

Curbing the Trusts. The Federal Trade Commission Act and the Clayton Antitrust Act of 1914, in Wilson's view, completed his program for "setting the business of this country free." They epitomized the limitations of progressive reform. Originally, Wilson had opposed the idea of a trade commission because it had become identified with Theodore Roosevelt's proposals for "regulating the trusts" in the interest of promoting a "New Nationalism." Wilson recognized the danger. A regulatory bureau might too easily become the agent of the interests it was supposed to regulate. But when it came time for designing the antitrust legislation he had promised, Wilson discovered how complicated it was to anticipate in a statute the kinds of business activities that were conducive to "destructive competition." He therefore agreed to a commission that could terminate specific "unfair" trade practices. The Clayton Act, meanwhile, would attempt to prohibit certain current business practices that were already acknowledged to have substantially reduced competition, such as discriminatory price policies, and tie-in contracts which required a business customer to buy or lease a complete line of products in order to get any single item.

As in banking reform, the fate of Wilson's antitrust program demonstrates the failure of nerve that characterized so much of progressive reform. "We are all agreed that private monopoly is indefensible and intolerable," Wilson told Congress when he presented his program. "We are agreed, I take it," he said, "that holding *companies* should be prohibited." (That, too, seemed clear enough.) "But what of the controlling private ownership of individuals or actually cooperative groups of individuals? . . . Enterprises," he noted, "are oftentimes interlocked, not by being under the control of the same directors, but by the fact that the greater part of their corporate stock is owned by a single person or group of persons who are in some way intimately related in interest. . . . Surely," he concluded, "we are sufficiently familiar with the actual processes and methods of monopoly and of the many hurtful restraints of trade to make definition [of antitrust policy] possible."

In view of such an apparently straightforward analysis of the problem, it is remarkable that no Wilsonian legislation fulfilled even minimal expectations. Wilson himself made impossible a reversal of the consolidation movement by exempting in advance those holding companies already in business. Nor was there even a hint of attempting to restore pre-1890 legal barriers against corporations owning equity in other corporations. Congress did prohibit the acquisition of a firm's *securities* by its competitor (where such action might tend "to substantially lessen competition" between those firms). But it left an inviting gap by permitting corporations to acquire the *physical assets* of their competitors. Congress thus seemed more concerned with protecting competitors against vaguely sneaky stock raids than with improving competition and limiting bigness.

Again, although Brandeis and others had argued that mere bigness afforded corporations many competitive advantages unrelated to economic efficiency or the public interest, proposals to limit the size of corporations met with easy defeat. Congress also turned down proposals to make corporate directors personally liable for certain illegal corporate practices (except where it could be proved that a particular director personally and willfully authorized the violation). And finally, Congress refused to make conviction of a firm for antitrust violations serve as *prima facie* evidence in individual suits by companies or persons claiming damages against the guilty firm.

Congressman Covington (D.-Ky.), who helped write the antitrust bills, inadvertently summed up the New Freedom's crippling ambivalence toward antitrust action:

> The equal and complete freedom in business, which is the way of peace and of success as well, is best promoted by the unrestrained and uncontrolled genius of the American business man. Consequently, it would be completely out of harmony with our present idea to establish a commission clothed with the effective power . . . to enforce fair competition, to prohibit unfair competition . . . and . . . to issue orders outlining the scope of unlawful operation of industrial business in this country.

For all the brave rhetoric about the need to inject an aggressive public policy into the economic processes, the Wilsonians proved squeamish about using "effective power." Perhaps it was because, despite the logic of their analysis, they remained timorous about shackling the institution they had identified for so long with "peace" and "success" and "genius." Perhaps, too, it was because they had discovered that "The General Interest" was an inadequate guide for the hard decisions about social priorities that an effective system of national regulation would require.

The Emergence of Group Interest Politics

As political crosscurrents buffeted progressive ideals, the Wilson administration approached the brink of acknowledging the legitimacy of group interests. In many respects, the legislation of 1916-20 seemed to follow the prescriptions of TR's "New Nationalism." Indeed, a number of historians have stressed this. Arthur S. Link, Wilson's most important biographer, has contended that in 1916 Wilson adopted the New Nationalism "lock, stock, and barrel." Arthur Schlesinger, Jr., has written in *The Crisis of the Old Order, 1919-33* (1957), that "The war completed Wilson's conversion . . . [to] the best New Nationalist of them all."

But a crucial difference remained. The "New Nationalism" offered official recognition to group interests in the nation's political life in exchange for a consensus on the subordination of all interests to the supreme interest of the nation. The war did produce that consensus, at least superficially: "The General Interest" simply was defined as "National Security." But within a month of the Armistice in November 1918, Wilson just about completely abandoned all the wartime programs that had coordinated industrial mobilization; the experiment in associated economic enterprise on behalf of The General Interest came to a stunningly abrupt end. Even for that reason alone it should appear plain that there had never been a genuine conversion to the "New Nationalism" but only an exercise in war emergency planning.

The war served Wilson's political needs. Without forcing him to abandon his commitment to the principle of individualistic competition, it enabled him to undertake certain political expedients that his principled opposition to the pressure of group interests would have denied him. The simulated New Nationalism of 1916-20 arose from political convenience in a period of international crisis, not from some ideological conversion on the part of the Wilsonians.

A brief review of the reform legislation of 1916 illustrates the point.

The Farm Loan Act. Early in 1916, Wilson proposed that Congress establish twelve Federal Land Banks authorized to grant five- to forty-year land-mortgage loans to members of "farm loan associations." The subsequent Farm Loan Act allowed any ten farmers to organize such an association—a farmer became a member by purchasing stock to the amount of 5 percent of his loan. The land banks raised their money by selling bonds—initially to the government, for which Congress appropriated $9 million.

Farm spokesmen had long argued that government had to underwrite long-term loans because private banks refused to assume the risks of most commercial agriculture. Farmers simply could not get long-term improvement capital to buy new land, to improve marginal land, to acquire expensive equipment, and the like at practical and amortizable interest rates. At stake (it was argued) was the family farm, and the ability of tenant farmers to acquire land of their own. In such terms, the intent of the measure seemingly fell well within the spectrum of progressive reform.

Yet, as already noted, Wilson had earlier rejected such proposals because they implied using federal credit on behalf of a special group of interests. Even at the end of 1914, when Carter Glass (D.-Va.), the powerful chairman of the House Banking and Currency Committee, once more urged Wilson to reconsider his position, Wilson had written him: "It is really my duty to tell you how deeply and sincerely I feel that Government should not itself be drawn into legislation for credits based on farm mortgages. . . . I have a very deep conviction that it is unwise and unjustifiable to extend the credit of the Government to a single class of the Community."

By 1916, however, Wilson was facing a campaign for reelection. He needed the votes of normally Republican midwestern farmers to convert his 42 percent popular plurality of the three-party campaign of 1912 into a popular majority in 1916. The rural credits proposal was designed specifically for that constituency. The war provided the rationale. To encourage farmers to expand production by clearing new land and using marginal soils, the government would assist by making credits more readily available.

The Warehouse Act. As the presidential election of 1916 drew closer, Wilson moved further to expand the farmers' access to credit. The demands of the war dovetailed with the political needs of an election year to justify for the Wilsonians the special treatment afforded farmers as against other kinds of businessmen. The Warehouse Act set up a system for licensing warehouses and standardizing crop grading procedures. This helped farmers to use their receipts for crops left in storage as collateral for short-term loans. It went a long way toward assuring farmers that crops would not spoil, or markets become suddenly glutted, as shipments suffered the irregularities created by the war. Although few noticed, this measure essentially enacted the Populists' "subtreasury" plan, once regarded as a radical thrust toward socialism.

The Adamson Act. Nothing could be more clearly a case of "special interest legislation" than the railroad arbitration act of August 1916. It was the first federal statute to intervene in the wage-bargain between private employers and their employees engaged in nongovernmental business. (Federal laws already governed the hours of labor of workers employed by the government or doing government contract work.) It dictated a settlement that established eight hours as the standard workday for interstate railroad workers, with extra pay for overtime. The measure was a "war emergency" bill, pure and simple. It did not signify a change in Wilson's philosophy but his response to the threat that a railway strike would paralyze the country at a critical time. On those grounds the Supreme Court decided, five to four (*Wilson* v. *New,* 1917), that the act was constitutional.

Toward a "Scientific" Tariff. In proposing a Tariff Commission, Wilson again gave the appearance of moving toward the "New Nationalist" brand of progressivism. "Taking the tariff out of politics" and "putting it in the hands of experts" seemed the most sensible, the most *scientific* thing to do, according to much progressive thinking. On the other hand, the idea seemed to concede the principle of *protectionism,* which Wilson and the Democrats avowedly opposed. What was the need for "experts" if not to compute the cost differentials between U.S. and foreign products and to apply a compensating protective duty? By 1916, however, Wilson was concerned not only about the votes of traditionally protectionist workers of some eastern states such as Pennsylvania and equally tariff-minded midwestern farmers, but also about the prospects of a sudden deflation when the war ended and the possibility that Europe might "dump" surpluses in the United States.

Labor's Toehold on "Legitimacy." Election year expediency, not a conversion to the New Nationalism, persuaded Wilson to sign the Kern-McGillicuddy Act on workmen's compensation. In scarcely any field was U.S. law more retarded. By 1900 every other industrialized nation in the world had begun to provide for compensation to workers injured in industrial accidents. In the U.S., in line with a social policy that generally acknowledged individual actions only, an injured worker or the bereaved family of a worker killed on the job had to sue for damages. Employers, in their own defense, could lawfully plead (a) that the worker understood in advance the risks of the job, (b) that the worker's own negligence contributed to the accident, and/or (c) that the negligence of a fellow worker, not of the employer, was responsible. Thus the law denied institutional responsibilities. That is, it refused to recognize that the nature of the industrial system itself created hazards for members of particular groups (e.g., factory, mine, and transportation workers) against which simple humanity demanded protection and recompense but for which no individuals—neither the victims nor the industrial proprietors—could be found justly responsible. By 1910, various states had passed employers' liability laws, reducing some of the pleas employers could use in their defense against damage suits; and the federal government had concocted an employers' liability law that applied to interstate railway workers. But the principle of having to prove liability in court remained, with all the delay, costliness, and frustration it implied.

In the spirit of the quest for social justice that conditioned conservative thought in the Progressive era, many large corporations began instituting accident insurance programs of their own. By 1908 business leaders and lawyers in organizations such as the National Civic Federation and the American Association for Labor Legislation began pressing for state and federal compensation laws. At least in part, motives included the hope of increasing labor productivity through improved morale, as well as deflating some of the current hostility toward corporations. In New York, stalwart conservatives such as Elihu Root helped enact a compensation law. But in March 1911 the New York Court of Appeals, with outrageously inept logic, declared the act unconstitutional (*Ives* v. *South Buffalo Rwy. Co.*, 1911). The decision was so unpopular it gave renewed impetus to the cause of popular judicial recall. To deflect this movement, conservatives joined reformers in pressing for new compensation legislation.

By 1914, despite the *Ives* decision, no less than fourteen states had enacted compensation laws, and within three years more only ten southern states, North Dakota, and the District of Columbia had no such law—offering to us another example of how the conservative impulse acted efficiently to produce a progressive reform. Even so, Wilsonian scruples resisted. In the first place, Wilson was apparently persuaded that workmen's compensation was unconstitutional (the Supreme Court would not "validate" it until 1917). Perhaps more important, Wilson remained committed to the principle of individual responsibility and reward. For these reasons Wilson repeatedly threatened to veto compensation bills in Congress—until 1916 when he signed the Kern-McGillicuddy Act.

Child Labor. Wilson's reversal on a federal child labor act, much like his conversion on workmen's compensation, seems to have been motivated by a bid for the support of the new, dynamic group of social workers, perhaps their clientele, and their urban progressive allies. Most of these people had been Republicans and had supported TR in

Street scene, early 20th century. A young entrepreneur on his way up? Or a victim of exploitation? How one answered that question was one way of separating progressives from conservatives. *Louis W. Hine, International Museum of Photography, George Eastman House*

1912. Wilson had objected to the federal government making social policy with respect to an employer's access to the labor market and a parent's right to send his children to work. But in 1916 he appears to have been willing to compromise his principles because he was so confident the Supreme Court would declare the measure unconstitutional anyway. Of course, the Court did just that in 1918 (*Hammer* v. *Dagenhart*) and again in 1922 (*Bailey* v. *Drexel Furniture Co.*) after Congress tried a second tack in 1918.

In any event, by 1916 Wilson was thoroughly preoccupied with the war. Nothing must be allowed to interfere with his ambition to mediate a just peace along the lines inspired by American progressivism—certainly not a defeat at the polls in November. Against this fact, everything appeared small—the nettlesome complexities of "social justice," the elusive nature of The General Interest, the enigma of maintaining an individualistic society amidst the growth of behemoth institutions, to say nothing of the expedients of partisan politics. Ironically, one fact obscured by the overwhelming importance of the war, even in 1916, was the failure of progressivism itself.

The Failure of Progressivism

To say that progressivism failed is not to deny that a remarkable number of social and political reforms made substantial contributions to a more humane and well-ordered society. Progressivism would have real, lasting effects toward the blunting of the sharper edges of self-interest in American life, toward the elimination of some of the cruelties suffered by the society's underprivileged—and therefore toward the heightening of civilized sensibilities in America.

On the Inadequacies of Mere Decency. Many changes during the Progressive era significantly improved living conditions for thousands who lacked effective bargaining power as individuals. Maximum hours laws now governed the employment of women and children; mine, factory, and tenement laws improved safety and sanitation; increased public expenditures for education and recreational facilities enlarged possibilities for good living. Efforts by employers to reduce industrial tensions gave rise to "industrial democracy" movements (sometimes referred to as "welfare capitalism"), whereby companies set up grievance procedures, employee stock-purchase programs, pensions plans, and company unions. Although the usual purpose was to undermine the independent labor union movement, many workers did enjoy immediate, if sometimes short-run advantages. At the very least, such things indicated that the "survival-of-the-fittest" doctrine was becoming bad form.

Such achievements deserve emphasis, not least because they materialized directly from the progressive habit of looking to standards of conventional morality and human decency for resolving diverse social conflicts. But the deeper nature of the conflicts confronting American society required more than the invocation of conventional standards. Many of the conventions themselves were at stake, especially as they bore directly upon how privileges and rewards were distributed among the American people.

To see this, it will be useful to refer once again to the Clayton Act. It is ironic, in view of the Wilsonian progressives' emphasis on competitive individualism, that the most dramatic features of the measure had to do not with its antitrust provisions but with those granting a kind of legitimacy to farm cooperatives and labor unions. It did this by giving those organizations specific formal *exemption* from the antitrust laws. The act declared that neither association of group interests should be viewed by the courts to be illegal in itself. "Nothing contained in the antitrust laws," read the act, "shall be construed to forbid the existence of labor, agricultural, or horticultural organizations . . . or to forbid or restrain individual members of such organizations from lawfully carrying out the legitimate objects thereof. . . ." Since the Supreme Court, in the Danbury Hatters Case (*Loewe* v. *Lawlor*), had held in 1908 that a union's actions were forbidden by the Sherman Act because they amounted to "combinations in restraint of trade," the Clayton Act seemed to have great significance. Gompers called it "the Magna Carta of Labor."

Events would prove Gompers mistaken. As he should have anticipated, the clinker lay in the words "lawfully" and "legitimate." Judges' interpretation of what actions were "lawful" and "legitimate" would continue for two more decades to be determined by their preference for a social policy that assigned highest priorities to the private commercial uses of property. Furthermore, neither Wilson nor Congress indicated at any time a wish to change that assignment of privilege. "The labor provision of the antitrust bill as agreed upon," Congressman Carlin (D.-Va.) confidentially advised

Wilson at the time, "gives labor the right to exist as an organization. . . . It does not exempt labor from specific acts which would constitute a restraint of trade or a conspiracy in restraint of trade." Indeed, in the 1920s, the courts applied antitrust sanctions against trade unions with unprecedented vigor. (See Chapter 5.) The Clayton Act "exemptions" would thus prove an illusion—a symbolic doffing of the hat to an interest group that Americans still preferred not to acknowledge.

On the other hand, before the Wilson administration was done, several sectors of the business community would win a longstanding quest for exemptions from the antitrust laws. Amendments to the Federal Reserve Act permitted banks to combine for overseas operations. The Webb-Pomerene Act of 1918 gave exporters collective pricing and marketing privileges, to make them more competitive with European cartels. The Esch-Cummins Transportation Act of 1920 virtually directed the railroad industry to consolidate the scores of separate lines into a few regional groups, to coordinate traffic policies, and to end most rate competition (ostensibly under the supervision of the ICC).

The Triumph of Big Business. Indeed, it would not be too much to say that, whatever the intentions, it was in the Wilson era that the corporate revolution fastened its hold on the American business system. Instead of producing conditions that would restore small unit business competition, the actions and inactions of the Wilson administration set the stage for a new merger movement in the 1920s that matched in its vigor and dimensions the movement that had subsided during the Roosevelt administration. To some degree, the resurgence of economic concentration proceeded for reasons having little to do with government. For one, several new giant industries, such as chemicals, rubber, and automobiles, matured during the period, and these industries followed the consolidating tendencies of the older ones at their comparable stages. But the new mergers also reflected the celerity with which corporate leaders exploited the loophole in the Clayton Act which permitted them to acquire the physical assets, though not the securities, of competing firms. Perhaps most of all, they exploited the Wilsonians' timidity in antitrust matters.

When the crunch came, the Wilson administration showed that it dreaded economic recession more than it feared business concentration. It drew back from effective action against trusts whenever it seemed such action might cause temporary economic distress. Thus, when his attorney general, James McReynolds, was pressing for penalties against the New Haven Railroad for gross antitrust violations, the president intervened, claiming he wanted to protect New England's rail system from further damage (that is, beyond what the Morgan interests had already inflicted). McReynolds proposed a special tax on the tobacco trust to put teeth in the Supreme Court's dissolution decree of 1911. But Wilson renounced the proposal at the first panicked outcry from corporate leaders that such a tax would mean Wilson really did intend to break up the big corporate structures and not merely prevent the growth of new ones, as Wilson had assured them in the 1912 campaign. In 1914, a recession threatened and financial leaders rallied to the time-honored practice of blaming it on reformers. Wilson responded with efforts to reassure corporation leaders not only by signing an ineffectual Clay-

RECORDED MERGERS OF LARGE MANUFACTURING
AND MINING CORPORATIONS, 1895-1929

These figures do not include every change of ownership or business transfer. They do include virtually all acquisitions involving corporations with widely held and publicly traded securities.

1895	43	1904	79	1913	85	1921*	487
1896	26	1905	226	1914	39	1922*	309
1897	69	1906	128	1915	71	1923*	311
1898	303	1907	87	1916	117	1924*	368
1899	1208	1908	50	1917	195	1925*	554
1900	340	1909	49	1918	71	1926*	856
1901	423	1910	142	1919	171	1927*	870
1902	379	1911	103	1919*	438	1928*	1058
1903	142	1912	82	1920*	760	1929*	1245

*Beginning with 1919, a more complete recording of smaller mergers is reflected in the larger figures. The two techniques are included for 1919 to suggest a rough basis for comparison of the pre-1919 and post-1919 figures.

SOURCE: *The Statistical History of the United States from Colonial Times to the Present.*

CONCENTRATION INDICATORS

Percentage Total Assets of all Nonfinancial Corporations (less taxable investments): largest 200 corporations

1909: 33.3   1929: 47.9

SOURCE: John M. Blair, *Economic Concentration* (1972).

Percentage Total Assets of all Manufacturing, Mining, and Distribution Corporations: largest 100 corporations

1909: 17.7   1919: 16.6   1929: 25.5

SOURCE: Norman R. Collins and Lee E. Preston, "The Size Structure of the Largest Industrial Firms," *American Economic Review*, December 1961, v. 51, p. 989.

ton Act, but also by appointing to the new Federal Reserve Board and the Federal Trade Commission men conspicuous for their sympathetic attitude toward the corporate revolution.

The Wilson administration's failure to act effectively against the ascendancy of giant corporations was matched by its positive aid to the trade association movement. In some measure, trade associations had arisen in reaction to the merger movement, and in this sense they served the objectives of the progressive decentralists by maintaining the viability of (relatively) small-unit business enterprise. The associations' policies typically were designed to keep all their members in business, even those competitively the weakest. On the other hand, insofar as such policies effectively gave sanctuary to inefficient firms, shut out new firms, set up production quotas, and indirectly implemented price fixing, they tended to violate the antitrust laws more clearly than did mergers.

The exigencies of war mobilization after 1916 depleted what was left of the Wilson administration's antitrust enthusiasm. In order to procure and allocate war matériel most efficiently, the administration authorized private business leaders to establish "war service committees." Each committee was composed of representatives selected by the firms and trade associations of each industry and was responsible for crucial decisions concerning what resources each industry needed, how war contracts should be distributed, what were "reasonable" prices, and what constituted "unfair labor practices" (mostly directed against employers who "raided" a competitor's work force, thus bidding up wages). Although nothing explicit was said about it, the government suspended the antitrust laws and created what amounted to government-authorized cartels.

The Denouement. Eventually a War Industries Board (WIB), War Labor Board, Food, Fuel, and Railroad Administrations, a Grain Corporation, and several other agencies were established to coordinate various resource mobilization activities. To "New Nationalist" progressives such as Herbert Croly, Walter Lippmann, and John Dewey, who had long deplored the centrifugal thrust and inefficiency of the competitive system, these agencies seemed almost the fulfillment of the scientific vision at work in social organization. The war agencies were to serve, moreover, as models for the industrial-code agencies and the principle of collective bargaining incorporated in the National Industrial Recovery Act of 1933—a fact that has led historians such as Link and Schlesinger to hail them as examples of how the Wilson administration moved to a position of "advanced progressivism" that would be adopted anew with the advent of the New Deal.

But the picture has been overdrawn. The wartime practices of consolidation and control not only would doom the decentralists' thrust for restoring an individualistic and competitive polity but Wilson would also disappoint the "New Nationalist," or so-called advanced progressives. It was the Wilson administration, not its reactionary successors, that dissolved the coordinating and planning agencies, returned the railroads to private control, planned the reduction in rates of the graduated income tax, and precipitously withdrew its endorsement of collective bargaining the moment the war ended. The reversal would do nothing to divert the consolidationist tendencies among business leaders, which federal policy had encouraged during the war; those tendencies accelerated in the business-can-do-no-wrong atmosphere of the 'twenties. The abandonment of the war agencies simply freed the now more highly concentrated and informed power of the private sector from whatever public-oriented constraints a progressive administration might hopefully provide.

In sum, the Wilson administration was ineffectual in stemming the tide of corporate ascendancy, group politics, and associational (as distinct from individualistic) behavior. Indeed, it would greatly contribute to the tide. Progressivism became caught up in its own timidities and ambiguities, in its failure to comprehend competing definitions of social justice, and, ultimately, in its preoccupation with a world at war.

SUGGESTED READINGS

Most textbooks, as well as the scholarly surveys of progressive reform, such as H. U. Faulkner's *The Quest for Social Justice* (1931), G. E. Mowry's *The Era of Theodore Roosevelt** (1958), and A. S. Link's *Woodrow Wilson and the Progressive Era** (1954), and Faulkner's volume in The Economic History of the United States series, *The Decline of Laissez Faire, 1897-1917* (1915), tend to imply without ever demonstrating that the legislative reforms of the period in fact solved the problems they were designed for. John Chamberlain, *Farewell to Reform** (1931), offers one early challenge to that view. More recently, Gabriel Kolko's *The Triumph of Conservatism** (1963) has gained much attention for its argument that progressive reform was all a shuck, that it was designed by Big Business in order to save inefficient capitalists from the perils of competition, and also to forestall real reform that might have benefited "the masses." The book has a great many flaws but gained a wide college audience in the 1960s and early 1970s because it expressed the popular urge to reject orthodoxy in scholarship as well as in politics and morals. Because it is often cited, it is worth a brief comment here. In general, Kolko claims that progressive reform enabled Big Business to put the federal government to work for it, to guarantee economic stability, social order, and high profits. In a sense, then, Kolko concurs in the view that progressivism succeeded, but challenges the view that progressivism was ever intended to benefit "the people." His book contains much worthwhile material, particularly the evidence that many different businessmen had a vital interest of one sort or another in the economic legislation of the day. But it is a one-sided, one-dimensional account that frequently misuses evidence, and in general is more likely to mislead than to inform a newcomer to the study of the period.

The point about business interest in reform was made earlier and with more accuracy in Robert Wiebe's "Business Disunity and the Progressive Movement, 1901-14," *Mississippi Valley Historical Review,* v. 44, March 1958, and Wiebe's *Businessmen & Reform** (1962); also, in many books concerned with special subjects, such as *The Decline of Agrarian Democracy** (1953), Grant McConnell, *Conservation and the Gospel of Efficiency** (1959), Samuel P. Hays, and *Railroad: Rates and Regulation* (1912), William Z. Ripley. R. M. Abrams, *The Issue of Federal Regulation in the Progressive Era** (1963), offers a brief introduction to the whole issue. For the story of how many of the regulatory agencies set up during the era often came to serve the businesses they were supposed to control, Marver Bernstein's *Regulating Business by Independent Commission** (1955) is well written and comprehensive, and G. Cullom Davis', "The Transformation of the Federal Trade Commission, 1914-29," *Mississippi Valley Historical Review,* v. 44, Dec. 1962, tells the story of what the Republican administrations did to this key progressive agency. S. P. Hays, "The Politics of Reform in Municipal Government in the Progressive Era," *Pacific Northwest Quarterly,* v. 55, Oct. 1964, makes the point that urban progressivism often operated to protect the dominant business and other elite groups; as does James Weinstein, "Organized Business

* Available in a paperback edition.

and the City Commission and Manager Movements," *Journal of Southern History,* v. 28, 1962. But J. Joseph Huthmacher, "Urban Liberalism and the Age of Reform," *Mississippi Valley Historical Review,* v. 49, Sept. 1962, attempts to locate urban reform energies in the ethnic lower classes, although mostly after 1912.

*Theodore Roosevelt** (1931) by Henry F. Pringle is an old, racy, and hostile biography that is still worth reading; the paperback version is abridged and lacks footnotes. William H. Harbaugh's *Power and Responsibility: The Life and Times of Theodore Roosevelt* (1961), reprinted in paperback as *The Life and Times of Theodore Roosevelt* (1975), is more scholarly and up-to-date. John M. Blum's *The Republican Roosevelt** (1954) is a brief and exciting essay. Although H. K. Beale's *Theodore Roosevelt and the Rise of America to World Power** (1956) focuses on foreign policy, it contains in the early chapters an exceptionally cogent analysis of TR's social and political views. But no one should overlook the brilliantly edited eight-volume collection of Roosevelt letters assembled and extensively annotated by Elting E. Morison, Alfred D. Chandler, and John M. Blum.

Pringle's highly favorable two-volume *The Life and Times of William Howard Taft* (1939) is amazingly still the best complete account of Taft's life and career. To fill the gaps: Kenneth W. Hechler's *Insurgency: Personalities and Politics of the Taft Era* (1940) and G. E. Mowry's *Theodore Roosevelt and the Progressive Movement** (1946) cover the political rebellion within Taft's party, the latter suggesting that TR's candidacy in 1912 cut the potential for radicalism in the progressive movement. James Pennick, *Progressive Politics and Conservation: The Ballinger-Pinchot Affair* (1968) discards the usual "people-versus-the-interests" approach for a sharp analysis of contending political and economic forces. For similar perceptivity on the tariff issue, L. Ethan Ellis', *Reciprocity, 1911: A Study in Canadian-American Relations* (1939) is especially noteworthy. On railroad regulation, whereas the older generation of historians told the story as "the people," or at least "the farmers," versus "the interests," now historians divide over whether regulation was deliberately designed to aid the railroad corporations, as in G. Kolko's *Railroads and Regulation* (1965), or resulted in the ruin of the industry, to the public's great loss, as in Albro Martin's *Enterprise Denied* (1971). Robert W. Harbison, "Railroads and Regulation, 1877-1916: Conspiracy or Public Interest?" *Journal of Economic History,* v. 27, June 1967; K. Austin Kerr, *American Railroad Politics, 1914-20* (1968); and Jordan Jay Hillman, *Competition and Railroad Price Discrimination* (1968), may help to put the issue in sensible perspective.

On Woodrow Wilson, Arthur Link's exhaustively researched multi-volume biography has reached volume 5 and the 1916 struggle to stay out of war. Arthur Walworth's two-volume *Woodrow Wilson* (1958) has the virtue of being complete and readable. John M. Blum's *Woodrow Wilson and the Politics of Morality** (1956), like his *Republican Roosevelt,* is a gem of analysis but is heavy on foreign policy; and John A. Garraty's *Woodrow Wilson* (1956) is a sharp, brief account. A few earlier works are exceptionally valuable: Harley Notter's *The Origins of the Foreign Policy of Woodrow Wilson* (1937) offers much about the premises of Wilson's thinking, as does William Diamond's *The Economic Thought of Woodrow Wilson* (1943).

The War Industries Board: Business-Government Relations During World War I (1974), Robert Cuff, "The 'Industrial-Military Complex' in Historical Perspective: World War I," *Business History Review*, v. 41, Winter 1967, Paul A. C. Koistinen, and, *Big Steel and the Wilson Administration* (1969), Mel Urofsky, are indispensable for the Wilsonian policies toward big business in the war period. Equally important for the crucial demobilization period, see R. F. Himmelberg's "The War Industries Board and the Antitrust Question in November 1918," *Journal of American History,* v. 52, June 1965 and "Business, Antitrust Policy, and the Industries Board of the Department of Commerce, 1919," *Business History Review,* v. 42, Spring 1968; while Susan Armitage's *The Politics of Decontrol of Industry: Britain and the United States* (1969) is a remarkably useful comparative study.

CHAPTER FOUR

AMERICA'S STAKE IN WORLD AFFAIRS: 1901-29

WORLD WAR I WAS UNQUESTIONABLY the crucial event of the first quarter of the century.* For some, it marked the transformation of Western culture, the end of an entire system of values that had once kept in check the baser passions of humankind. All the self-acknowledged heralds of global progress fell upon each other with murderous zeal. At its conclusion nearly eight million of Europe's and America's most promising youth lay dead from battle. Millions more suffered death from disease and starvation. The German, Austro-Hungarian, Russian, and Ottoman empires had shattered. Great Britain, long the chief organizer of the world's peace and one of the "victors" in the Great War, faced a future of economic and imperial decline, part of the price it had paid for its victory. Revolution ravaged eastern Europe; the specter of "atheistic bolshevism" haunted the West. Civil war stalked the continent. And across the Atlantic, in the New World, the ranks of the perennially self-satisfied, self-seeking, and cynical gained fresh recruits from among those once so hopeful and now grown suddenly weary of crusades, doubtful of enlightenment, disenchanted with the possibilities for human uplift, unsure of all they only recently had believed eternal and true.

In some ways it would be more accurate to say that the war merely confirmed the irrelevance of conventional wisdom for the social facts of twentieth-century life. Traditionalists, lingering on the notion that there was still such a thing as "civilized warfare," were unprepared for the loosing of mass passions. The horrors they witnessed goaded them to justify and to mandate a wide assortment of barbarities before it was over. As Charles de Gaulle would reflect many years later: "The Great War was a revelation. . . . The mass movements and mechanization to which men and women were subjected by modern life had preconditioned them for . . . the war of peoples." This was a war in which rational human restraints, supposedly developed during civilization's long progressive conquest over barbarism, failed to make a noteworthy appearance. After the war, only the most willfully insensitive could deny the demise of the old order.

The Shaping of Foreign Policy

Meanwhile the power of tradition continued to govern how leaders viewed the problems confronting them. In examining the decision to intervene in the European conflagration in 1917, one can discover all the main elements of United States foreign policy in the first quarter of the century. The discussion here first takes up, in detail, President Wilson's decision to intervene, then moves back in time to the "Dollar Diplomacy" of the Roosevelt and Taft administrations to show how intervention in 1917 grew out of historical commitments and value choices made by the American people, and finally follows the course of American foreign relations through the postwar period.

* The principal belligerents in the war were Great Britain, France, Russia, Belgium, Italy, Serbia, Rumania, and Japan (the "Allies") on the one side, and Germany, Austria-Hungary, Bulgaria, and the Ottoman Turks (the "Central Powers") on the other.

The inglorious massive horror of the World War is captured in this black and white sketch, "Shadows." *Library of Congress*

Three principal considerations guided the foreign policies of the major powers early in the century, and in varying intensities still do: missionary ambition, economic advantage, and national security. In periods of great confidence, Americans have tended—as they did at the turn of the century—to give the missionary motive extraordinary emphasis. In more recent times, national security has predominated. After 1919, when no power seemed capable of threatening U.S. security and when the American electorate buried missionary politics beside Wilson's League of Nations, economic advantage would remain the inspiration for the foreign policymakers—insofar as there was inclination at all to make policy regarding foreign affairs.

All three concerns entered into Woodrow Wilson's deliberations as he developed his response to the perils of the international situation created by the outbreak of war in August 1914. The weight to be given each of those concerns is a matter of historical judgment that depends crucially on a detailed examination of the facts Wilson himself surveyed in coming to his decision to ask Congress to declare war on Germany in April 1917.

Like all but a few Americans, Wilson had not thought much about foreign policy before becoming president, which allows us to assume that his reactions arose from values widely shared in the nation. From the beginning, public opinion appeared overwhelmingly pro-Allies, but not so strongly as to indicate willingness to get into the fray. On the other hand, millions of Americans with Irish or Scandinavian or German background—perhaps half the first- and second-generation American population—sympathized in some measure with the Central Powers, though hardly anyone imagined the possibility of war between the U.S. and Britain. President Wilson, keenly aware of these clashing preferences, implored the public to remain "impartial in thought as well as action" and to "put a curb upon our sentiments as well as upon every transaction that might be construed as a preference of one party to the struggle before another." Within three years, however, he made the decision to intervene.

The Road to War

German U-Boat Campaign. It is common knowledge that German U-boat policy at the start of 1917 provoked the U.S. declaration of war that spring. From the beginning of 1915, the U.S. had strongly protested the torpedoing of merchant and passenger ships without provision for the safety of noncombatants. By mid-1916 that policy had achieved measurable results. After the death of an American passenger aboard the English packet, *Sussex,* in March 1916, Wilson's warnings to the German government had brought a (somewhat ambiguous) pledge of compliance. Then, in December 1916, the German High Command decided it would risk American intervention by launching an unrestricted submarine attack on all shipping destined for Allied ports. Even if the Americans rose to the bait, the Germans reckoned, they would be unable to lend substantial aid to the Allies for at least a year, by which time the Allies, weakened by disruption of their supplies, would have lost the war.

The High Command announced its decision to the world in January 1917, and by February the U-boat fleet began sinking vessels at a rate exceeding even German expectations. President Wilson responded to these acts with a well-conditioned sense of outrage. In view of the "Sussex Pledge," the renewal of unlimited submarine warfare appeared to be little less than a treacherous move by an irredeemably savage nation. ("I was for a little while unable to believe that such things would in fact be done," Wilson reflected.) As Wilson saw it, not only had the Germans reneged on their word, their U-boat program meant they intended to deliberately "murder" thousands of human beings whose specific activities embodied no belligerent purposes. Meanwhile, the discovery in February that the Germans had attempted to secure an alliance with Mexico against the United States brought home to Americans the potential dangers of a German victory in Europe. With American shippers afraid to forward cargoes from Atlantic ports, and with export goods backing up in midwestern depots, President Wilson went before Congress in April, asked for and, four days later, got a declaration of war. The approving American press wondered only what had taken the president so many months to act, while most historians have acknowledged there was little else Wilson could do at that point.

The Debate Over Intervention. Controversy persists, however, over the propriety and wisdom of Woodrow Wilson's policies leading up to the denouement of 1917. Was it necessary to insist that American citizens had the right to travel into a war zone on the ships of belligerent nations? Was it worth risking war to demand safe passage of U.S. merchantmen bearing noncontraband cargoes to belligerent nations? Should the U.S. government have permitted American bankers to tie significant portions of the country's credit resources to the Allies' cause by making loans to the British and French governments? Was it truly neutral to accept British interception of American cargo ships enroute to neutral ports while issuing ultimatums to Germany?

These are telling questions, but they have greater force in the abstract and in retrospect than when placed in the specific historical setting in which Wilson's neutrality policy developed. For example, if Wilson had forbidden the belligerent nations to borrow from American citizens, that would have been not only a form of government intervention in private business practically without precedent in the recent history of the country, it would also have contravened international precedents. Much has been made of the fact that at the outset of the war the government did temporarily prohibit foreign loans, and then rescinded the ban in 1915 when, because of British control of the Atlantic, only the Allies could make practical use of American funds. The matter became controversial largely because Secretary of State William Jennings Bryan, in announcing the prohibition, commented somewhat irrelevantly that "Money is the worst of all contraband." At a time when animus toward "The Money Trust" still ran high, it was a popular thought. The ban originated, however, not as a foreign policy decision but as an emergency measure to stem the sudden outpouring of domestic funds as the European belligerents dumped their American securities in exchange for cash. Actually, the Germans protested the loan embargo the most emphatically, accurately claiming that the move violated international law. Neither they nor Bryan protested the lifting of the ban in 1915 when the danger to the U.S. monetary system had passed, and when the immediate future of the nation's exports appeared to depend directly on American financing of European purchases.

The issue of the right of Americans to travel, or to send shipping, into the "war zones" is a highly complicated one. At the time, it was additionally clouded by a series of events laden with emotion. For present purposes it may be sufficient to note that the United States did warn both sides that it would hold them accountable for losses sustained because of what the United States regarded as illegitimate wartime practices. But it was immeasurably more difficult to conceive of an appropriate postwar settlement of such claims when they concerned the loss of human life than when they arose over property damages. No Americans lost their life because of British actions, while about two hundred died before April 1917 from U-boat attacks. Most of the American fatalities occurred on May 7, 1915, when a U-boat sank the British luxury liner, *Lusitania.*

Impact of the Lusitania. In large measure the *Lusitania* incident accounts for the limited political options available to the Wilson administration. When the war began there were few precedents on which to base a neutrality policy. Among western countries it had become the practice—and therefore was widely accepted as "international law"—for warships to give warning to nonmilitary vessels flying an enemy flag or carrying contraband before sinking them, so as to permit the crew and passengers a chance to find safety in lifeboats or aboard the warship itself. This may have been practicable enough for surface cruisers. But tiny and vulnerable U-boats faced an obvious problem. Even an unarmed merchantman could, and in at least one early case did, sink a surfaced submarine by ramming it. Americans, however, conceded nothing to the Germans on this score. To begin with, the weapon itself, dependent on stealth and surprise, seemed unworthy of a civilized nation. Moreover, the chosen victims were not enemy warships, but noncombatant vessels carrying supplies. But if reasonable men might eventually acknowledge that modern weaponry and the phenomenon of total war made the old rules of belligerency irrelevant, the sinking of the *Lusitania* when the conflict was still less than ten months old and at the cost of 128 American lives aroused passions which conditioned U.S.-German relations thereafter.

"Too Proud to Fight". President Wilson did his best to deflect the blow to American sensibilities and to preserve the country's equanimity. He pleaded with the public to temper its response. "The example of America must be a special example," Wilson said, appealing to the very conviction—some would call it a conceit—which the American nation bore so boldly into the Progressive era. "The example of America," Wilson continued, "must be . . . [one] of peace because peace is the . . . elevating influence of the world and strife is not. There is such a thing as a man being too proud to fight. There is such a thing as a nation being so right that it does not need to convince others by force that it is right." It was indeed a noble effort, one worthy of a man who had been a member of the American Peace Society.

Some may argue nevertheless that there was less logic and nobility in the speech than usually is attributed to it. Wilson might have observed, for instance, that American

OCEAN STEAMSHIPS.

CUNARD

EUROPE VIA LIVERPOOL
LUSITANIA

Fastest and Largest Steamer
now in Atlantic Service Sails
SATURDAY, MAY 1, 10 A.M.
Transylvania, Fri., May 7, 5 P.M.
Orduna, - - Tues.,May 18, 10 A.M.
Tuscania, - - Fri., May 21, 5 P.M.
LUSITANIA, Sat., May 29, 10 A.M.
Transylvania, Fri., June 4, 5 P.M.

Gibraltar—Genoa—Naples—Piraeus
S.S. Carpathia, Thur., May 13, Noon

NOTICE!

TRAVELLERS intending to embark on the Atlantic voyage are reminded that a state of war exists between Germany and her allies and Great Britain and her allies; that the zone of war includes the waters adjacent to the British Isles; that, in accordance with formal notice given by the Imperial German Government, vessels flying the flag of Great Britain, or of any of her allies, are liable to destruction in those waters and that travellers sailing in the war zone on ships of Great Britain or her allies do so at their own risk.

IMPERIAL GERMAN EMBASSY

WASHINGTON, D. C., APRIL 22, 1915.

The German Embassy notice appeared directly under the Cunard advertisement in New York newspapers. But the "fair warning" did nothing to assuage popular wrath when the *Lusitania* went down off Ireland. *Culver Pictures*

citizens had no business traveling on a belligerent's ship, especially one probably carrying munitions as the Germans had claimed in paid newspaper advertisements before the *Lusitania* set sail. Because of the strength of the argument, Congress in February 1916 only narrowly defeated a joint resolution sponsored by Senator Thomas Gore (D.-Okla) and Representative Thomas McLemore (D.-Tex) which would have renounced diplomatic responsibility for such citizens.

But even if Wilson personally could have accepted that position in May 1915, it was scarcely a useful or even credible argument to make at that moment. The Germans had already offended a broad spectrum of European and American opinion by violating Belgian neutrality at the very outset, by the heedless bombardment of thickly populated cities, and by the deliberate sack of Louvain. These were tactics reminiscent of Attila the Hun, not expected of a nation which had laid claim to the leadership of civilization. And so, although Wilson may be faulted for uncritically sharing the popular view that the sinking of the *Lusitania* was an act of unmitigated barbarism, it must be noted that even *his* plea for calm met a hostile public. In fact, Wilson was forced to retract the import of his message the following day. "I was expressing a personal attitude, that was all," the president told reporters. "It should not be regarded as any intimation of policy."

When policy took form it did so in a series of tough protests which, to all effects, would have required the Germans to give up their submarine weapon altogether. The Germans in response chose to brazen it out, a tactic that won few friends anywhere. Whatever second thoughts anyone in the administration may have had later—and by 1916 Wilson began to have some—the crush of popular opinion in the U.S. after *Lusitania* inhibited their practical expression for at least the rest of the year.

Ever-Constricting Options. Once committed, moreover, the U.S. could not easily back down. The Germans retreated first. Aware that they had too few submarines to do more than harass Atlantic shipping while they provoked the Americans, German leaders decided to put the pack on a tight leash following the *Sussex* incident in the spring of 1916. When President Wilson interpreted the German message to that effect as a firm pledge, he drew a still more constricting noose around the policy options that remained. The message contained only qualified assurances, but by claiming that they embodied a solid and permanent promise Wilson left room for little choice but to regard any new transgression as further evidence of German disregard for honor, requiring the most drastic response. In some respects Wilson recognized his self-constructed trap. "Any little German lieutenant can put us into the war at any time by some calculated outrage," he remarked to a friend. That was during the presidential campaign that year in which the Democrats boasted of Wilson, "He kept us out of war." As it turned out, the German High Command did the job when it decided in December it finally had enough operable U-boats for a decisive blockade.

That Wilson refrained from asking for war for two months after the sinkings began suggests some policy options remained available. The president of the United States wields enormous persuasive power. If the administration's diplomatic posture, or "international law," or national pride were all that was at stake—not to belittle the power of pride, especially in that confident era—and if Wilson had declined to ask Congress for war, one may fairly guess that Congress would not have ventured on its own responsibility to demand it. If the response to the past crises could serve as a guide, the American public appeared eager to beat war drums while standing ready to support the president, even with some enthusiasm, in whatever he decided to do. The partisan opposition would have hurled a new barrage of epithets at Wilson, but the president would have had equally militant partisan defenders and some good arguments about Americans' lives and other costs of war on his side. He had withstood two years of bellicose vitriol (since early 1915 Theodore Roosevelt, for instance, had been denouncing him almost monthly as representative of all "professional pacifists . . . flubdubs and mollycoddles . . . every soft creature, every coward and weakling"), and his reelection in November 1916 seemingly endorsed his antiwar position.

Wilson Vulnerable. That Wilson did not follow this course left him exposed to the charge that he betrayed the mandate of 1916 and had opted for war out of a wrong-headed, moralistic willfulness. The terms in which he couched his war message, and the substance of the sustaining rationale thereafter, tend to confirm this view. "The recent course of the Imperial German Government," he told Congress on April 6, 1917, was "nothing less" than a war against the people of the United States, and indeed, "a war against all nations." "The challenge," he continued, "is to all mankind. . . . It is a fearful thing," he confessed, "to lead this great peaceful people into war, into the most terrible and disastrous of all wars, civilization itself seeming to be in the balance." But he buoyed himself up with the thought that America would be fighting "for the things which we have always carried nearest our hearts,—for democracy, for the right of those who submit to authority to have a voice in their own governments, for the rights and liberties of small nations, for a universal dominion of right by such a concert of free peoples as shall bring peace and safety to all nations and make the world itself at last free." Finally, that long remembered and much derided passage: "The world must be made safe for democracy. Its peace must be planted upon the tested foundations of political liberty."

Although the speech contained no more than the usual amount of cant for a war message, and probably a good deal less, it exposed the weak side of the war rationale. To a certain degree, Wilson himself perceived the frailties of the argument. "It would be impossible," he said privately, "for men to go through the dark night of this terrible struggle if it were not that they believed they were standing for some eternal principles of right." It was as if he were personally acknowledging that the whole intellectual progress of the era had already thrown into doubt the very notion of "eternal principles of right," but that *little else remained* to rally the necessary enthusiasm for effective war mobilization. The motivations he addressed still had profound meaning for that generation of Americans; the ideals of the progressive movement could still be invoked to martial support for a political cause. Nevertheless, too many people had already observed the imperfect honor Americans paid at home and abroad (especially in the western hemisphere) to the very ideals their president now professed to sanctify as the overarching purpose of the war. In the aftermath, as democracy suffered one body blow after another throughout Europe, the cause to which Wilson had dedicated American "lives and . . . fortunes, everything that we are and everything that we have" would come to seem both pompous and profligate.

The worst of it was that Wilson not only used those ideals to promote an efficient mobilization, he still mostly believed in them. Although he may have conceded that his rhetoric contained some license, there was precious little guile in his summons to war. Had it been otherwise, he might still have worked to prepare Americans for the tough choices that the postwar settlement would demand. Instead, he breathed new life into the progressive faith that the old consensus and harmony could be restored in America and exported abroad. Nor was he alone among progressives in hoping that the war might yet serve, where the progressive movement had faltered, to unite the country behind the values which America had historically cherished—to revitalize the force of such ideals in the nation's own life, and thereby to lend impetus to their dissemination throughout the world. The whole tragic story of Woodrow Wilson's postwar peacemaking struggle, at Versailles and on Capitol Hill, would follow inexorably from his having mounted this chimera.

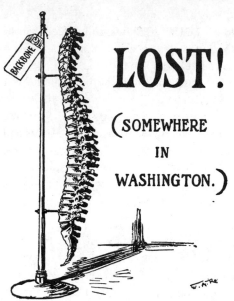

LOST!

(SOMEWHERE IN WASHINGTON.)

President Wilson's restrained protests to the German government, designed to establish a principle while keeping the nation out of war, often brought vicious characterizations by Republican partisans and the Anglophile press. Cartoon by Rogers in the *New York Herald*

Wilson Vindicated. But before one pursues too avidly the retreating ghost of Woodrow Wilson the Wrongheaded Idealist, one should pause to note that in the most important sense Wilson's neutrality policies had been successful: they had protected American shipping while keeping the U.S. out of war for more than two and a half years. When one reflects that at the outset practically no one expected the war to last longer than three months, that achievement demands full credit. One should consider furthermore that as late as February 1917—after he had learned of the new U-boat policy—Wilson continued to insist that the U.S. could best serve civilization by *staying out* of the war. We were the last of "the great white nations" to be free of the war, he repeated to different intimates on separate occasions over the course of a month. "It would be a crime against civilization," he said, for the U.S. to get into it. Even after he found it necessary to respond to the German action by severing diplomatic relations in February, he refused to concede that war should follow. "The President was insistent," his closest adviser, Colonel E. M. House, wrote in his diary, "that he would not allow it to lead to war. . . . He reiterated his belief that it would be a crime for this Government to involve itself in the war . . . [so] as to make it impossible to save Europe afterward."

In this perspective, it becomes evident that Wilson was determined to keep the U.S. at peace as long as it was possible to do so without jeopardizing what he conceived to be the nation's paramount interests. He pursued this determination even at the cost of what nearly all his own closest advisers as well as his pro-British social peers throughout the country presumptuously called "Honor." Wilson was convinced not only that the U.S. would wield greater power in shaping the postwar world if it conserved its strength while Europe fought; he also seems to have been more aware than most Americans of the domestic dangers that lurked behind the ardor of a nation at war. He knew that the passions of conflict would cut through the tolerance that sustained normal social relations among America's polyglot population. He had highlighted the point in his first message to the country following the outbreak of the war in 1914. In 1915 he had ordered transferred any officers found to be drawing up plans for a war with Germany. Well into 1916 he had resisted the preparedness campaigns sponsored on a national scale by private associations and encouraged by his political opponents, because he was convinced that war preparations would produce "a reversal of the whole history and character of our polity." He had maintained this position despite his belief that Germany had become infused with militarism, and that if it won the war Americans would "be forced to take such measures of defense here as would be fatal to our form of government and American ideals."

It becomes evident, further, that however much the president was convinced of the rationale he himself ultimately offered to the public for intervening in "The Great War," more urgent imperatives dictated (can one say "justified"?) his decision in April 1917. It may well be that in the rationale he offered Wilson merely put what he and probably most of his generation thought to be the best possible face on a bad situation. There were more crucial stakes in question besides those threatened by Germany's affront to "democracy," to the U.S. diplomatic posture, and to the sensibilities of "civilized nations."

The submarines struck at the vital nerve. By the end of March 1917, President Wilson was forced to conclude that unless the U.S. forcibly broke the German blockade, it would be in a poor position to adopt the very responsibilities to "civilization" for which he had persistently hoped its nonbelligerent status would best prepare it. Those tasks depended on the maintenance of American economic strength. Just before his reelection in 1916, he had told audiences that American postwar economic power would enable the U.S. to "determine to a large extent who is to be financed and who is not to be financed," and this would help the U.S. "to determine the politics of every country in the world." If Germany succeeded in blockading American ports—which is what shutting off trade with the Allies amounted to, given the volume of goods then crossing the Atlantic—it would have meant severe economic dislocations, probably a depression, at home. It would have left the U.S. desperately preoccupied with its own troubles at the very moment that Europe would most need help toward postwar reconstruction. Furthermore, Japan alone among the world's powers would emerge from the war with enhanced and possibly unopposed capabilities for international expansion. For a race-conscious Christian militant such as Wilson, that prospect demanded serious attention, as his reference to "great white nations" suggests. Altogether, acquiescence in the German U-boat policy would have reduced the United States to secondary status as a world power. That implied not only a negligible role in the postwar peacemaking negotiations, but also greatly diminished access for Americans thereafter to the world's markets, resources, and business opportunities.

It constituted, in brief, a more fundamental as well as a more immediate threat to American institutions and ideals than that which Wilson had fearfully foreseen in war mobilization itself. For it was axiomatic in American thought that any serious constriction of economic opportunities would jeopardize not merely the country's prosperity but the very qualities of its business sytem which made a free, democratic society feasible. If industry and agriculture could not continue to grow, if large-scale unemployment such as the country had experienced in the 1890s were to become chronic, if all the hopeful promises of American life were to be thus shut off, the electorate would force their government to take over functions conventionally consigned to the marketplace and to private contract. Such a situation would mean an end to the American social system as contemporaries had come to understand it.

American Stakes: The Long View

For Woodrow Wilson, the American stakes in international leadership had become clear long before World War I, and indeed before he entered politics. In an article called "Democracy and Efficiency" written for *Atlantic Monthly* in 1901, Wilson had stressed the serious problems confronting American democracy since the apparent "closing" of the frontier. The significance of the frontier for American liberal institutions had become a major contemporary theme after Wilson's fellow historian, Frederick Jackson Turner, had introduced it at an American Historical Association convention in 1893. In Wilson's view, the raison d'être of any form of social organization consisted in its contribution to the building of personal character. Liberal political and economic institutions were valuable precisely because they depended on self-help, constructive competition, and sympathetic intelligence—the chief ingredients of good character. Conversely, if demographic changes constricted individual energies and thereby undermined the development of character, liberal institutions would necessarily suffer. The nation, he observed, would have to look abroad to find new outlets for its energies and its produce.

Wilson went on to make a still more important point. The United States had to export its goods and its capital not so much to solve its own problems, but because it stood before the world as a herald of progressive democracy. America's example of a successful organization of social energies obliged it to assist less successful peoples. For Wilson, as for probably most of his American contemporaries, the United States had something special to bring to the world. That was not merely its republican institutions. It was rather the way in which private voluntary associations (governed by private contracts) had progressively taken over from the state the function of defining the relationships of individuals to one another.

Whereas most other peoples in the early twentieth century were still learning to conceive of liberty as a civil function privileged by the law of the nation-state, Americans had moved beyond that in the nineteenth century to define liberty in terms of the individual's access to economic opportunity. Wilson so defined it when he said, "If there is no free enterprise there can be no freedom of any kind." Louis Brandeis so defined it when he wrote, some years later, ". . . only through the participation by the many in the responsibilities and determinations of business can Americans secure the moral and intellectual development which is essential to the maintenance of liberty." Yet neither Wilson nor Brandeis was "probusiness." For them the essence of a man's liberty consisted in his ability to use his energies freely and to employ his property creatively to provide for his own sustenance and independence.

In the context of his time, when international politics still turned on the mock-heroic ambitions of monarchial dynasties and on nationalistic zealotry, Wilson's emphasis on business and commerce has extraordinary enlightened and humanistic qualities. Most of all, it had a special *relevance* to the pressing, everyday needs of the masses of humankind. It indicated a hardy, pragmatic optimism such as John Dewey expressed in 1920 in his book, *Reconstruction in Philosophy,* where he speculated "whether the national state . . . is not just another instrumentality for promoting and protecting the other and more voluntary forms of association," and might soon become merely the coordinator of "the activities of voluntary groupings . . . [which] have become the real social units."

Such optimism energized American expansion in the early twentieth century. It conditioned the thinking of the policymakers from 1901 to the end of the World War and lingered long after in various forms. The foreign policy it helped shape was called "Dollar Diplomacy" first by its advocates. Later, when commercial interests seemed to be dictating national policy, rather than the other way around, "Dollar Diplomacy" acquired a more sinister meaning.

The Partnership of Nationalism and Commercialism: 1901-14

But it would be a mistake to assume that most Americans early in the century thought much at all about foreign affairs. Domestic business opportunities and social issues took up about all the attention Americans could spare for public policy. This meant that those who sought support for a vigorous foreign policy had to pitch their appeal to concerns that might attract other groups. Businessmen were not often moved by appeals from ministers and politicians to help "spread Christianity" to the un-enlightened parts of the world, and at least until World War II they usually viewed with a cold eye the likely costs of advancing American power abroad. But when they had some specific objective overseas they knew well how to use the appropriate for-mulas about "national honor" and "Christian obligation." American nationalists, like Theodore Roosevelt, on the other hand, often railed against "men of mere wealth to whom the stock market is everything and whose short-sighted vision is bounded by the horizon of a material prosperity" that would render the country incapable of achieving "the position to which it is entitled among the nations of the world." But TR and his expansionist friends had to appeal to the business community for support in building a big navy, and for such purposes "the need of American producers for foreign markets" became a forensic standby. Civil servants in the commerce and state departments meanwhile staked their careers on extending the nation's commitment to international affairs. They developed a strong professional interest in publicizing the strategic and economic costs to the U.S. of permitting foreign governments and businesses to preempt opportunities in various territories over the globe.

On the whole, it is safe to say that despite the nearly ubiquitous references to "foreign markets" in the rhetoric of expansion, the nation's leaders at the turn of the century sought primarily to direct the United States toward the paths to greatness. To put it less grandly, they wished to make the United States count for more in the decisions that governed the world's progress. It seems clear that the commercial motif largely served as handmaiden to such nationalist ambitions. As the late Howard K. Beale observed in his remarkable study, *Theodore Roosevelt and the Rise of America to World Power* (1956): "Economic factors were important in imperialism and were to become important in American expansionist foreign policy of the twentieth century. But the primary concern of Roosevelt and his fellow expansionists was power and prestige and the naval strength that would bring power and prestige."

The expansionists had to cope with the fact that other nations already dominated the course of world developments, and were bent on expanding their influence still further. To gain admission to the councils of power, the United States had to make its strength evident. But more than that, it had to make believable its willingness to assert its power. This required more than building a navy and putting it on display as Theodore Roosevelt did when he sent "The Great White Fleet" around the world in 1908. Rather, the United States had to establish real stakes in international developments in defense of which Americans could be expected to use force.

Dollar Diplomacy and Power Politics in the Far East. Thus, beginning with Theodore Roosevelt's administration, and for the next twenty-five years, the State Department encouraged American bankers to invest in China, in order to establish that maintaining "the Open Door" was not merely an empty statement of principle but an assertion of substantial intentions:

> The nations that finance the great Chinese railways and other enterprises will be foremost in the affairs of China [a State Department memorandum reported in 1909] and will give the voice of the United States more authority in political controversies in that country which will go far toward . . . the prevention of the establishment of predominant interests and influences at Peking on the part of other powers.

The department also used what influence it had to persuade the Chinese government to contract with the Bethlehem Steel Corporation for the construction of warships. The Taft administration employed various forms of cajolery to induce J. P. Morgan and other American financial houses to join an international consortium of bankers then organizing to underwrite development programs in northern China—principally to deter the Japanese there. Investment prospects in China, however, were never very bright, and when Woodrow Wilson entered the White House and denounced the consortium for binding China to subserviency, he had already been told by a delegation of the American bankers that they would be relieved to be done with it. Within five years, however, again fearing Japan's unchallenged power in China, Wilson urged American bankers to participate in a new consortium as a patriotic duty!

Actually the policymakers recognized from the beginning that even the establishment of some economic stakes in the Far East would not suffice to deter any nation, such as Japan, that chose to employ force to gain its objectives there. Roosevelt, who had been directly instrumental in the acquisition of the Philippines from Spain in 1898, began to regard those islands as America's most vulnerable defense problem soon after he became president. Japan's own expansionist ambitions constituted enough of a worry, especially after Japan's astounding victory over Russia in 1905. But in addition the Americans, particularly San Franciscans and Californians generally, persisted in provoking Japan by a series of legislative outrages designed to make life in America unbearable for Japanese immigrants. Federal, state, and municipal statutes deprived Orientals of the privilege of becoming naturalized citizens and of the right to own land, and their American-born children, U.S. citizens by birthright, were denied access to public schools. These measures were supposed to protect American working standards, such as they were. Just how was not altogether clear, but it assuredly exposed U.S. interests in the Far East to some form of retaliation by Japan. "Our vital interest," Roosevelt told Taft in 1910, "is to keep the Japanese out of our country and at the same time to preserve the good will of Japan." He was even willing to sacrifice the "Open Door" for the purpose, especially since he recognized that "the 'open-door' policy, as a matter of fact, completely disappears as soon as a powerful nation determines to disregard it, and is willing to run the risk of war rather than forego its intention."

Three times before 1920 the U.S. was forced to acknowledge "that territorial contiguity creates special relations" between Japan and the countries washed by the Yellow Sea. In 1905 the United States became the first nation to recognize Japan's hegemony over Korea, in exchange for Japan's renunciation of any interest in the Philippines. The accommodation was reaffirmed in 1908 when Secretary of State Elihu Root and Ambassador Kogoro Takahira agreed that each country would respect the other's Far Eastern interests, including Japan's recent penetration of Manchuria. In 1917, by a protocol that was to remain secret for sixteen years, Secretary of State Robert Lansing and special minister Viscount Kikujiro Ishii agreed that "Japan has special interests in China, particularly in the part to which her possessions are contiguous."

The Monroe Doctrine Twentieth-Century Style. In the western hemisphere, meanwhile, the United States had of course long asserted its own special prerogatives by means of the Monroe Doctrine, which was seventy-eight years old when Theodore Roosevelt became president. In the new century, the doctrine acquired new characteristics. For one thing, with the growth of German naval power it became evident that the Americans could no longer depend on the British to prevent potentially hostile powers from securing military footholds in Latin America. The Americans in fact bristled as much at the British approach as at any other nation's—as when England threatened force against Venezuela in a boundary dispute with British Guiana in 1895, or again in 1913 when His Majesty's navy lowered its guns toward Nicaragua and forced the government there to honor its debts to foreign creditors, mostly British. In the latter case, Secretary of State Philander Knox protested to the British ambassador that it was time London understood that Central America "lay especially in our sphere of influence." But on the whole, the British were pleased to turn over to the Americans responsibility for policing the New World.

Cuba. Besides building a navy commensurate with the new tasks, U.S. policymakers worked to remove the conditions that invited Old World intrusions into the hemisphere of the Americas. The special relationship with Cuba provided the model. In going to war against Spain in order to end that country's barbaric repression of Cuban patriots (at least as the Americans viewed the issue), and also to eliminate the unsettling disorders in the nearby island, the United States had underlined its missionary objectives by declaring in advance its commitment to Cuba's full independence. But if the United States was to prevent a recurrence of disorders that would likely serve as an invitation for some other European power to replace Spain on the island, it would have to exercise some control over what happened there.

The Platt Amendment signified the Americans' belated recognition of the fact. In drafting the treaty recognizing Cuba's independence, preliminary to the withdrawal of the American military administration on the island in 1903, the Americans tacked on a special proviso, named after Senator Orville H. Platt of Connecticut, Chairman of the Senate Committee on Foreign Relations, who wrote the provisos originally into the Army Appropriations Act of 1901. According to the terms of the amendment, which the Cubans had to incorporate into their constitution as well, Cuba pledged to make no treaties or financial agreements with any foreign country that might impair its self-government, and it granted to the United States the right to intervene to quell any disorders that likewise might threaten its independence. The United States also received the right to oversee Cuba's debt management so as to preclude threats of intervention by foreign governments on behalf of their bondholders' just claims.

Apart from brandishing its club, the United States adopted special measures to aid the Cuban economy. In 1903, President Roosevelt pressured Congress into accepting a reciprocity tariff treaty which opened the U.S. market to Cuban sugar on a preferential basis, at some cost to U.S. sugar producers. The purpose was to avoid the necessity of fulfilling the commitments specified in the Platt Amendment by helping the Cubans to stabilize their economy and hence their politics. It could be argued, surely, that by encouraging Cuba's commitment to a staple crop economy, reciprocity served poorly the end of enhancing Cuban self-sufficiency and independence. But then Cuba had been wedded to such an economy for half a century before it became a "client" of the United States, and it has not rid itself of the condition in the years since Fidel Castro severed the client relationship in 1959.

The Spread of Intervention. Meanwhile, the facade of legality afforded by the Platt Amendment proved quite unnecessary. The United States exacted less extensive treaty privileges from the Dominican Republic, Haiti, Panama, and Nicaragua during the next fifteen years. By the terms of the Washington Convention of 1907, the United States attempted to establish, in tandem with Mexico, unofficial status as international policeman for the Central American republics; and, in fact, in 1910 Mexico sent warships to settle disturbances between Nicaragua, Honduras, and Guatemala. But with or without benefit of treaty rights, the United States intervened militarily in at least a half-dozen Latin American countries. The plea of national self-interest and security, as well as the need to protect life and American-owned property where no effective local government could or would, provided sufficient justification.

The rationale for intervening in the affairs of weaker countries rested essentially on the assumption that as a principal agent of civilization the United States was obliged to use force on behalf of its own security and in the name of social order and progress. For the record, and in order to avoid setting inconvenient precedents in international law which might complicate the relationships of the greater powers to one another, the official explanations for each intervention stressed the protection of lives and property, and also treaty "obligations" where they might reasonably be inferred. But in fact, all the powerful nations of the world assumed their right to knock heads together on behalf of higher causes usually associated with the more powerful countries' national interests.

TR's Canal and His "Corollary." In 1903, Theodore Roosevelt had resolved the problem of an isthmian canal through foreign territory by applying precisely such a principle. When Colombia declined to act on a United States offer to purchase canal rights across the isthmus of Panama, which at the time was a Colombian province, Roosevelt proceeded to help Panamanian patriots to wrest their independence from Colombia and then concluded the deal for the canal zone with their spokesmen instead. "The United States," he wrote privately in 1903, "is certainly justified in morals, and therefore . . . in law[!] . . . in interfering summarily in Panama and saying that the canal is to be built and that they [the Colombians] must not stop it." Officially, for the benefit of congressional critics, Roosevelt denied any American role in the final, successful rebellion of Panama against its parent country. But years later, when bravado seemed appropriate, he declared: "I took the Isthmus, started the canal and then left Congress not to debate the canal, but to debate me."

Possession of the canal heightened Americans' sensitivities about "defense perimeters." Creating outposts beyond U.S. borders required new measures for protecting them. In the dual interest of liberating Latin Americans from the threat of European domination and the United States from the anxieties caused by a powerful European presence nearby, the State Department adopted a policy of encouraging American bankers to replace European investors. The premise was that if Latin American governments defaulted on their debts they would have only the United States to answer to. Presumably, the United States would give fairer treatment to its neighbors than European governments customarily did. But in addition, Americans would face no threat of armed intrusions by European powers into countries that sat astride U.S. commercial and naval routes. Alternatively, the United States would have to assume responsibility for guaranteeing "justice" to European bankers in the event of defaults.

These considerations gave rise to Roosevelt's "Corollary" to the Monroe Doctrine. Originally TR had argued, as in a letter to a German friend in 1901: "If any South American State misbehaves toward any European country, let the European country spank it." In 1904, the Dominican Republic failed to make its debt payments—

because of the usual "revolutionary" disorders—and several European nations prepared to despatch warships to the Caribbean, Roosevelt remained aloof. "If I possibly can," he said, "I want to do nothing. . . . If it is absolutely necessary to do something, then I want to do as little as possible." But then an international court of arbitration, deliberating on the claims of European creditors against Venezuela, granted the best awards to bondholders whose government—specifically Germany—had sent warships to bombard Venezuelan cities. Roosevelt finally realized that unless the United States interposed its own "good offices" (or at least its power) in such disputes, the Caribbean would likely become the scene of major naval activity for European powers.

"We must make it evident," Roosevelt announced to Congress that December, "that we do not intend to permit the Monroe Doctrine to be used by any nation on this Continent as a shield to protect it from the consequences of its own misdeeds against foreign nations." The United States, said the president, would not go to war to prevent a foreign power from collecting a legitimate debt from an American nation; on the other hand, it would seriously jeopardize U.S. interests if a foreign power took over an American republic's customhouse to ensure payments, because even a temporary occupation might become a permanent one. "The only escape from these alternatives," Roosevelt concluded, "may . . . be that we must ourselves undertake . . . [to see to it that] a just obligation shall be paid." In 1907, when local disorder again threatened payments on the Dominican Republic's foreign debts, the United States took over the San Domingo customhouse.

The United States thus became committed to a two-headed policy that soon proved unmanageable, although none of successive administrations through 1929 fully learned the lesson. On the one hand, to avert military interventions in Latin American nations the State Department encouraged American businessmen to extend their interests into their economies. The theory was that a steady, prosperous economy might indeed help to stabilize and even liberalize Latin American governments. But on the other hand, U.S. policymakers could not expect American businessmen to venture south on a large enough scale unless their government first assumed some responsibility for maintaining political stability in those countries. Beyond such minimal assurances of a stable environment in the host countries, U.S. diplomats felt called upon to assist American investors, at least in some small way compared to what the European and Japanese governments afforded their businessmen. "Today, diplomacy works for trade," remarked Secretary of State Philander Knox in 1909, "and the foreign offices of the world are powerful engines for the promotion of commerce of each country. With the expansion of American commerce it becomes imperative that American exporters should have equally efficient support from their government." And in 1915, Secretary of the Treasury William G. McAdoo wrote to Secretary Robert Lansing: "I think it is essential, if we are to accomplish anything at all [toward replacing European capital in Latin America with U.S. capital], that this Government shall give such assurances to the American bankers and investors such as Great Britain gives the British bankers and investors, namely that the Government will see to it that the bonds and obligations of foreign governments, bought in good faith . . . are protected."

Logically, the McAdoo proposition should have required some government restraints on American business operations abroad in order to ensure that they did proceed "in good faith"—that they were not exploitive, monopolistic, corrupt, or corrupting. But the idea of supervising business ventures abroad departed even more sharply from traditional American government functions than did active promotion; and so logic went begging. By the time McAdoo urged his views upon the State Department, U.S. troops and warships had already seen action in Panama, Nicaragua, Honduras, San Domingo, Haiti, Mexico, and, once again, Cuba.

Actually, few if any of these interventions either protected or were designed to protect the interests of a foreign investment or any general U.S. trade policy. Indeed, few of them arose directly from economic issues of any sort. Political concerns in each case predominated.

Cuban insurgents, for example, learned quickly that the best way to overturn an entrenched domestic political faction was to provoke a visit from the United States marines. In view of the "obligations" stipulated in the Platt Amendment, this was achieved by instigating civil war. "We prefer a new American intervention that will guarantee future legal elections," declared a rebel leader in 1906. "We would much rather trust Roosevelt," he continued, "than [President Estrada] Palma." Badly informed about the true situation in Cuba, Roosevelt too hastily sent the troops, then regretfully kept them there for three years to preserve American "prestige" until a settlement was achieved in 1909. Of course, ruling factions were equally adept at luring U.S. marines to their assistance. American troops spent the better part of twenty years in places like Panama, Haiti, and Nicaragua at the invitation of the host governments.

The Mexican Revolution. A brigade or two of U.S. marines and a warship anchored in the harbor of a principal port city usually sufficed to intimidate insurgents and governments in the weak Caribbean and Central American countries. But Mexico presented a different problem. Its territory is too vast, its society too well organized, its elite too large and advanced, to permit such casual intrusions. Until 1911, in any event, no such action was called for. Mexico had experienced remarkable stability for more than forty years, as the result of the effective dictatorship of Porfirio Díaz. In addition to imposing authoritarian order on the country, Díaz encouraged national economic growth by liberalizing Mexican law in order to invite extensive foreign investment in Mexican land and resources. Then, in 1911, Díaz was overthrown, and his successors declared their intention of carrying out broad economic and social reforms. The proclaimed revolution directly threatened the land holdings of the Catholic Church, and the subsoil rights of the mostly foreign-owned mining and petroleum companies.

Although the Mexican Revolution differed from all other Latin American insurgencies of the period in that it offered genuine prospects of social change, in two consequential respects it followed the more common pattern: the new government prepared to default on the country's foreign debt; and factional warfare quickly erupted among various contenders for power. Only shortly before Woodrow Wilson entered the White House in 1913, the revolutionary government's first president,

Francisco Madero, was overthrown and murdered by counterrevolutionaries led by General Victoriano Huerta. Greatly indignant over such barbarism, Wilson departed from the usual diplomatic practice of granting recognition to new governments that merely gave evidence of firm governing control and without regard for the character of such governments; he refused to recognize Huerta's government and, moreover, vowed to depose him. To this end, he secured British aid in isolating Huerta, lifted an arms embargo whose purpose was to deprive insurgents of weapons for use against the constituted government, and found an excuse to land marines in Vera Cruz.

From the point of view of Wilson's diplomatic objectives, the Vera Cruz adventure had mixed results. The Mexicans resisted the landing, many men were killed, and the intervention seriously compromised the United States' diplomatic posture of benevolence. Indeed few incidents have had such a thoroughly souring influence on Latin American attitudes toward the U.S. On the other hand, it contributed to Huerta's overthrow by General Venustiano Carranza's "Constitutionalists," and this encouraged Wilson to hang on to the belief that "moral diplomacy" might work.

It was not until 1916 that Wilson began to discover his error. Only belatedly he recognized that the strongest support in the United States for intervention came from the most reactionary and self-serving sectors of American society, particularly from certain mining and petroleum companies that sought to use U.S. power to protect their special interests. "The foreign diplomacy with which she [Mexico] has become bitterly familiar," President Wilson told the American public in October 1916, "is the 'dollar diplomacy' which has almost invariably obliged her to give precedence to foreign interests over her own. . . . Most of the suggestions of action come from those who wish to possess her, who wish to use her, who regard her people with . . . a touch of contempt, who believe that they are fit only to serve and not fit for liberty of any sort." These domestic forces would spoil Wilson's intentions of using U.S. power for ensuring responsible, constitutional government in Mexico for as long as he continued to meddle there.

For their part, Mexicans of every faction resisted all *norteamericano* interference. Carranza's assumption of power did not end civil war in the country, and to hold his position Carranza could scarcely appear to be "Wilson's choice." Indeed, each faction readily exploited the political benefits of appearing to be the special target of U.S. ire. On that principle, Pancho Villa, whose efforts to overthrow Carranza had been foundering, chose the ultimate provocation. In January 1916 he stopped a train in northern Mexico and executed sixteen of seventeen American engineers whom he found on board. When that evoked no immediate response, Villa's troops crossed the border into New Mexico and shot up the town of Columbus, killing nineteen people.

The uproar in the United States that followed finally overcame Wilson's resistence, especially since 1916 was an election year. When Carranza could not (or, as some Americans believed, would not) bring Villa to book, Wilson sent Brigadier General John J. Pershing with six thousand troops to do the job. But Villa proved elusive and Pershing unimaginative. The "punitive expedition" penetrated more than three hundred miles into Mexican territory, clashed with Carranza's army, nearly triggered full-scale war, yet failed to find Villa.

Pershing's troops, in pursuit of Pancho Villa, were swallowed up by the vast desert hills of northern Mexico. Wilson withdrew the "Punitive Expedition" when German resumption of unlimited U-boat activity brought the U.S. to the brink of intervention in Europe. *U.S. Army Photograph*

Because the troops failed in their mission, they remained for nine months. Long before the Vietnam War, it was a weakness of United States presidents to persist in an ill-chosen policy after its futility had been demonstrated. Carranza's repeated denunciations of U.S. "aggression" exasperated President Wilson, who seemingly could not appreciate why Carranza could not understand that he intended no conquest but only to capture Carranza's own mortal enemy. Yet as a matter of pride rather than of principle or tangible interest, Wilson found it impossible to back off. Americans generally found it inconceivable that their purposes might be successfully thwarted by "lowly" Mexicans. In fact throughout the Carribbean, when Americans met resistance, they responded by trying harder and by staying longer and longer: in Haiti from 1915 to 1932, in the Dominican Republic from 1916 to 1924, in Nicaragua from 1916 to 1926.

Impending war with Germany at the end of January 1917 finally gave Wilson the opportunity to "save face" according to his own lights—while recalling Pershing from

Mexico. And although after Germany's defeat many political leaders, as well as spokesmen for the oil industry and others for the Catholic Church, resumed demands for intervention, Wilson's better judgment finally prevailed. His successors in the presidency showed similar restraint. In the 1920s, an accommodation with Mexico over settlement of Mexico's foreign debt and the treatment of foreign investors was worked out with the aid of an international bankers' committee headed by Thomas Lamont of J. P. Morgan and Company.

The Maturing of Wilson's Foreign Policy. After 1917 the war turned Wilson's attention almost entirely to matters of foreign policy. Wilson appears to have conceded, at least privately, the futility from every vantage point of military intervention in Latin American countries. But in the interest of preserving America's military security and promoting its future economic advantages, Wilson brought to maturity his predilection for using American business as a political tool. To this end, he fully developed his predecessors' policy of encouraging American financiers and industrialists to establish themselves abroad, to displace the Europeans and Japanese wherever possible and to preempt newly developing opportunities. The Bureau of Foreign and Domestic Commerce began large-scale operations—which Herbert Hoover would augment still further during his term as secretary of commerce (1921-29)—as advance agent and drummer for American business interests overseas. The State, Commerce, and Treasury Departments, aided by war agencies such as the U.S. Shipping Board and the War Trade Board, arranged to withhold funds and supplies made scarce by the war until various Latin American governments agreed to reorganize their finances and trade patterns in ways advantageous to American venturers. New administration-sponsored legislation encouraged American banks to open branches overseas, to deal in international acceptances, and to combine among themselves with immunity from the antitrust laws in order to operate abroad. Export companies gained similar immunity in the Webb-Pomerene Act of 1918.

All these things reveal some of the paradoxes and ironies of the Wilsonian foreign policy, as well as the roots of its failure. Somehow, despite his fine perceptions about the threatening growth of monopolistic power in the domestic economy, Woodrow Wilson continued to behave as if the economic model of liberty that had worked apparently so well in the nineteenth century would continue to work in the twentieth century; and, moreover, that it would work in the international scene without even the frail safeguards that he attempted to construct domestically by means of the New Freedom program of his first administration. In contemplating the possibility of war, Wilson had remarked in 1915 that all he stood for as a reformer would be lost: "The people we have unhorsed will inevitably come into the control of the country," he predicted, "for we shall be dependent upon steel, oil, and financial magnates." On another occasion he said, "We shall have to get the cooperation of big businessmen and, as a result they will dominate the nation for twenty years after the war comes to an end." How curious, then, that insofar as Wilson's international objectives depended on the expansion of American business overseas, even his peacetime policies implied that outcome!

The trouble was, Woodrow Wilson never thought through the linkages between his reform objectives and the means for achieving them. His foreign policy, like his domestic policy, suffered from a failure of nerve. He wanted to promote a new society but could not yield on principles that continued to sustain the old. He distrusted bankers and accused them of using other people's money to become rich without performing useful work; yet he turned to them all the same to implement his policies in Latin America and Asia. In 1914, when Secretary of State William Jennings Bryan suggested using U.S. government credit to refinance Central American republics that had been perpetually victimized by private European financiers, Wilson declined. He cited the principle that the U.S. government could not usurp the economic role of American private bankers—whose services he proceeded to press upon the Latin nations to the south. The principle made even less sense when Wilson applied it to the postwar reconstruction of Europe.

We have noted how important it was to Wilson's plans for shaping the new postwar diplomacy that the U.S. preserve its economic strength, and that it use its financial leverage to gain diplomatic advantages against the major powers in the interest of a lasting peace. "When the war is over," he had told Colonel House, "we can force [the Allies] to our way of thinking, because by that time they will . . . be financially in our hands." Yet the moment the war ended, Wilson cut off all Treasury loans to foreign governments. For some reason, just as the opportunity arrived for the United States to use its economic leverage in accord with publicly determined policy, the administration came to view European reconstruction solely in terms of the future of Europe's ability to buy American goods. And from that skewed angle, Wilson and his advisers could only express their unwillingness to subsidize the American export industry! "Governmental financial assistance in the past," declared Secretary of the Treasury Carter Glass in 1919, ". . . has apparently led our industrial concerns to the erroneous expectation that their war profits, based so largely on exports, will continue indefinitely without effort or risk on their part. . . . Those industries which had been developed to meet a demand for great exports, paid for out of government war loans . . . [must now] create . . . the means of financing [their own] export business." The anti-special interest attitude seemed admirable. But in the meantime it caused the government to surrender a major diplomatic weapon to private bankers, whose international interests were only coincidentally congruent with those of Woodrow Wilson's postwar hopes.

Toward a "New Diplomacy": Preparing for Peace

Paradoxically, Wilson's preoccupation with the war itself may have distracted him from his prewar diplomatic strategies. First, the assertion of clear-cut war aims and, later, the mechanics of drafting the peace treaty at Versailles took about all the energies Wilson could spare on diplomatic strategies.

The Fourteen Points. Wilson set forth American war aims in a series of declarations, published in January 1918 and quickly dubbed the Fourteen Points. At the time, he purported to speak for the Allies as well. What inspired the Points was the Russian Bolshevik coup in November 1917, and the revelation by the new Russian leaders of secret treaties among the Allies for postwar territorial annexations. The Soviet government, on the brink of a separate peace with Germany, called upon the peoples of the world to repudiate their imperialistic governments and to end the war. Wilson sought to clarify the liberal-humanist objectives of the nations united in the effort to defeat the autocratic Central Powers.

Without repudiating the war treaties, Wilson proposed a new, postwar diplomacy based on "open covenants, openly arrived at," with "no private international understandings of any kind" but rather a concert of all nations participating without discrimination in the world's trade and resources. Although Wilson opposed colonialism in principle, he shared the contemporary European assumption that most of the peoples in the poorly organized regions of the world were unprepared for self-government. He demanded, however, that "the interests of the populations concerned must have equal weight" with the rival claims of the imperial powers to sovereignty over them. The largest number of points concerned the safeguarding of the right of European peoples to self-determination in nationhood. These alluded in particular to the founding or reconstitution of nations, such as Poland, Yugoslavia, and Czechoslovakia, that were formerly provinces of Austria-Hungary, Germany, and the Russian empire. For Wilson, the key proposal was the fourteenth, which stated the Allies' commitment to international collective security under the aegis of "a general association of nations," whose power would afford "mutual guarantees of political independence and territorial integrity to great and small states alike."

The U.S. Role in Ending the War. By the time the United States entered the war, it had apparently settled into a devastating stalemate. Germany's plan to win in six weeks by sweeping through undefended Belgium and capturing Paris foundered in the Fall of 1914. First, the Belgians unexpectedly put up a fierce struggle. Then Russian assaults on Prussia in the northeast forced the Germans to pull troops from France. This affected the balance enough to permit the reeling Belgian, British, and French forces to stop the German army just short of Paris. Both sides then literally dug in, constructing hundreds of miles of trenches and underground tunnels, a defense technique first observed by European military strategists during the American Civil War. Newly perfected machine guns and quick-loading rifles made such defenses virtually impregnable against even the most massive ground attacks—although that didn't stop the generals from trying, in spite of *millions* of casualties. (Both sides employed airplanes and armoured tanks as offensive weapons for the first time by 1916, but neither side had either weapon perfected or enough of them to make a difference. Both sides also used poison gas on offense, but it proved ineffective even while raising casualty figures.) So the struggle degenerated into a war of attrition which, by mid-1917, the Germans appeared to be winning.

The United States' entry came just in time for the Allies. Until the American navy began successful convoys of cargo ships across the Atlantic, German submarines were effectively strangling the Allies' lifeline. Meanwhile, the eastern front collapsed. By

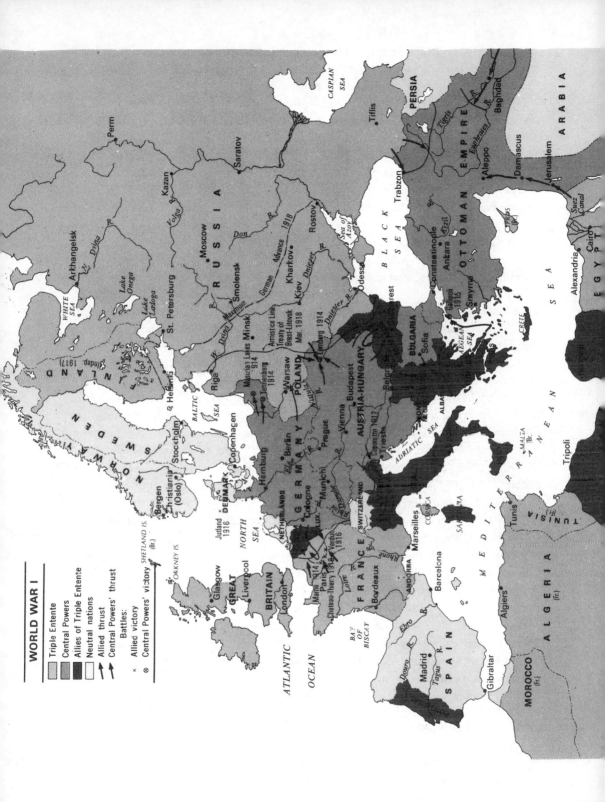

WORLD WAR I

Triple Entente
Central Powers
Allies of Triple Entente
Neutral nations
Battles:
↑ Allied thrust
↑ Central Powers' thrust
× Allied victory
⊗ Central Powers' victory

autumn of 1917, Russia, Serbia, and Rumania were knocked out of the war. With Italy staggering after the Austrian breakthrough at Caporetto (October/November 1917), Germany readied a final offensive on the western front.

If the war had ended then, as the new Soviet government assumed it would and as even many Allied leaders feared it might, Germany would have achieved virtually all its war aims in Europe. It occupied nearly all of Belgium and a substantial corner of northeastern France. Most of the Balkans, the Black Sea, and the Baltic lay within its power. By the Treaty of Brest-Litovsk (February 1918), which formally concluded Russia's part in the war, Germany acquired all of Russian Poland, further territories on the Baltic, and effective protectorates over Lithuania, Finland, Estonia, Kurland (Latvia), and the Ukraine, which were severed from the Russian empire.

By this time, however, the Central Powers had expended their resources about as completely as had the Allies, and whereas the Central Powers had little prospect of revitalization, massive reinforcements in men and supplies had just begun flowing to the Allies from America. In late spring 1918, the first contingents of the American Expeditionary Force (AEF) helped the Allies beat back new German thrusts in France. The AEF grew to two million that summer and played a major role in blunting the last German offensive and in finally turning the tide.

With food and matériel exhausted and morale on the home front low, first the Austrians, then the Turks, and finally the Germans capitulated. By the end of the summer of 1918, the German High Command called on the civil authorities in Berlin to arrange for a ceasefire. During the month of negotiations which followed, the Germans sought to bargain directly with President Wilson for terms that would include the Fourteen Points and a "peace among equals." At Wilson's insistence that he would deal with "the German people" and not with their autocratic rulers, Kaiser Wilhelm abdicated and fled to Holland where he remained in exile until his death twenty years later. The fact that that gesture forced a republican German government to sign the capitulation would play an important role in the discrediting of the Weimar Republic by German militarists over the next fifteen years.

Armistice. On November 11, 1918, in the cities and villages of Italy, Belgium, France, Britain, and the United States, millions of people greeted the signing of the Armistice with jubilation. But the joy was brief and cut by ambivalence. The war, for all its diabolical brutalism, had brought—at least for those at home, remote from the actual agonies, the dying, the terror, the despair—a sense of exalted purposefulness. Ordinary men and women, and the less than ordinary too, had brushed intimately with heroic events, had glimpsed or thought they had glimpsed the nobility of devoted service to humankind. From various letters and diary entries of that day, we learn that the conclusion of The Great War, long anticipated and so long in coming, must have jolted many contemporaries nearly as badly as its outbreak more than four years earlier. One Briton reflected:

> I was stunned by the news, as if something highly improbable and difficult of belief had happened. . . . There was relief that the war was over . . . I sorrowed

Woodrow Wilson embarks for Versailles, January 1919, to negotiate with the Allies for a just peace and a League of Nations. He was the first U.S. president to leave the country during his term in office. *Brown Brothers*

for the millions of young men who had lost their lives; and . . . for the bereaved . . . whose reawakened grief must in this hour of triumph be unbearably poignant. But . . . a melancholy took possession of me when I came to realize, as I did quickly and keenly, that a great and unique episode in my life was past and gone, and, as I hoped as well as believed, would never be repeated. Our sense of the value of life and its excitements, so vividly heightened by the war, is, with one final leap of its flame today, about to expire in its ashes. Tomorrow we return to the monotonous and the humdrum.

The monotonous and the humdrum would not in fact follow so soon. The heroics and the exhilaration of noble causes were gone, but misery remained in extraordinary dimensions. An influenza epidemic that may have begun in the United States in the fall of 1918 quickly spread to Europe with the last arriving contingents of American troops, and by January 1919 some army units were reporting more than two hundred deaths per day from the virulent disease; civilians, weakened by hunger and malnutrition, dropped in numbers that may have surpassed those of the medieval plagues. Revolution and counterrevolutionary warfare racked central and eastern Europe. Disruption of supply lines and general disorder brought on catastrophic food and medical shortages. An estimated 200,000 Russian prisoners of war died in Germany of starvation in January 1919 alone, while an additional million remained in the camps too debilitated to walk out the open gates for home—presuming that "home" had survived the continuing devastation. Well into the spring of 1919, until Germany signed the treaty of peace and the war was officially ended, the Allies continued to blockade central Europe, allowing only minimal food staples to pass through. Political warfare among the Allies themselves worsened the calamity. For example, to press their claims for suzerainty over Slavic territories at the head of the Adriatic Sea, the Italians stopped relief shipments through Trieste, which was the only port with rail facilities to Vienna, Belgrade, and Prague. They also drove non-Italians out of the city, leaving a labor shortage for the handling of cargoes. When American threats to cut off food to Italy got the Italians to relent, the French intervened to prevent food from getting to Hungary, where Communist forces had temporarily seized the government.

Intervention in Russia. The French were especially fearful that the Bolshevik Revolution would prove contagious and sweep westward across the Continent. It was largely at their insistence that Britain and the United States agreed to despatch thousands of troops to northern Russia under British command in the summer of 1918. Ostensibly, the troops were directed to prevent tons of war matériel recently delivered to the Arctic ports of Murmansk and Archangel from falling into German hands. But in fact, the Allies' real objectives differed sharply: France openly sought to topple the Bolshevik government, and to that end sent additional military expeditions to the Baltic, Odessa, and the Ukraine; Wilson, who foresaw plainly that intervention for such purposes would backfire, wished only to placate the French in anticipation of winning them over to a liberal peace treaty; British objectives remained unclear, and they were therefore left to the practical discretion of their field commanders in the Baltic territories as well as in the Arctic.

In 1918 an additional nine thousand American troops joined French and British units in Siberia, supposedly to rescue a Czech army that had been fighting beside the Russians before the revolution and now had got stalled on its eastward trek to Vladivostok, enroute to join the Allies on the Western Front. Actually, the United States and Britain were more concerned to deter Japanese expansion into Siberia. Although the British and French forces there did tangle sporadically with Bolshevik government troops in their efforts to aid counterrevolutionary elements, the Americans, under their own command, carefully obeyed President Wilson's orders to stay clear of the Russian civil war throughout their eighteen-month stay.

From the viewpoint of American, French, and British foreign policies—and they differed among themselves—the interventions in Russia proved catastrophic in every respect, with the possible exception of restraining Japanese ambitions on the Asian continent. They exacted huge costs in lives and money; they magnified and prolonged the misery of the Russian people; they tended to rally Russian support for the Bolshevik government, which was far from popular but stood as the only evident barrier to the restoration of the Czar by the counterrevolutionary armies drawing sustenance from the Allied forces. Furthermore, when Wilson withdrew the American troops because he could no longer defend their role in Russia in terms commensurate with his New Diplomacy, he antagonized the Allies, who felt the United States had deserted them.

Meanwhile, there was nothing monotonous or humdrum about life in America either. Although certain objective realities lent substance to fears of imminent revolution in Europe, the hysteria that infected the United States throughout 1919 had no such basis. There was no prospect of political revolution in the United States. Nevertheless various politicians, business groups, and militant radicals, each group for reasons of its own, vied for attention in cultivating and manipulating apprehensions of impending upheaval.

Cultural Crackup. The war had had the effect of heightening sensitivities to the transformed culture and of polarizing rival ethnic and economic groups. In mobilizing the nation for war, Woodrow Wilson's administration had endorsed the popular view that social, economic, or political insurgency of any sort was tantamount to disloyalty. Protests against American entry into the war, objections to military conscription, resistance to low wages and poor working conditions all came under the category of "Aiding the Enemy." When the Bolshevik Revolution took Russia out of the war, it became easy to equate "the Bosch" with "the Bolshies." And insofar as Marxian communists rejected Christian ethics and religion, it became clear to traditionalists that all those who, for a generation or more, had been challenging the society's commercial, sexual, ethnic, and racial conventions had always in fact threatened the nation's "security."

For those inclined to read them that way, there were indeed some signs of cataclysm. The war's end spurred on a runaway inflation. Businessmen, with the tacit consent of the government, felt no longer constrained to obey price controls. But the government continued to enforce wage-rate ceilings on the improbable theory that the nation must remain officially at war until the Senate ratified a peace treaty. A rash of major strikes inevitably followed, accompanied by strident proclamations by various socialist and communist groups that the moment for revolution was at hand. The fact that more than four million able-bodied workingmen trained in the use of military weapons were being mustered out of the armed forces gave flesh to the spectre of potential class insurrection. More than 200,000 of those servicemen, moreover, were black, whose kinsmen had migrated during the war by the hundreds of thousands into northern industrial cities where they threatened to preempt white men's jobs permanently.

In the course of 1919 and well into 1920, many American communities experienced a virtual reign of terror. Government agents conducted massive raids on various radical organization headquarters, invaded private homes, rounded up thousands of "dangerous agitators," jailed some, deported others whose alien status left them especially vulnerable. Constitutional guarantees of personal liberties went begging for aliens and citizens alike whenever federal or local agencies tarred them as "undesirables." Vigilante groups—many of them organized during the war by the government itself, such as the American Protective League, to help enforce conscription, rationing, wage and price controls and the like—contributed vigorously to the campaign against "the reds." So, too, did newer groups, such as the American Legion, whose raison d'être included directing the energies and inclinations of the recently discharged war veterans into

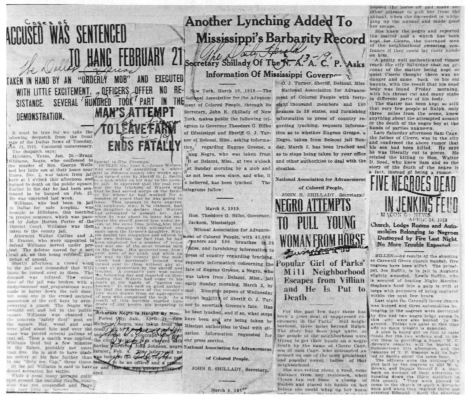

In 1919 race riots erupted in many large cities where large numbers of blacks had migrated to take war-created jobs. But as this collage of clippings suggests, the horrors of living in the rural South had by no means abated.

"patriotic" channels. Others took into their own hands the solution to the problem of postwar race relations: the "Red Summer" of 1919 gets its name not only from the nation's ferocious struggle with "revolution" that year but from the blood spilled in the streets of half a dozen big cities as the result of race riots.

The Demise of Wilson's New Diplomacy. It was amidst this supercharged atmosphere in the spring of 1919 that Woodrow Wilson returned from Paris with a peace treaty and a charter for a League of Nations. He had been the first United States president ever to leave the country during his term of office. The ship on which he had sailed was named the *George Washington,* but ironically, the New Diplomacy that Wilson passionately hoped he had inaugurated was dedicated toward ending a century and a quarter of adherence to President Washington's "Farewell" plea to avoid "entangling alliances" for the defense of other nations' security. Article X of the Treaty of Versailles was designed to commit Americans to the principle of international collective security. This was to be the key sanction for enforcing a new world order based on a "universal dominion of right."

There was irony, too, in the sensational popularity that Wilson personally enjoyed at home and especially abroad during the first few months following the Armistice. His arrival in Europe for the peace talks was greeted with massive enthusiasm, almost as if he were some sort of past and future savior. He could hardly have been faulted for believing that his ideals were also those of the European people, and that the world's future could be safely shaped by democratic forces. All the same, the flaws in the much-flawed treaty to which Wilson asked American commitment in 1919 owed much to just those forces—in particular, the still rising power of populistic nationalism throughout the world.

There was, after all, a fatal contradiction in the notion of creating a transnational authority while insisting on independent nationhood for Europe's mutually distinctive and distrustful populations. There was something incongruous about the idea that national sovereignty should yield up some of its exclusivist prerogatives to an international organization charged with enforcing the peace just when Europe's great transnational empires were being dismantled by the demand for "self-determination." Apart from the covetous zeal of the war's revitalized nations such as Poland, Greece, Serbia, Czechoslovakia, and Rumania, Wilson failed to reckon with the spirit of *revanche* and the passion for war spoils among the masses in the victorious nations—the Italians' scramble for Fiume in Slavic Croatia, for the Greek Dodecanese Islands, and for the Austrian Tyrol; the French demands for crippling reparations from Germany and control of the industry-rich Saar; the division of the Turkish empire between the British and French Syria and Lebanon to France, Palestine and Mesopotamia (Iraq) to Britain.

While the peoples of Europe cheered Wilson wildly, they helped sack the peace he stood for. Wilson might parade triumphantly down the streets of London, Paris, and Rome before enthusiastic crowds, but Lloyd George had promised Britons he would make the Huns pay, Clemenceau had sworn to the French to make Germany forever impotent through dismemberment and reparations, and Orlando's Italy had entered the war on the Allies' side specifically for territorial gain. Not the Fourteen Points, the League of Nations, nor even Woodrow Wilson could persuade them to return to their constituencies without their prizes.

Back home, politics-as-usual crippled Wilson's purposes still further. Historic issues of war and peace may have preoccupied the president, but the American electorate ruminated on more mundane matters, like wheat prices, corporate profits, war contracts, labor insurgency, "uppity" blacks newly settled in northern neighborhoods. Prideful ethnic identification with Old World nationalist causes shattered Wilson's political coalition. For example, Irish-Americans, who could usually be counted on to swell the Democratic party vote, were furious with Wilson for having taken the country to war to "save England," and then for having declined to insist on a "Free Ireland" clause in the peace treaty.

In 1918 Wilson had asked the public to elect a Democratic Congress that he could claim as a "mandate" so that he might negotiate a peace treaty from a strong position.

But the American electorate does not customarily vote for congressmen on the basis of national, much less international, issues. And however popular President Wilson personally may have been, the Democrats were still a minority party that had wrung out only tiny congressional majorities in 1914 and 1916. Divisions within the GOP, shrewd legislation that attracted normally Republican farmers in the Midwest, and the appeal of Wilson's own leadership qualities had produced the small Democratic successes. By 1918 those factors prevailed no longer. Entry into the war in 1917 cost the Democrats large numbers of German-, Scandinavian-, and Irish-American voters, especially in the Midwest, on the force of ethnic affinities alone. Wartime price controls on grains—while southern cotton went unregulated—plus new policies initiated by the wartime railroad administration that wiped out gains only recently awarded by the ICC to midwestern shippers, cost the Democrats further in that region. In the elections of 1918, the Midwest reverted to its pre-1914 Republican voting habits. Wilson failed to gain his mandate, though the vote showed the force of regional and ethnic interests and had nothing to do with the president's program for world peace, or, for that matter, with his ill-advised call for a Democratic Congress.

Wilson's inattention to domestic politics thus foredoomed his efforts at Versailles. Not that he did not have an impressive initial advantage with the public, as well as in the Senate which would have to consent to the treaty. Rather, he failed to reckon wisely with his opponents' ability to exploit the glaring weaknesses of his political position. Possibly he also failed to measure accurately the full force of Massachusetts Senator Henry Cabot Lodge's personal antagonism, and the lengths to which Lodge already had gone to undermine his negotiating posture at home and abroad.

Lodge had become chairman of the crucial Senate Foreign Relations Committee as a result of the Republican victory in 1918. That December he wrote confidentially to certain English friends, including Lord Arthur Balfour and officials in the British government, advising them not to take Wilson seriously. The Senate, Lodge suggested, would support Britain and France if they stood fast for their terms against Wilson's plans for a liberal settlement. In the Senate, Lodge posed as a "reservationist"—one who supposedly favored the League but with some reservations—while he worked wholeheartedly with "irreconcilables," such as Senator William E. Borah of Idaho, to defeat the League entirely.

The League's opponents carefully cultivated a variety of political forces with potential for killing the president's hopes for a New Diplomacy. Many opponents, such as Borah, were instinctive isolationists whose vision rarely extended beyond the American scene and who especially shunned Europe, the way one might recoil from acknowledging a habitually dissolute parent. Others, such as Lodge and Roosevelt, were militant nationalists who opposed the League not so much because it might entangle the U.S. in foreign commitments but because it might delimit the character and scope of American ambitions. In coalition, these forces proved unbeatable, especially as they were able to exploit many different kinds of grievances with the proposed peace settlement. They nurtured fears that commitment to the League would emasculate American nationalism ("denationalize the Nation's manhood," is the way ex-Progressive Senator

Albert Beveridge put it to Theodore Roosevelt) and threaten American exclusivist prerogatives in the western hemisphere as asserted in the Monroe Doctrine. They also played heavily on ethnic sensitivities, stressing—in the appropriate districts—the denied ambitions of the Irish and the Italians, while shedding tears over the "vindictive" peace terms forced on Germany. At the same time, they formed an alliance of convenience with liberal humanists who had become disenchanted with Wilson for having yielded too much to the British and French, to the conservatives at home, and to nationalists abroad. Wilson, the liberals charged, betrayed China by acquiescing in Japan's occupation of Shantung, and then betrayed Japanese friendship by refusing to support Japan's insistence on a clause in the League covenant asserting the equality of the races. Wilson also failed to lend support to Europe's insurgent progressive forces; instead he helped sustain Europe's Old Guard, meanwhile promoting a world organization that under the circumstances, many liberals believed, would likely serve only counterrevolutionary purposes within as well as beyond the borders of individual nations—as evidenced by the presence of United States and Allied troops in Russia.

Beyond these sources of opposition, there remained the country's profound and always potent isolationist proclivities—the general desire to withdraw from explicit international responsibilities, to retreat to the world that was, to get away from causes and complications, and from the imponderables of a new, high-risk international diplomacy.

This last probably had the greatest force of all. Wilsonian ideals had a momentary lustrous appeal. But 1919 was not a year for promoting generous schemes for world progress, no matter how enlightened or impelling they might have been. This is not to say that American interests shrank back behind the continental borders. The sheer force of American economic vigor would carry Americans abroad in major commercial and capital ventures. Trade and investment by Americans in Latin America, Europe, the Middle East, China, and even Africa multiplied many times during the 1920s. The growth of American business interests abroad would have inevitable political implications which the leaders of the Harding and Coolidge administrations had to handle. But after 1918 the American public strenuously resisted all efforts to direct American energies abroad by means of any effective political process or public policy.

The Return to Isolationism

In the 1920s, Americans by and large rejected the burdens of a nation committed to the cause of human progress. The few political leaders who, like Hiram Johnson and Robert La Follette, strove to maintain the progressive faith struck responsive notes with the American public only when they denounced proposals to extend the American commitment overseas. The plainest fact about American popular attitudes toward international affairs after 1919 is that they were willfully, profoundly, self-consciously isolationist. Whatever one may say about the continuing expansion of American overseas concerns, no other word adequately describes the prevailing public spirit.

International Charades. The consequences were sometimes ludicrous. Having strained, successfully, to persuade the European powers to accept a New Diplomacy based on an international system of law and the principle of collective security, the American government then turned its back on both the Permanent Court of International Justice (the World Court) and the League of Nations. Popular pressures grew beyond merely endorsing Congress' rejection of the League; they virtually forbade the State Department to concede its existence. Until September 1921, the U.S. government refused even to acknowledge official letters from the League. Nevertheless, the government maintained an "unofficial observer" at the League. It is one of the features of the 1920s that invites historians to look back in ridicule.

Constrained by the prevailing isolationism, American diplomacy worked mountains to produce mice. The great "triumphs" of the era included the Four-Power and Five-Power Treaties of the eight-week-long Washington Conference of 1921/22, and the Kellogg-Briand Peace Pact of 1928. The "Four Powers" were the U.S., Britain, France, and Japan, who agreed on December 13, 1921 that for ten years they would try to be nice to each other. The "triumph" in it was that the U.S. got the British out of renewing a formal alliance with Japan that some professional Anglophobes in America found menacing to Anglo-American amity while presumably reassuring the Japanese that there were no hard feelings. The "Five Powers" were the U.S., Britain, France, Japan, and Italy, who agreed on February 6, 1922 to the principle of "naval disarmament." This they did by arranging a coordinated scrapping of already antiquated battleships and by agreeing not to build more than a specified number of new ones for ten years— or at least until it became politically and financially convenient once more to do so. Of course, the latter was not in the treaty; it was merely obvious.

Did the Washington Conference produce any tangible consequences? Perhaps. The Japanese did agree to withdraw their troops from the Russian half of Sakhalin Island and from eastern Siberia, which they did gradually over the next three years—and probably would have anyway for reasons having little to do with pressures brought to bear in Washington. (Russia was not even invited to the Conference.) Second, the Japanese yielded certain privileges to the Americans on the use of the communications cables anchored on Yap Island in the central Pacific, formerly a German possession and mandated to Japan at Versailles; in exchange for this, the U.S. (and Britain) promised not to fortify any Pacific islands west of Hawaii or much beyond the Australian, New Zealand, and Canadian coasts.

But the historical importance of these matters pales compared with the significance of grown men of much advertised dignity spending weeks and months engaged in such piddling charades. The treaties contained no hint of a practical mechanism for enforcing their terms beyond the very measure—the unilateral use of violence—that the treaties were supposed to forestall. History has properly tossed them in the junkyard; only historians unaccountably continue to give them attention beyond their value.

It is also remarkable that as innocuous as they were, the treaties still caused an uproar in the bowels of the U.S. Senate where isolationists espied signs of entangling alliances. Borah, predictably, led the assault on the Four-Power Pact, entirely unappeased by President Harding's pathetic "assurance that nothing in any of these treaties commits the United States or any other power to any kind of alliance, entanglement, or involvement," or by Senator Lodge's assertion that the treaties required not even a *moral* commitment by the signers to force compliance in any way. The Four-Power Treaty passed the Senate by a scant four votes. It would be comforting to believe that the small margin owed to the inanity of the treaty and not of the Senators, but we must do without such relief.

There were many disarmament conferences and peace agreements in the 1920s, but the capstone to the "Parchment Peace," as some historians have called it, was the Kellogg-Briand Peace Pact. It began with an effort by Aristide Briand, the French Premier, to get the U.S. to make a declaration of support for French security (which the Americans would not even consider doing), followed by an incredibly complex succession of international posturings designed for domestic political effect, and ended with an orgy of pious pacifist platitudes officially given the stature of an international treaty that affected to do nothing less than declare war "outlawed." Eventually, it was signed by sixty-two solemn nations—each and every one of which then solemnly denied it was bound in any way to enforce what it had agreed to. The pact's chief historical consequence is that it became the torment of all young students required to memorize the "outstanding diplomatic events" of the 1920s.

Actually, all that is worth remembering about these pseudoevents is that they won a lot of attention at the time. And by remembering that, one may understand the lengths to which Americans were prepared to go in order to affirm their own virtue while evading the responsibilities of world power.

As part of its general aversion to the realities of power, the U.S. also refused to acknowledge the Soviet government. Until 1933, the United States insisted that the Bolsheviks did not deserve recognition because (1) they had repudiated all prewar debts, (2) they had confiscated foreign properties without compensation, and (3) they were financing propaganda campaigns internationally to subvert existing governments. But although England and France had greater financial and property stakes in Russia (almost $2 billion in repudiated war debts alone), both followed the traditional international practice of giving diplomatic recognition to the Moscow government soon after it gained stable control of the country. American protestations on that score rang hollow. Few cared to note, moreover, that the U.S. had virtually pioneered in international subversion by propaganda with several missions into Russia beginning in the summer of 1917. As George Kennan writes in his book, *The Decision to Intervene* (1967): "The United States government, uninhibited by any firm attachment to the traditional principles of diplomatic intercourse, appears to have been one of the first to embrace this new type of activity with breezy candor and to conduct it openly, as an avowed governmental operation."

European Financial Troubles. More serious was the unwillingness of Americans to recognize their crucial role in the political economy of the world. The U.S. government's refusal in 1919 to continue its wartime practice of making direct loans to foreign governments keyed the difficulties. Europe was forced to negotiate for capital with private American bankers, whose immediate concern for maximum profits inevitably failed as a substitute for long-view planning on behalf of the national interest or world peace.

When England was the world's chief creditor—for more than a century before 1914—British bankers often self-consciously moved capital around for purposes of stimulating international trade and restraining sharp fluctuations in currency exchange rates (the ratio of one nation's money to another's). But Britain had a relatively small domestic market, and depended on international trade and investment for domestic prosperity. Its own interests and international economic stability had much in common. By contrast, foreign commerce accounted for scarcely 10 percent of the U.S. Gross National Product, and the enormous domestic market offered ample opportunities for high returns on investments right at home. Furthermore, Americans had little experience in international finance, an additional deterrence to venturing abroad. With government officially out of the scene, responsible officials (such as Secretary of State Charles Evans Hughes and Secretary of Commerce Herbert Hoover) had to use indirect, sometimes even covert means for encouraging American participation in international settlements.

As a result, it was not until 1924 that Europe gained substantial access to the American loan market. By that time Mussolini had led his Fascist troops into Rome, German inflation had soared completely out of control, Hitler had established a political base in Bavaria, and French troops had reoccupied the industrial regions of the Rhineland in a desperate effort to stabilize France's critical economic and political condition. It is unlikely, of course, that wiser deployment of American finance would have prevented all these things. But the absence of American leadership was sorely felt. The troubles described were not only predictable, they had been predicted. In pondering the decision to intervene, Wilson and his advisers had foreseen Europe's postwar desperation and the urgent role America would have to play in Europe's peaceful reconstruction.

Among other things, the war had left Europe in a tangle of unpaid accounts arising from war loans, credit advances, and post-Armistice shipments of supplies. Britain and France owed the U.S. government $4.7 billion and $4.0 billion respectively, and France owed Britain $3.0 billion. Various other nations owed the United States $3.1 billion, Britain $8.1 billion, and France $3.5 billion. In addition, according to the terms of the Versailles treaty, Germany owed Britain, France, and Belgium reparations usually figured at about $31 billion. Very possibly these nations could have paid their debts, especially if they were amortized over a long enough period of years. But the economic costs to them would have had immediate political repercussions that neither they nor, in the last resort, the Americans really cared to contemplate. Moreover, the Allied nations, especially France, reacted bitterly to "Uncle Shylock's" insistence on war-debt payments; except for money, America had suffered few losses compared to those sustained by the Europeans. Debt obligations had the effect of hobbling the Europeans in their competition with the Americans for economic opportunities at home and abroad.

In 1920, in view of the massive economic confusion rendered critical by shortages in capital, growing unemployment, and paralyzing uncertainties about if, when, and on what terms international indebtedness would be liquidated, Britain formally proposed a general cancellation of all war debts. The United States refused. The lame-duck Wilson administration took the position that it had no authority to cancel foreign obligations without congressional approval. And the bipartisan nationalist-isolationist coalition in Congress precluded any such thing. In February 1922 Congress wrote its rejection of cancellation into law and demanded, moreover, an interest rate of "not less than 4.25 percent"—a figure substantially higher than prewar borrowing rates in London. Eventually American negotiators arranged settlements that departed greatly from the terms set by the War Debts Act; and Congress tacitly accepted them. But few of the agreements survived the worldwide economic collapse after 1929, a collapse due in no small measure to America's refusal to accept a leadership role.

The Dawes Plan. While the Americans took a hard line on the war debts, they adopted a "generous" attitude toward German reparations. At Versailles the United States declined all indemnities from Germany for itself. It proceeded, furthermore, to press its wartime allies to reduce their claims. As the U.S. viewed it (with some support from British leaders) Germany could not pay large sums, and to force it to comply would prolong reconstruction and further endanger the political and economic situation. The British and especially the French, of course, viewed reparations as essential for their postwar rehabilitation and for their ability to pay their American debt. The U.S., however, officially refused to acknowledge any connection between reparations and the war debts.

In 1924, with calamity spreading in Germany and threatening the rest of Europe, American officials helped arrange for a multilateral settlement that stepped down both reparations and war debt payments and committed American bankers to underwriting a $200 million loan to Germany. The French were required to withdraw their troops from the Ruhr. The German central bank was severed from the German government and placed under loose supervision by an international commission which, it was agreed, an American would head.

The "Dawes Plan," named for Chicago banker Charles G. Dawes who became the first chairman of the commission created by the arrangement, gave some American bankers but still not the American government something of a leadership role in European economic affairs. Officially, the government remained aloof; it took the position that Dawes—like the Americans serving as "unofficial observers" at the League of Nations and on the Inter-Allied Reparations Commission—was merely a private individual. The situation exemplifies the contorted postures that America so often adopted in the 1920s. Dawes, S. Parker Gilbert of J. P. Morgan & Company, and other "private" persons who took on comparable responsibilities in Europe continually acted in close association with the State and Treasury Departments and the Federal Reserve Board. Expenses and some salaries were drawn from the State Department's "emergency funds." But the Harding and Coolidge administrations steadfastly maintained the fiction that the government took no part in the European arrangements. The isolationists in Congress were ever vigilant to keep it that way.

Unfortunately, there was substance to the fiction. The indirect means by which members of government attempted to look after the country's international interests poorly served the needs of public policy. Forced to act through private "experts," the government was impelled to accept the expertise of bankers—no other *private* agents could command the respect their roles required. Consequently, the bankers' policies became the government's policies rather than the other way around.

The Dawes Plan launched a brief era of extravagant American lending abroad, especially to Europe and Latin America. With the government helping to promote the German loan, American investors began buying European bonds beyond all expectations and wisdom. Since the government was not doing the lending itself, it could only encourage, or discourage, the market; it could not release or shut the flow at the optimal moments. Investment behavior was governed by private speculative appraisals of profit opportunities in the money market rather than by principles of long-range management. In 1924 American annual long-term lending abroad rose abruptly from a four-year plateau of $500 million to a new two-year plateau of over $900 million, and then still further to $1.25 billion in 1927 and 1928. At that point, speculative opportunities in the booming New York stock market suddenly brought capital rushing back to the United States. The shock to the international economic system contributed in a major way to the world depression that followed.

America, the Coy Imperialist? There is a school of historians who argue that America was not isolationist in the 1920s—that in fact the U.S. actively promoted American hegemony throughout the world. The theme was keyed by William Appleman Williams' essay, "The Legend of Isolationism" (1954), and has been elaborated on in works such as *Heir to Empire* (1969) by Carl Parrini. The thrust of the argument is that *expansionism* rather than isolationism has been the dominant theme of American history from its very origin, and that the theme persisted through the twenties in spite of the popular rejection of the League, of the World Court, and of other formal ties with the rest of the world. The only difference in the 1920s was the reliance on economic rather than military power. Notwithstanding this limitation, the revisionists insist, American leaders worked strenuously to enlarge American "control" of foreign nations, especially through the resources of the great investment bankers and industrial corporations. "What emerged," writes Williams, "was an American corporatism. The avowed goals were order, stability, and social peace"—both at home and abroad.

Part of the truth to the argument is that many government leaders and lesser officials, notably a group of activists in the Bureau of Domestic and Foreign Commerce (BDFC) and in the State Department, adopted strongly nationalist policies designed, indeed, to enhance American interests abroad. Roosevelt's "Corollary" to the Monroe Doctrine continued to govern U.S. relations with Latin America, and in 1927 marines intervened once more in Nicaragua to thwart a so-called communist takeover there. For the most part, however, U.S. "agressiveness" was economic, and directed at Europe. BDFC agents throughout the world alerted American businessmen to investment opportunities, informed them of foreign trade practices and consumer preferences, and kept Washington apprised of "unfair" foreign business tactics. The State Department vigorously intervened to impel Britain and France to permit American oil companies a share in the development of petroleum resources in Iran and Iraq. It also worked to prevent the British from monopolizing transoceanic cable lines, especially those linking South America to the United States and to Europe and Africa—although it did not always have the cooperation of the American cable companies which preferred their own arrangements with the British. Secretary of Commerce Herbert Hoover protested, and took retaliatory steps against, a British plan to constrict rubber supplies so as to raise prices on this resource essential for the booming American auto industry. A Brazilian valorization, or price-fixing, scheme for coffee evoked a similar response from the U.S. The Fordney-McCumber Tariff of 1922 was one of the weapons the U.S. sometimes used for international leverage in the 1920s. It empowered the president to raise or lower tariffs with individual countries in order to obtain the most advantageous trade relations.

Even as they struggled with their European rivals, American policymakers worked to rehabilitate the European economy. It is not clear that American business urgently needed European markets and investment opportunities, as revisionists argue, but there is no question that a European collapse would have jeopardized the American economy, just as the American collapse in 1929 helped bring down Europe. Some Americans also worried that unless Europe recovered, Bolshevism would sweep westward from Russia. Given the American commitment to liberal institutions, a communist triumph in Europe (or Latin America) could not be viewed with disinterest, for moral as well as strategic and economic reasons.

It would be a foolish historian who failed to observe that the custodians of American interests in world trade and politics strove to promote such "order, stability, and social peace" as they believed would best serve American strategic, economic, and ideological or moral interests. The crucial question has always been how one defines those interests, and how the country pursues them. By focusing on the expansionist activities of American government and business, revisionists perceive more continuity than change in the postwar decade: America remained committed as always to maximizing opportunities for private economic venture. The emphasis has the virtue of correcting a possible misinterpretation of "isolationism" as suggesting that America withdrew all its international activities. Even in the 1920s, Americans did not do that. Nevertheless, the revisionist focus distorts even more than does the error it corrects. By stressing the continuities, it blurs the differences that were at the center of contemporary controversy and that virtually define the special ethos of the 1920s.

For one thing, the reliance on economic power rather than military action is not to be dismissed as merely another form of "imperialism." In a world that took for granted that nations had the right to improve their economic chances by whatever the means, it is no small matter that American expansion took on economic rather than political form. But more than that, what has needed explanation is how *little* American economic resources spread abroad. Given the weakness of the country's rivals and trading partners, one would have expected American capital to have flooded into Europe and Europe's colonial system. But that didn't happen. And this requires attention to the striking insularity of American thinking, in politics, in most of the business world, and in the American public at large. The sheer size, vigor, and complexity of American industrial and financial institutions sufficiently explain the growth of American trade and overseas investments during the 1920s and the concern of those in government charged with influencing international affairs. For America to have been *less* expansive would have required active government discouragement, and perhaps an abrupt, massive reversal of the nation's commitment to the private uses of capital for private gain.

What has also been at issue is why American resources were used so poorly in foreign policy. American capital flowed to Europe in inappropriate amounts and at less than optimal moments. The loan terms which foreign governments were impelled to accept may not have served well either their or America's long-run interests. American leaders too often lumped social-democratic political movements with "communism," thereby committing the U.S. in advance against virtually all significant social reform and complicating our foreign relations. But if all this is true about American foreign policy, at least some of the responsibility must lie in the fact that virtually all the forces for liberal progress in America had abandoned the field.

By a policy of deliberate neglect, the American public in the 1920s took no responsibility for the growth in American stakes overseas. By abandoning politics in the disenchantment that followed the war, American intellectuals offered no guidance and only sniping criticism. Without pressure from sectors of the society that might have offered a broad definition of the nation's international interests, U.S. policy-makers responded all too readily to the pressures of the businesses that had stakes abroad. Left otherwise alone in the field, a relatively few American financiers and industrialists defined American international interests in a framework that narrowed the possible options to those compatible with their own profits and ideological preconceptions. Most Americans in the 1920s appear to have wanted it no other way.

SUGGESTED READINGS

Charles C. Tansill's *America Goes to War* (1938) is still the best detailed critique of President Wilson's neutrality policies and the eventual U.S. intervention in the war. N. Gordon Levin, Jr., *Woodrow Wilson and World Politics: America's Response to War and Revolution** (1968), puts Wilson's foreign policy generally against the background of a liberal progressive's defense of capitalism in a revolutionary world, especially America's alleged need for economic expansion overseas. This perspective became popular among revisionist historians during the 1960s. But John Milton Cooper, Jr., "The Command of Gold Reversed: American Loans to Britain, 1915-17," *Pacific Historical Review,* v. 65, May 1976, thoroughly disposes of the argument that American loans gave the U.S. a stake in Allied victory that impelled intervention. Levin developed for the American case the thesis put forward in Arno J. Mayer's brilliantly argued *Political Origins of the New Diplomacy, 1917-18** (1959) and his monumental

* Available in a paperback edition.

*Politics and Diplomacy of Peacemaking** (1967), both of which focus on European politics and put Wilson in a comparatively favorable light.

Beyond the Anglophobia that helped inform critics such as Tansill and critiques founded in Marxian premises about the supposed needs of capitalism and liberalism, the most persuasive challenge to Wilson's decision to intervene has stressed Wilson's abandonment of domestic concerns in his anxiety to remake world politics. This argument appears in many general accounts of the period, such as W. E. Leuchtenburg's *The Perils of Prosperity, 1914-32** (1957), and most pointedly in Otis L. Graham, Jr., *The Great Campaigns** (1971), where Graham writes: "Given the circumstances—the uncontrolled passions of Europe and the ignorance that gripped his [Wilson's] own great democracy—there was one *sure* way to pursue American security, a familiar way, without staggering risks, and without death. It was by an intensification of that surge of internal reform to which he had already become committed." Graham concedes, "Had Wilson acted along these lines the result would almost certainly have been a German victory." But he confesses that with the benefit of hindsight, he does not regard that prospect with the apprehension contemporaries like Wilson felt at the time.

On the other hand, other historians tend to view Wilson's decision as in accord with a correct, longview assessment of U.S. national interests. A. S. Link's *Wilson the Diplomatist: A Look at His Major Foreign Policies** (1957), the relevant chapters in his biography of Wilson, vols. 3, 4, and 5, and "The Higher Realism of Woodrow Wilson," *Journal of Presbyterian History*, v. 41, Mar. 1963; Ernest May in *The World War and American Isolationism, 1914-17** (1959), and E. H. Buehrig in *Woodrow Wilson and the Balance of Power* (1955), all argue the danger to U.S. national security if Wilson had not intervened. May, whose book offers the most detailed account of the diplomatic deliberations on both sides of the Atlantic and of the Western Front, also contends (in a way not inconsistent with Levin and other revisionists) that intervention squared well with the American people's expectations of their government's responsibility to look after their long and short term economic opportunities. Ross Gregory's *The Origins of American Intervention in the First World War** (1971) intelligently captures the fine points of the problem in sharp essay form.

Since there is no room here for a full historiographical account, readers are advised to see the bibliographies of the cited works as well as three especially well-done historiographical essays: *The American Revisionists: The Lessons of Intervention in World War I* (1967), Warren I. Cohen; "The Problem of American Intervention, 1917: An Historical Retrospect," *World Politics*, v. 2, April 1950, Richard Leopold; and "National Interest and American Intervention 1917," *Journal of American History*, v. 52, June 1965, Daniel M. Smith. See also J. M. Cooper, Jr., "World War I in American Historical Writing," in Cooper's anthology, *Causes and Consequences of World War I** (1972).

For the link between national and commercial interests in the fashioning of American foreign policy, readers may find R. M. Abrams' "United States Intervention Abroad: The First Quarter Century," *American Historical Review*, v. 79, Feb. 1974, a reasonably up-to-date introduction to the historiographical issues. The most important work on postwar economic policies is only now beginning to appear in print, after developing in the form of doctoral dissertations. Samples of the new scholarship have emerged in the journals, such as: Benjamin D. Rhodes' "Reassessing 'Uncle Shylock': The United States and the French War Debt, 1917-29," *Journal of American History*, v. 55, Mar. 1969; Melvyn Leffler, "The Origins of Republican War Debt Policy, 1921-23," *Journal of American History*, v. 59, Dec. 1972, and "Political Isolationism, Economic Expansionism, or Diplomatic Realism: American Policy Toward Western Europe, 1921-33," *Perspectives in American History*, v. 8, 1974 (derived from his work on American policy toward France, 1921-33, completed in 1972); and Frank Costigliola, "The Other Side of Isolationism," *Journal of American History*, v. 59, Dec. 1972, and "The United States and the Reconstruction of Germany in the 1920s," *Business History Review*, v. 50, Winter 1976. Stephen A. Schuker's *The End of French Predominance in Europe: The Financial Crisis of 1924 and the Adoption of the Dawes Plan* (1976) is a brilliant analysis of international politics and finance that makes extensive use of France, Germany, Britain, Belgium, and U.S. archives.

Otherwise, see Carl P. Parrini's *Heir to Empire: United States Economic Diplomacy, 1916-23* (1969), which is flawed by a zealous desire to berate "American imperialism"; Joseph Brandes' *Herbert Hoover and Economic Diplomacy: Department of Commerce Policy, 1921-28* (1962), which pioneered in a now-crowded field; and Joan Hoff Wilson's *American Business and Foreign Policy, 1920-33* (1971), which provides nearly exhaustive coverage of American trade journals. William Appleman Williams, *The Tragedy of American Diplomacy** (2d edition, 1972), like Parrini, grinds several hostile axes and never makes clear what alternatives Williams believes were available to U.S. policymakers but his book is very popular on college reading lists. Herbert Feis' *The Diplomacy of the Dollar: First Era, 1919-32** (1950), is a short essay by a historian who served for many years in the State Department. The first hundred pages of Charles P. Kindleberger's *The World in Depression, 1929-39** (1973) presents an exceptionally lively and informative account of Euro-American financial relations in the 1920s. Mira Wilkins' *The Emergence of Multi-national Enterprise* (1971) and her *The Maturing of Multinational Enterprise* (1974) are the definitive volumes on the expansion of American investments abroad. Wilkins writes with almost clinical detachment to place before the reader the basic data on the subject.

Some specially focused studies worth particular attention for present purposes include: Walter V. and Marie V. Scholes' *The Foreign Policies of the Taft Administration* (1970) is pretty straightforward; Jerry Israel's *Progressivism and the Open Door: America and China, 1905-21* (1971) is revisionist in approach; Paul A. Varg, "The Myth of the China Market, 1890-1914," *American Historical Review*, v. 73, Feb. 1968, points out that American capitalists were less interested than American foreign service zealots in expanding across the Pacific; Akira Iriye, *After Imperialism: The Search for a New Order in the Far East 1921-31** (1965), is especially good on the variety of forces at work in fashioning policy in the Pacific; Dana G. Munro's *Intervention and Dollar Diplomacy in the Caribbean, 1900-1921* (1964) is an excellent detailed account by a former State Department officer, a second volume by Munro has brought the story into the 1960s; Joseph S. Tulchin's *The Aftermath of War: World War I and U.S. Policy Toward Latin America* (1971) actually begins around 1916, carries forward to about 1926, and presents an excellent view of the inner workings of the State Department; Waldo Heinrich's *American Ambassador: Joseph C. Grew and the Development of the United States Diplomatic Tradition* (1966), especially Part Two, offers further perspective on the State Department in the 1920s, as does Robert D. Schulzinger's *The Making of the Diplomatic Mind: The Training Outlook & Style of U.S. Foreign Service Officers, 1908-39* (1975); P. Edward Halsy's *Revolution and Intervention: The Diplomacy of Taft and Wilson in Mexico, 1910-17* (1970), and Robert Freeman Smith's *The United States and Revolutionary Nationalism in Mexico, 1916-32* (1972) are both excellent, as is Smith's *The United States and Cuba: Business and Diplomacy, 1917-60** (1960). Smith's revisionist approach adds much to the perspective Munro presents. The quotation in the text about President Estrada Palma by the Cuban insurgent is from Allan Reed Millett's *The Politics of Intervention: The Military Occupation of Cuba, 1906-09* (1968), which, together with James H. Hitchman's *Leonard Wood and Cuban Independence 1898-1902* (1971) and Hans Schmidt, *The United States Occupation of Haiti, 1915-34* (1971) provide "inside" details on U.S. policymaking and implementation. John Silverlight's *The Victors' Dilemma; Allied Intervention in the Russian Civil War* (1970) is a fascinating narrative from a European's perspective; and Christopher Lasch, "American Intervention in Siberia: A Reinterpretation," *Political Science Quarterly*, v. 78, June 1962, offers excellent historiographical coverage as well as a provocative thesis, namely, that "intervention was directed against neither [the Bolsheviks nor the Japanese], but against the Germans." (Read the article and find out why!)

David Burner, "The Breakup of the Wilson Coalition of 1916," *Mid-America*, v. 45, Jan. 1963, and Seward W. Livermore, "The Sectional Issue in the 1918 Congressional Election," *Mississippi Valley Historical Review*, v. 35, June 1948, will help readers understand the political weaknesses that undermined Wilson's foreign policy ambitions.

CHAPTER FIVE

BETWEEN WAR AND DEPRESSION

AMERICAN POPULAR LITERATURE, the entertainment media, and probably most history textbooks still treat the 1920s as "The Jazz Age," a disorderly, libidinous, money-oriented, antiintellectual period given to revelry, to crudity and corruption, to flappers, fads, fancies, and follies. With the emphasis on goldfish swallowing, rumble seats, raccoon coats, stunt flying, shimmy dancing, speakeasies, cloche hats and rolled-down stockings, it has appeared as a slaphappy interlude starkly set off from the preceding era by Warren G. Harding's proclamation of "Normalcy" in 1920 and from the succeeding era by The Great Crash of 1929. It has the aspect of a perpetual carnival, a perennial silly season, the sunny summer of everybody's adolescence when the more important events are all light-hearted ones, and the horrible appear at least in retrospect just divertingly pathetic, always a trifle funny and unreal, like grotesquerie. Think of Prohibition, and "bathtub gin," and men and women literally drinking themselves blind with poisonous bootlegged alcohol. Think of "Scarface" Al Capone and the "St. Valentine's Day Massacre" that left seven thugs of a rival Chicago gang dead against a garage wall, decoyed by their assassins masquerading as policemen. Think of the Ku Klux Klan, grown men careering about in bedsheets, calling themselves Kleagles and Cyclops, using whips and fagots and tar and feathers to keep America pure.

Think of Warren Harding as President of the United States.

Rapture Turns to Gall: Descent into Mediocrity

On Election Day, 1920, the voters punished Woodrow Wilson for his failure to achieve the better world he had envisioned and had done so much to make popular. They took to their bosom two men who virtually caricatured insular, "old-fashioned," homespun, small-town mediocrity. Both major parties presented candidates who had been no one's first choice, and whose chief virtues were that they stood for nothing very clearly and came from Ohio. The ticket of Warren Gamaliel Harding and Calvin Coolidge crushed the Democratic slate of James Cox and Franklin Delano Roosevelt (assistant secretary of the navy at the time) with the greatest popular majority since the development of the two-party system. Harding, the undistinguished senator from Marion, Ohio, swept into the presidency with sixteen million votes to nine million for Cox, the colorless governor of Ohio. When he took office in March 1921, the country seemed to have been set back twenty years. In the drop seats of the limousine that bore the president-elect and the glowering Woodrow Wilson to the inaugural ceremonies sat William McKinley's attorney general, Philander Knox, now the newly designated majority leader of the Senate, and white-bewhiskered "Uncle Joe" Cannon, once again Speaker of the House and fully recovered from his humiliations at the hands of the progressive insurgents way back in 1910. It was as if the progressive movement had never occurred.

Woodrow Wilson and the Democrats had tried to make the election of 1920 into a "Solemn Referendum" on the League of Nations, but by then Americans were a little

Opening game, 1924 World Series. Fun and games replaced progress and politics as the great American pastime in the twenties. But the "serious" stuff of the decade is reflected in the unyieldingly businesslike aspect of President Coolidge. Mrs. Coolidge is seated to his right. *Culver Pictures*

En route to Warren Harding's inauguration, March 4, 1921, President Wilson, partially paralyzed from a stroke, rode beside the president-elect and behind old Joe Cannon and Philander Knox, two symbols of the incorrigible Old Guard, restored to power after ten years. *UPI*

sick of solemnity. The Great War was over. Its toll—37.5 million military casualties alone, including 321,000 Americans—mocked all pretensions of achievement or glory. Some of the casualties, shells of men bereft of their sanity and various parts of their anatomy, had become enduring testimony to modern warfare's triumph over valor. The president himself had become a casualty of the war, invalided by a stroke in August 1919 while touring the country in a foredoomed effort to build popular pressure for the treaty the Senate was determined to defeat. Isolated and bitter, Wilson did nothing while his attorney general, A. Mitchell Palmer, recklessly trampled over the legal rights and liberties of striking workers, dissenters, radicals, and aliens. He did nothing while industrial prices soared, real wages plummeted by 16 percent, and unemployment climbed to four million by mid-1920. Worse, he let farm price supports lapse while the Treasury cut off the government loans that had been enabling Europeans to buy American foodstuffs. Depression hit in July 1920, and by fall wheat prices had dropped 41 percent; beef steers, 51 percent; cotton, 62 percent; corn, 62 percent; farmers suspended mortgage payments, and country merchants and bankers closed their doors. Wilson himself had become a pariah, "personification of the rapture that had become gall," wrote Mark Sullivan. All he touched became tainted: the League, the peace treaty, the Democratic party, progressive reform itself.

The Disenchanted Generation. It was the first national election in which women could vote, as provided by the newly ratified Nineteenth Amendment, but not even a third of the women eligible took the trouble. The progressive achievement held little charm for moderate-income and lower-class families, most notably among the more recently arrived Americans. Male "superiority"—at least as defined by traditionalist assignment of family roles—remained an important source of personal dignity for men whose predominant experience was one of continual submission to authority, on the job, at church, or perhaps as recent subjects of a monarchial state. Among women in the same groups, role-playing offered the comforts of stability in lives often filled with anxiety, forced change, tumult, and physical danger. In any event, considering the mediocrity of the major candidates in 1920, it is little wonder that few more than those women who had actively campaigned for the voting privilege showed an interest in the franchise.

The best candidates for the presidency simply were not for the choosing in November 1920. The most obvious intelligent choice was Herbert Hoover. Born in a two-room blacksmith's shack in the farming village of West Branch, Iowa, and orphaned at the age of nine, Hoover became a millionaire before he was thirty-five as one of the world's leading mining engineers. In 1912 he retired to devote himself to "public service," a calling quickly tested when he found himself in Belgium at the outbreak of World War I. By the end of the war no American besides Wilson and TR was better known, and none was better respected. During and immediately after the war, Hoover headed the Belgian and Russian relief agencies and the Federal Food Administration. The word "Hooverizing" entered the American language, meaning conserving food and fuel and in general doing things in the most efficient way possible. But Hoover had no political organization behind him and little political know-how. He torpedoed his own chances for nomination by prematurely announcing he was a Republican. Without the threat that the Democrats might name him (as Louis Brandeis and Franklin Roosevelt earnestly hoped at the beginning of 1920), the Republican politicos were free to ignore him.

Other possibilities also evaporated early. William G. McAdoo, an outstandingly able and progressive individual, was "tainted" by his association with Woodrow Wilson; he had served as secretary of the treasury (1913-19) and was Wilson's son-in-law besides. A handful of old Bull Moosers gathered in June to consider the Progressive party's future; they resolved to keep in touch with each other, and disbanded. The Socialists nominated once more the aging Eugene V. Debs, who was entering his third year in jail for having spoken out against the war in 1917; Woodrow Wilson had refused repeated pleas by eminent Americans, including some leading Democrats, that he commute the sentence. A. Mitchell Palmer, who had once been a leading Pennsylvania progressive, in 1919 staked his presidential ambitions on leading the antiradical campaign while attorney general. But by mid-1920 his popularity as the country's chief red-baiter backfired on him; not that the country condemned his excesses, but rather had grown weary of the game.

"The Jazz Age," wrote F. Scott Fitzgerald, who invented the name, "began about the time of the May Day riots in 1919. . . . When the police rode down the demobilized country boys gaping at the orators in Madison Square," Fitzgerald explained, "it was the sort of measure bound to alienate the more intelligent young men from the prevailing order. . . . But, because we were tired of Great Causes, there was no more than a short outbreak of moral indignation."

"Great Causes" had a way of falling into the hands of demagogues, prigs, bigots, and authoritarians. Fitzgerald's generation had watched benign Americanization efforts turn into xenophobic outrages and the brutalizing of dissenters. It had witnessed the humane fight against alcoholism and other exploitive features of the liquor industry degenerate into the intolerant absolutism of Prohibition. It had seen government power, augmented by reformers to regulate industry for the National Good, become perverted to serve the industrial tycoons instead. It had observed altogether too many old-time progressive leaders—Miles Poindexter of Washington, Ralph Easley of the National Civic Federation, Jonathan Bourne of Oregon, Albert Beveridge of Indiana, A. Mitchell Palmer, Woodrow Wilson himself—turn into vicious activists for "law and order," which, translated, identified nearly every dissenter, labor leader, or critic of corporate management with communism, anarchism, treason, and immorality. It had watched reform movements abroad, frustrated, turn into revolution and then terror, with menacing reverberations around the world and utter calamity in Russia.

Worst of all, the same generation had witnessed the Great War for Democracy, which had featured calculated mass carnage as standard battle tactics; and, finally, the peace rendered stillborn by feckless leaders and mindless nationalism. "The War and the [Russian] Revolution," Hiram Johnson, California's progressive Republican Senator, commented in 1920, "has set back the people for a generation. They have bowed to a hundred repressive acts. . . . They are frightened at the excesses in Russia. They are docile; and . . . the interests which control the Republican party will make the most of their docility." There was nothing left on which to base a common effort for the improvement of the human condition. As the British economist John Maynard Keynes observed near the end of 1919: "Our power of feeling or caring beyond the immediate questions of our own material well-being is temporarily eclipsed. . . . Never in the lifetime of men now living has the universal element in the soul of man burnt so dimly." The editors of *The New Republic,* the advanced progressive journal that had urged American entry into the war as early as 1916, wrote in October 1919 of "The Discrediting of Idealism." "The implications . . . come home to every one who favored . . . the war on what are termed idealistic grounds. It comes with especial force to those who . . . broke with the pacifists because they saw in this war a means of realizing pacific ideals." Five years later, in 1924, the independent progressive William Kent remarked: "The war and the radicals in Russia have set back the course of democratic progress at least 20 years." The mood was enduring.

The Harding Years. The country in 1920 was ready for Warren Harding. It wanted calm not crusades, not tocsins but tranquility. Or as the man put it so memorably himself: "not heroism but healing, not nostrums but normalcy, not revolution but restoration, not agitation but adjustment, . . . not experiment but equipoise," and so on and on. William McAdoo was moved to remark that Harding's speeches "leave the impression of an army of pompous phrases moving over the landscape in search of an idea." But who wanted ideas? America's business was business. Get back to fundamentals. The country needed cooling off. "We have builded the America of today," said Harding, "on the fundamentals of economic, industrial, and political life which made us what we are, and the temple requires no remaking now." It also could do with less hysteria over the red menace. He who had joined in the clamor of 1919 to despatch "to Russia or some other land of tragic experiment" all who did not "subscribe heartily and loyally to the Constitution" freed Debs the first chance he got in 1921 and invited him to visit the White House. Some government officials, he complained, had become just too preoccupied with "reds" and "bolsheviks."

Harding recognized his limitations. He knew the job was too big for him and he promised to get the "best brains" to run the country. But although he made a few good, obvious selections—such as Charles Evans Hughes for secretary of state and Herbert Hoover for commerce—by and large he was a poor judge of either intelligence or character, and he lacked the simple competence to decide among competing views. "God! What a job!" he complained. "I listen to one side and they seem right, and then, God! I talk to the other side and they seem just as right." Heaven for Harding was strolling on a golf green, playing poker with hometown cronies, smoking good cigars, and drinking moderate amounts of hard liquor—an indulgence not even national Prohibition and the Volstead Act deterred. It also included escape from his austere, matronly wife—The Duchess, he called her—through covert liaisons with the adoring young Nan Britton, who had secretly borne him a child in 1919. He had always had an undownable appetite for sexual dalliance. It had entangled him for years in an anguished affair with the wife of one of his hometown friends; and it drove him to a number of "one-night stands" as well. He continued to satisfy all these cravings while campaigning for the presidency and after he came to reside in the White House. He was, as someone said, just "an average sensual man"; handsome, crude, heartily sophomoric, a joiner who hadn't the slightest capacity for solitary recreation, everyman's good fellow who hated to say no.

He was an adulterer and a dissembler; he lied to the delegation of Republican leaders who had asked him before his nomination if there was anything that might embarrass him (or them) as president; he solicited bootlegged liquor while president; he appointed incompetents and men with little character to positions of national authority out of loyalty to their friendship; and he probably collaborated in concealing some crimes in high places. Yet he was a man of basically decent motives and small pretensions. "Harding was not a bad man—just a slob," said Alice Roosevelt Longworth. The crown of hypocrisy rests on those who promoted him; the badge of corruption belongs to those who betrayed his simplicity and naive loyalties.

In the light of the criminal acts of the Nixon administration half a century later, the scandals of Harding's administration seem like peccadillos, reinforcing still further the view of the twenties as a frivolous era. Only a few of the offenses concerned the abuse of power by high government officials. None victimized private individuals for partisan political gain. Some, relatively at least, might today come under the heading of petty theft. Many had their origins in the final acts of the Wilson administration.

The Volstead Act, for example, passed over Wilson's veto in 1920 and set the stage for large-scale corruption. The act specifically exempted the Prohibition enforcement unit, which was placed within the Internal Revenue Service, from civil service rules. This fact, together with the low salaries that Congress provided for enforcement officers, virtually guaranteed that many agents would accept or solicit payoffs from liquor manufacturers, bootleggers, and operators of speakeasies. By 1926, 752 prohibition agents had been dismissed from the 2000-member IRS unit; 141 were convicted of various criminal acts.

The president did not yet know that his own political mentor, Attorney General Harry Daugherty, had apparently been selling immunity, pardons, paroles, and government appointments from an apartment he shared in Washington with Jesse Smith, a hometown friend and accomplice. Although Daugherty was never convicted, friend Smith committed suicide in May 1923, shortly after Harding had received warnings of what was going on from close associates in the White House. Daugherty was also implicated, at least through Smith, in the corruption of the Alien Property Custodian's Office, which was charged with selling or returning mostly German-owned properties confiscated during the war. The agency's chief, Thomas Miller, went to jail. But in spite of the most brazen defiance of congressional probers—whom Daugherty secretly ordered the FBI to investigate—and despite mounting evidence against him, Daugherty hung on as attorney general until President Calvin Coolidge had to fire him in March 1924. Eventually Daugherty eluded jail by pleading that his confidential relationship with the late president and Mrs. Harding prevented him from offering a proper defense in court.

Except in a few cases, such as the conduct of Harry Daugherty, the corruption of the Harding years seems tinged as much with pathos as with true villainy. About the time of Jesse Smith's suicide, Harding learned that his old crony, Charles R. Forbes, whom Harding had made chief of the Veterans' Administration (VA), had been taking kickbacks on hospital contracts he had awarded and had sold off at bargain prices nearly a quarter of a billion dollars of "surplus" government medical equipment and supplies. Harding sent his friend quietly into retirement abroad, but a month later the suicide of Charles F. Cramer, legal aide to the VA, broke open the case, and Forbes went to jail in 1925.

Albert Fall, a former Senate colleague whom Harding named secretary of the interior in 1921, became the first cabinet member ever to go to jail for crimes committed in office. Using the discretionary powers that Congress had authorized during the Wilson administration, Fall leased drilling rights at Elk Hills Naval Reserve (Los Angeles) to Edward Doheny of Pan American Oil Company, and at Teapot Dome, Wyoming, to Harry Sinclair of Mammoth Oil Company. His problems began when conservationist senators Thomas Walsh and Burton Wheeler of Montana caught him lying about who gave him $100,000 on an unsecured personal note. Further investigation showed that Sinclair had presented Fall with $260,000 in cash and in Liberty Bonds, and that the $100,000 cash had come from Doheny, delivered personally by his son. Fall was convicted of accepting a bribe, but both Doheny and Sinclair were acquitted. Doheny's son committed suicide.

The Coolidge Era. When Warren Harding died suddenly in August 1923—some say of a broken heart over the disloyalty of his friends—the country once again found itself with a Puritan president. John Calvin Coolidge and Thomas Woodrow Wilson were profoundly similar men, especially in their stern view of life and in their emphasis on personal duty and service. But though they resided in a common Puritan cosmos, they stood at polar ends. Where Wilson represented Calvinism with all the force of its social imperatives, Coolidge's righteousness remained strictly personal, even antisocial. Though both were college-educated their separate training was symptomatic of their divergence—Wilson emerging from Princeton and scholarly, internationally oriented Johns Hopkins looking out upon the Atlantic; Coolidge imbibing a "classical" learning at Amherst, the tiny elite college tucked away in the Connecticut Valley. Wilson's sense of mission, which so thoroughly conditioned his commitment to public service, suggested the "errand into the wilderness" quality of American culture—an attribute that arrived somewhat later than the Puritans, perhaps just as Wilson's Scotch-Irish forebears arrived a century later than Coolidge's Puritan ancestors had. Coolidge's Calvinism was indeed of the more antique variety, introspective and separatist in emphasis, given to facing up to the hardness of life, uninspired by the promise of a bounteous continent or by the more generous potentials of the Puritan ethic.

This antique quality in Coolidge has always invited caricature. He was the squarest of squares, a remarkably insensitive man, and yet never uninteresting. There is something almost titillating about him; he appears always so awkward, so simple, so incongruous, that he emerges a veritable spectacle. He looked, said Alice Roosevelt Longworth, like a man who had been weaned on a pickle.

Named for John Calvin, and after his father, Coolidge was born in Plymouth Notch, Vermont, on July 4th, in 1872. He named his sons John and Calvin. "He was born and raised," writes Donald McCoy, his best biographer, "in one of the backwaters of America. . . . He came from among those who were content to make do with what they had, those who held to high moral standards, those of low metabolism who had little interest in seeing what lay beyond the nearest ridge, those whose prosaic thoughts often seemed profoundly expressed and who had little truck with ideas that were not prosaic." He not only was of mediocre abilities; he deliberately sought mediocre men around him. As president, he insisted that his subordinates do their jobs without involving him, pleading that the president must not be made to look foolish since he was not free to leave whereas they could resign if they blundered. With his family, he sulked openly, had tantrums, delighted in playing practical jokes. He daydreamed habitually, fretted constantly about his health, and though he possessed a sharp wit it characteristically took the form of the "put-down."

A small-town lawyer who had settled in Northampton, Massachusetts, after graduating from nearby Amherst, Coolidge climbed the political ladder in the Bay State to become governor in 1918. He gained national renown in 1919 when, in reply to a telegram from Samuel Gompers that supported a strike by Boston police, Coolidge declared: "There is no right to strike against the public safety by anybody, anywhere, any time." Amidst the antiradical hysteria that the conservative press and politicians had cultivated in 1919, Coolidge's words qualified him for instant eminence. And when California's progressive Senator Hiram Johnson declined the second spot behind Harding, GOP leaders gratefully chose Coolidge.

Coolidge suited the times well. "He aspired," wrote Irving Stone, "to become the least President the country had ever had. . . . By the very act of sleeping with his feet up on the desk he sincerely believed he was making his most valuable contribution to the American way of life." "Four-fifths of all our troubles in this life would disappear," said Coolidge, "if we would only sit down and keep still." Appropriately, he slept late, retired early, and worked about a five-hour day in between. "Keep Cool With Coolidge" helped win him a term in the White House in his own right in 1924, with a substantial popular majority (15.7 million) over both John W. Davis, a right-wing Democrat who was J. P. Morgan & Company's lawyer (8.3 million), and "Fighting Bob" LaFollette, nominated by a rag-tag alliance of old radicals, progressives, and farm-bloc interests to head a new, short-lived Progressive party (4.8 million). "While I don't expect anything very astonishing from [the president]," wrote Justice Holmes at the time, "I don't want anything very astonishing." And William Howard Taft, whom Harding had made Chief Justice of the Supreme Court, gloated that America had become the most conservative country in the world.

The Business Side of the Jazz Age

"Teapot Dome" came to stand for all the corruption and ineptitude of the Harding administration, much the way "Watergate" came to mean so much more than the actual burglary of the Democratic party's headquarters by men hired by the Nixon White House. More important than the oil leasing affair itself was the general impression offered by the administrations of both Warren Harding and Calvin Coolidge that the government was for the taking by special interests in and out of office. It had been the mark of a progressive in the Age of Theodore Roosevelt to fight for strong government agencies to regulate private economic power. But with progressivism out, even passé, the old question, "Who will regulate the regulators?" returned as a torment. Teapot Dome was only the prime case in point.

TR's and Gifford Pinchot's conservation program had depended heavily on a strong executive with much discretionary power. Even after Pinchot had come to suspect the intentions of Wilson's secretary of the interior, Franklin K. Lane, he continued to support measures designed to enlarge the secretary's power to issue leases and to determine fraud in claims disputes. The Leasing Act of 1920 confirmed such power. Unfortunately for the conservationist cause, after 1920 the political climate had changed and the "wrong people" held power. The environment that had encouraged Albert Fall to believe he had done no wrong in accepting $360,000 in "gifts" already led Lane, William G. McAdoo, and other high officials of the Wilson administration to accept lucrative positions with the oil companies immediately upon their premature resignations from office in 1919 and 1920. As in the "Gilded Age," from Grant to McKinley, the line blurred between the public responsibility of officeholders and the prerogatives of private enterprisers.

The public did not seem to care, and this fact, for most practical purposes, removed considerations of "the public interest" from the political arena. Certainly the old issues of the Progressive era—conservation, corruption, regulation of the corporations—did not exercise most voters. "It was characteristic of the Jazz Age," Fitzgerald wrote in 1931, "that it had no interest in politics at all." "We're not out to benefit society . . . or to make industry safe," a college coed told a poll-taker. "We're not going to suffer over how the other half lives." When Senators Walsh and Wheeler began their oil leasing investigations, the leading newspapers in the country attacked them as "character assassins," "mud-gunners," and "scandalmongers." "A reformer," wisecracked New York's popular high-living mayor Jimmy Walker, "is a fellow who takes a pleasure cruise in a sewer in a glass-bottomed boat." So the field was clear for those with special interests at stake, and who did care about who decided what in government. The public's political apathy provided their opportunity.

In the circumstances, the character of government agencies became transformed. Although originally designed to shift priorities in national policy toward public and consumer interests, the regulatory bureaus under the new order restored the primacy of producer interests. The progressives had fought to activate government on behalf of social and economic interests that had been served poorly by the marketplace. But after 1918, government acted chiefly to affirm and reinforce the ascendancy of the already-powerful.

Encouraging Big Business. Noting the unfashionable vigor with which the four-year old Federal Trade Commission (FTC) had pursued wartime profiteering in the meatpacking industry, the Republican Congress in 1919 transferred jurisdiction over the industry to the more friendly, producer-oriented Agriculture Department. Harding's first appointment to the FTC was Vernon W. Van Fleet, who had served the National Association of Manufacturers (NAM) as its chief lobbyist. And Coolidge's choice in 1925 for chairman of the FTC was William T. Humphrey, who opposed government regulation on principle and who had complained that the FTC in particular had served as "a publicity bureau to spread socialistic propaganda." Under Humphrey, the FTC began offering businessmen advice on how to circumvent the antitrust laws. Eventually, the old progressives still in Congress began a fight to abolish the commission, charging that the FTC had become, in George Norris' words, "a refuge for monopoly, unfair competition, and unfair business methods."

The retreat from competition in the nation's business proceeded with a new energy. We have already noted how the Wilson administration encouraged "cooperative" business practices during the war years while suspending antitrust suits. In the same spirit Congress in 1920 passed the Transportation and Merchant Marine Acts, extending immunity from the antitrust laws to the railroad and shipping industries. In 1922 the Capper-Volstead Act, in response to pressures from agricultural interests, gave the same immunities to farm cooperatives which were, for all essential purposes, instruments for reducing competition in what farmers bought and sold. Throughout the 1920s, Secretary of Commerce Hoover helped organize business associations which he encouraged to set up self-enforced codes of "fair business practices." These practices included standardizing the quality of products and "price leadership" for reducing price competition. In 1925 the Supreme Court approved these anticompetitive devices, ruling that they did not violate antitrust statutes as long as they were used openly and avoided the appearance of collusion.

The Supreme Court launched the era with a remarkable decision in 1920 that defeated the government's ten-year-old on-again, off-again prosecution of United States Steel Corporation. "We are unable to see," declared the court, "that the public interest will be served by . . . dissolution of the company or the separation of it from some of its subsidiaries; and we do see in contrary conclusion a risk of injury to the public interest." And since "the public interest is of paramount regard," the Court asserted its power to lay aside "the policy of the law and its fortifying prohibitions." To clinch the matter, when Harry Daugherty took over the Justice Department in 1921, he reassured the corporation managers: "As long as I'm Attorney General, I'm not going unnecessarily to harass men who have unwittingly run counter with [sic] the statutes."

Small wonder then that the 1920s witnessed a new wave of business consolidations that seemingly belied the very existence of the Sherman and Clayton Antitrust Acts. In 1921 the number of mergers of industrial firms already approached a level nearly

BUSINESS ACTIVITY, 1890-1930

Solid line = wholesale price index.   1926 = 100
Shaded configurations represent measures of business prosperity, comprised by indices of activity in sectors of services and production such as pig iron consumption, rail production, imports, exports, coal output, cotton consumption, government expenditures, and freight ton-miles.

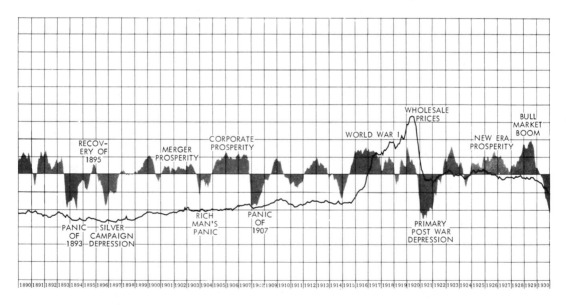

Except for the period between 1879 and 1883, the price index declined throughout the last quarter of the 19th century, until 1897, then rose steadily till 1914 and sharply to 1920. Steady prices during the 1920s and (except for 1923) consistently positive growth in business activity gave that decade its sense of well-being. Monthly fluctuations in activity can readily be correlated with political events.

SOURCE: *The Cleveland Trust Company.*

twice that for the high year of the Taft administration. By 1929 the annual merger figure reached four times the 1921 total (see chart page 93). Between 1919 and 1930 nearly 12,000 public utility, banking, manufacturing, and mining companies disappeared as the result of 2100 mergers, swallowing more than twice the number of operating plants as had been absorbed in the Great Consolidation Movement of 1897-1904. Moreover, concentration of economic power followed the consolidation curve. Whereas in 1909 the top 100 nonfinancial firms accounted for 17.7 percent of the assets of all such companies, by 1929 that figure was 25.5 percent. By 1925 a mere 95 manufacturing firms (0.1 percent of all such firms filing tax returns that year) accounted for 44.5 percent of aggregate manufacturing income. And the proportion of all corporate income going to the top 200 companies rose from about one third in 1920 to almost 40 percent by 1927.

Overall, corporate profits soared, rising twice as fast as productivity (measured by man-hours of input per unit of production) and eight times as fast as real wages. Management of many large corporations found it convenient to return as little as half the profits to the stockholders in the form of dividends, leaving huge surpluses for reinvestment and giving them an independence of commercial banks—almost unique since the development of corporate capitalism. One result of the increased "internal financing" of corporate growth was a decline of bank loans that caused more than 5000 of the smaller banks in the country to shut down; 17 percent fewer banks did business in 1929 than in 1921. The spread of branch banking further concentrated the country's financial power. By 1929, 744 commercial banks operated 3500 branches, and one percent of all banks controlled 46 percent of the country's banking capital. A second effect was that commercial banks turned increasingly to real estate loans, to investments in high-risk corporate equity (stocks as opposed to bonds), and to making short-term loans to securities brokers. Brokers loans grew by more than 300 percent between 1921 and 1929 ($800 million to $2.6 billion), amounting to a substantial portion of the money Wall Street used to reorganize the finances of the country. The redirection of the nation's business capital into the stock market helped to encourage speculation, which became increasingly reckless after 1926 and eventuated in the great crackup of 1929. Stock market price averages rose 180 percent between 1923 and 1929.

The nation that began the century with conscience pangs over what it deemed an inequitable distribution of wealth witnessed without evident dismay a worsening drift in the 1920s. By 1928, 5 percent of the population possessed more than one third of the disposable income in the country, up from 24 percent at the start of the decade. Less than 2.5 percent of all income recipients—or all those earning $10,000 or more annually—accounted for two thirds of all savings. The wealthiest 36,000 families in the country earned as much as the poorest 12 million (42 percent of all families).

Tax policies contributed to the drift. Taxes on excess profits died with the final two years of the Wilson administration, while the Harding and Coolidge administrations did everything legal and some things extralegal to reduce income taxes especially in the upper brackets. Surtaxes on the highest incomes dropped from 65 percent to 20 percent. Moreover, a congressional committee checking on the Internal Revenue

Service in 1924 discovered that many large corporations had received huge tax rebates during the first few years of Andrew Mellon's term as secretary of the treasury. As it turned out, the rebates were legal, though requiring an exceptionally generous interpretation of IRS rules. President Coolidge soon throttled the investigations by charging the committee with "fishing" for scandal. Given the prevailing consensus that sanctified Business and damnified Politics, the investigators, not the IRS or the corporations, retreated under fire. It was not until 1930, when The Crash removed some of the glow from business sacrosanctity, that a more complete picture of tax manipulations emerged. A new inquiry then revealed that Mellon had had the IRS draft a list of "ways by which an individual may legally avoid tax," five of which he readily confessed he used personally, and all of which he made available to friendly corporations. In addition, between 1921 and 1929 Mellon awarded $3.5 billion to individuals and corporations in the form of direct refunds, tax abatements, and credits; conspicuous among the beneficiaries were many who had contributed large sums to the Republican party.

Congressional Democrats and a group of midwestern Republicans representing farm districts fought Mellon's tax policies with some success until 1924, but it should be noted that no one in the antiadministration forces in Congress ever advanced constructive proposals for using tax revenues. Virtually no federally supported welfare, employment, education, or research programs of any significance gained a hearing in Congress during the entire period. About the only "new" program that Congress pursued with any interest was road building, in order to accommodate the exuberant growth of automobile and motortruck transportation. Extending paved roads beyond city limits consumed as much as 75 percent of federal construction outlays in the period. Congress expended less on public works in 1929 than in 1919. Under the circumstances, there was substance to the conservatives' argument that a higher tax on the wealthy would amount to a tax on savings, and ultimately on the nation's prosperity. That is, since wealthier people typically invest what they save after buying consumer goods, to tax higher incomes more heavily without investing the revenues in public works, education, health, research, or the like would have had the effect of reducing the total capital available for investment.

The Attack on Labor. The government's partnership with the country's financial and industrial leaders went beyond helping them evade the antitrust and tax laws. The Judiciary and the Executive branches especially turned their resources against the labor movement. Harry Daugherty, who had generously promised that he was "not going unnecessarily to harass" businessmen when they ran afoul of the antitrust statutes, showed no such magnanimity to union leaders. Harding's attorney general set the keynote for the decade when he declared: "So long and to the extent that I can speak for the government of the United States, I will use the power of the government to prevent the labor unions . . . from destroying the open shop." And he did. The high (or low) point of the Justice Department's antiunion activities came in September 1922 when Daugherty obtained an injunction against striking railway workers that was breathtaking in the scope of activities it prohibited. Even cabinet members Herbert Hoover and Charles Evans Hughes were moved to protest to the president that the injunction (in Hoover's words) "was outrageous in law as well as morals," and an "obvious transgression of the most rudimentary rights of the men." Although Harding eventually forced Daugherty to withdraw some of the more obnoxious features of that particular court order, labor took a bad beating throughout the decade.

It should be noted once again, however, that the retreat of the movement for social justice began in the Wilson years. In part this was because the Wilsonian progressives never favored unionism and were pleased to see it beaten down once the Armistice ended the need for a union-disciplined workforce. In spite of the government's official recognition of organized labor during the war, most Americans still refused to grant to unionism the legitimacy accorded to corporations. Partly for that reason, in 1919 the outbreak of major strikes over frozen wages amidst rocketing prices served mainly to heighten popular hostility to the unions. Especially since most other Americans were also victimized by runaway prices, the work stoppages appeared to add to the cost of living, aggravate shortages, and—in those hysterical months—raise the specter of "insurrection." For shallow partisans like the Harry Daughertys, even the outrages perpetrated in 1919 by Woodrow Wilson's Justice Department to break the steel and coal strikes and to head off a railway walkout appeared both too little and too late. They appeared "too late" because, as many voters had come to believe, Wilson's "capitulation" to unionism embodied in the Adamson Railway Labor Act of 1916 had already inspired union leaders to levels of arrogance that signified social revolution.

Throughout the final years of the Wilson administration, leaders of both parties vied with each other in putting down that "revolution," in condemning labor, in endorsing The American Plan—meaning the open shop—and in praising "Industrial Democracy" programs concocted by some corporations to replace AFL locals with company unions. "Labor . . . was never more alone than it is at the present time," wrote the editor of the rail unions' journal, *Labor*, in late 1919. "Congress and the administrative agencies of the government have joined with capitalism in a war upon labor."

But the real body blows to the labor movement came from the courts, and the responsibility for this lay much more with Chief Justice and President William Howard Taft than with Wilson. Between 1910 and 1923, Taft had a direct role in the elevation of no less than eight justices to the Supreme Court. In four years as president (1909-13), Taft had put five on the Court and had promoted Associate Justice Edward D. White to chief justice. (By contrast, Theodore Roosevelt named three in seven years; Wilson, three in eight years; and Franklin Roosevelt none at all until the start of his second term in 1937.) In less than three years, Harding named four to the Court, including Taft himself as chief justice in 1921 on White's death. From the center seat on the bench, Taft successfully influenced at least two of Harding's other three nominations.

As in all times of changing social priorities in America, the Supreme Court in the early twentieth century took on major policymaking functions. Although jurists of Taft's mental set were incapable of describing the issues in that way, Taft at least saw clearly that "the times are out of joint" and that it was of "the greatest importance" that the right kind of judges be appointed. Of course, a good judge was one who had fairly specific, "safe" views on property. "There is no greater issue," Taft said in 1920,

" . . . than the maintenance of the Supreme Court as the bulwark to enforce the guaranty that no man shall be deprived of his property without due process of law." "Our primary conception of a free man," he wrote in 1922, "is one who can enjoy what he earns, who can spend it for his comfort or pleasure if he would. . . . This is the right of property." For Taft, then, freedom consisted primarily in the protected ability to use property, but not necessarily in the ability to gain property (wages)— unless one already possessed property capable of generating more property (profits). When he became chief justice, Taft announced to his new associates that he had been chosen "to reverse a few decisions." He singled out labor as the main trouble. "That faction," he confided, "we have to hit every little while."

Altogether, Taft, his judicial appointees, and his spiritual colleagues throughout the American court system succeeded in sending the law on labor relations reeling backward into the nineteenth century. By expanding the use of court injunctions in labor disputes beyond every precedent in Anglo-American law and by voiding an also unprecedented number of state and federal laws, the judges took into their own hands the shaping of America's labor policy. Mostly the same judges on the Supreme Court who decided in 1920 to lay aside "the policy of the law" when it came to the Steel Trust also found that "the public interest" demanded using the antitrust laws against unions. As already suggested in Chapter 3, the protection labor was supposed to get from the Clayton Act (1914) never materialized because although the act exempted unions per se from the antitrust laws, what unions might *lawfully do* remained subject to determination by the judges. In *Duplex Printing Co.* v. *Deering* (1920), the first Supreme Court test of the Clayton Act exemptions, the Court majority decided that Congress intended to exempt only local, not national, unions from antitrust restraints. In *The Lean Years* (1960), the best study of labor in the 1920-33 period, Irving Bernstein writes: "In their impact the antitrust laws were much the most important labor relations statutes on the books. The manipulation of the Sherman and Clayton Acts to restrict union activities, emerging slowly for thirty years, reached a climax in the Supreme Court in the twenties."

What it amounted to was that the privileges the majority of the Court readily granted to organized capital assets (corporations) they found unthinkable for organized labor. Corporate management, for example, could legally coerce workers into signing "yellow-dog" contracts in which employees pledged as a condition of their continued employment not to join a union, but striking workers could not attempt to intimidate potential strike breakers even solely by the act of peaceful picketing. In *American Steel Foundries* v. *Tri-City Central Trades Council* (1921), the Court majority virtually outlawed picketing: "All information tendered, all arguments advanced and all persuasion under such circumstances," declared the judges, constituted "intimidation." "The very word picket," said Taft, implied threats. And when Arizona in 1913 attempted to guarantee the right to peaceful picketing by forbidding any state court from issuing an injunction against it, the Court (in *Truax* v. *Corrigan,* 1921) struck down the statute on the grounds that picketing was an act of coercion that both violated the rights of individual workers and threatened "irreparable damage" to employers' profit opportunities (here defined as "property," for constitutional convenience).

In *Adair* v. *U.S.* (1908) and *Coppage* v. *Kansas* (1915), the Supreme Court had ruled that neither the federal government nor any state could forbid an employer from discriminating against employees on the grounds of union membership. Although the *Adair* and *Coppage* decisions gave a kind of moral support to yellow-dog contracts, their enforcement remained a matter of the relative strength of employers versus union organizers. The *Hitchman Coal* decision of 1917 changed that; for the first time the high court placed the law of the land behind the contracts. The Court majority claimed —in spite of the Clayton Act—that labor organizers, by their "unlawful and malicious" efforts to induce workers to unionize, incited workers to commit "concerted breaches of contract" in violation of the common law ban against conspiracies or combinations in restraint of trade. Until the *Hitchman* case, the yellow-dog contract had been little more than a troublesome hurdle for union organizers. Thereafter it threatened the very existence of the independent labor movement. By 1929, 1.25 million workers had been forced to sign yellow-dog contracts, and there was virtually no legal means by which labor leaders could even approach them. For this and related reasons, union membership declined from its high of 5.1 million in 1920 to 3.4 million in 1930.

The courts hammered the labor movement on every front, showing little regard for legal traditions or for social preferences expressed in legislation. Of the 1845 injunctions ordered by American courts between 1880 and 1930, 921 were issued in the 1920s. No previous era approached the twenties in the number of statutes voided by the Supreme Court. Twelve congressional acts alone were struck down, or one fourth of all such acts invalidated up to 1925.

By 1930 no industrial nation in the world had labor practices so retrograde as the United States. Not only had the courts explicitly privileged the power of employers to discriminate against workers who belonged or wished to belong to unions of their own choosing, the judge-made laws also empowered employers to form company unions and to force employees to belong to them. Employers were also free to hire spies and to infiltrate workers' associations for espionage purposes; they could employ and arm industrial police, and in many localities invest them with the authority of public law by deputizing them. By 1921, because of Supreme Court vetoes, the country had no national child labor regulations, in spite of two congressional enactments; by 1923 it had no minimum wage law, despite fifteen state laws and one congressional act (for the District of Columbia) passed during the Progressive era. By voiding state laws that prohibited (or even attempted only to regulate) fees charged by private employment agencies, the judges asserted their own preference for the priority of profit-making over employees' interests, and left the country unique among modern nations in requiring the unemployed to purchase access to jobs at "open market" prices. America was also unique in having no unemployment insurance, and no pension system.

As Taft reflected on his career in 1930, he told his brother that his objective on the Court had been "to prevent the Bolsheviki from getting control." Actually, there had been little danger of that, even allowing for the fact that Taft's definition of "Bolsheviki" covered an extraordinarily broad spectrum of social critics. What Taft and his fellows did achieve was an environment in which the labor movement could make little progress by legal or peaceful means. As Bernstein has remarked: "It is a commentary on the state of labor relations in the late twenties to note the appallingly large number of arrests for felonies. . . . No other advanced nation in the world conducted its industrial relations with such defiance of the criminal law." Inevitably, especially in the big cities, union racketeers and extortionists infected the labor movement where the legitimate leadership had been blocked.

Agriculture. Progressive era efforts to save "the family farm" met with a fate comparable to that of the Clayton Act and the FTC. "The farmer who owns his own land," the progressive and pioneer conservationist Gifford Pinchot had written, "is still the backbone of this Nation and one of the things we want most is more of him." In the Smith-Lever (Agricultural Extension Service) Act of 1914, Congress had appropriated funds for experiment stations and local farm bureaus which various private banking and commercial groups had begun financing during the first decade of the century. An important goal was the bypassing of the militant farmer movements such as had caused great political turmoil in the last quarter of the nineteenth century and— as the progressives saw it—had emphasized "class interests" over the general interest. Under the partial supervision of the Department of Agriculture, a small army of agents advanced into farm counties to educate farmers in modern agriculture and in economical purchasing and marketing arrangements. The agents were instructed to work through local farm bureaus and community leaders. Their organizing efforts culminated in 1919 in the coalescence of state federations of farm bureaus into the American Farm Bureau Federation (AFBF), the most powerful farm group the country has had.

From the very beginning, the AFBF represented not the small-unit marginal farmers struggling to compete in the complex system of modern commercial agriculture, but the interests of the already dominant farm and merchant groups through which the country agents had been working. The rhetoric of the earliest AFBF conventions left

DECLINE OF THE FARM SECTOR

IN U.S. ECONOMY

Years	Farm Product Value Billions ($) (Constant 1929 Dollars)	Percent of GNP
1879-88	5.8	28
1897-1901	8.4	25
1902-06	8.9	20
1907-11	9.2	21
1912-16	10.1	17
1917-21	9.7	14
1921	9.0	13
1922	9.6	13
1923	10.2	12
1924	9.7	11
1925	10.4	12

SOURCE: *The Statistical History of the United States from Colonial Times to the Present.*

no doubt as to the path the organization would take. It disowned long-standing farmer-labor unity movements, blamed the high cost of living on "the curtailment of production through short hours, lessened efficiency of labor and strikes," and placed itself with the most strident union-busting exponents of the day. It vowed to fight any policy "that will align organized farmers with the radicals of other organizations." It pledged "unqualifiedly" to support "the government's determination to suppress radicalism." Above all, it set out in single-minded pursuit of government aid to agriculture while preserving intact the prevailing structure of advantage within the industry.

In a few words, the progressive legislation of 1914 that had aimed to quell special-interest pressures from farmers and to preserve family farming culminated in the creation of a massive pressure group. This group advanced, within the very governmental processes that had created it, the special claims of the dominant agricultural interests. Although many historians still treat the AFBF's campaigns as evidence of progressivism's continued vitality in the 1920s, it should be apparent that they expressed the progressive spirit as poorly as did the FTC during the Coolidge administration.

By early 1922 more than twenty senators and a varying number of congressmen from the farm states became persuaded that their political survival depended on their endorsement by the AFBF. The Farm Bloc, as the group called itself, pursued farm legislation without a hint of the embarrassment that would have attached to such dogged "class" commitment in the Progressive era. As late as 1918 agrarian spokesman Liberty Hyde Bailey protested "organized efforts that seek to gain their ends by force of numbers, by compulsion and strategy." "I trust," Bailey said with typical progressive hopefulness, "that we shall avoid class legislation by farmers." His trust proved vain. The AFBF counted among its political achievements in the 1920s: (a) removing packer and stockyard regulation from the FTC; (b) establishing federal regulation of the grain exchanges; (c) extending the War Finance Corporation's charter in order to make loans at low interest for grain and cotton exports (passed over President Wilson's veto in 1921); (d) raising tariff walls against farm imports; (e) exempting farm cooperatives from the antitrust law; and (f) creating the Intermediate Credits Act (1923), which permitted solvent farmers and country banks to apply for government-endorsed loans.

Through its allies in Congress, the AFBF also pushed through the McNary-Haugen bill after a six-year fight, only to have Coolidge veto it twice. The measure would have established a dual price system for major crops, whereby produce unsellable in the United States at prices pegged higher than those in the world market would be "dumped" abroad at the lower prices. The federal government would assume responsibility for distributing the costs of this program among the farmers on a pro rata basis. Coolidge, Hoover, Mellon, and other leaders pointed out that such a policy would raise domestic food prices unnaturally high, impinging especially on the mass of the urban working population. If manufacturers raised prices to compensate for the higher wages that would become necessary, they would become uncompetitive in international markets; and if they did not raise prices, lower net profits would mean less savings and investments—and ultimately fewer jobs. At the same time, since the measure imposed no limits on crops, there could be no restriction on the amount of commodities dumped overseas, therefore no lower limit to international food prices, and so no curb on the unfavorable differential between labor costs of foreign manufacturers and those of American manufacturers. Finally, the practice of dumping surplus commodities abroad has always provoked economic warfare in the form of retaliatory tariff barriers.

Farmer advocates argued that Coolidge's vetoes once again proved "Wall Street's" domination of America. They noted the continuing agricultural recession and the unwillingness of the federal government to do for agriculture what it did readily for other economic groups. As one Missouri congressman complained: "I would not for a moment be in favor of [McNary-Haugen] or in favor of putting the Government into business. . . . But the Government has already gone into business. It went into business when the first tariff law was passed . . . when the first immigration law was passed, because it decreased the supply of labor . . . [and] when the Adamson law and the Cummins-Esch law [the Transportation Act of 1920] were passed. . . . There is only one industry in the United States for whose benefit the Government has not yet gone into business, and that is our greatest industry—agriculture." Real farm income during the 1920s rose at a much slower rate than did corporate profits. The parity index, determined by comparing the cost of a mix of products farmers had to buy with the price of what farmers sold, dipped from 101 in 1913 and 110 in 1919 to a low of 80 in 1921 and an average of about 90 for the twenties.

On the other hand, by using 1913 and 1919 as points for measuring farmers' welfare meant citing agriculture's *most* prosperous years as the standard. Between 1900 and 1910, farm prices increased almost 50 percent and farm land values about the same, while nonfarm prices rose only 18 percent. This fact had much to do with the negligible increase in real income for factory and mine workers during the same period. In the 1920s most farmers continued to enjoy a rising standard of living, but now argued that urban employment brought more rapid growth. They were also no longer content with the spartan rural values they had traditionally held up over city life-styles. "One reason the farmer of today feels himself less fortunately situated than his father was," observed the *Indiana Farmer's Guide* in 1927, ". . . is that he has acquired a new standard of living. . . . He demands for himself and his family any number of things which his father never dreamed of having."

In addition, the troubles of agriculture arose in large measure from farmers' unwillingness or inability to adjust to important changes in the American scene that had reduced demand for the major commercial crops. A shift in dietary habits and sartorial

Percentage Distribution of the Gainfully Employed by Industry*

	1900	1910	1920	1930
Agriculture	37.9	31.6	27.4	22.1
Manufacturing	21.6	22.5	26.1	23.0
Trade	8.9	9.6	9.9	12.7
Government	2.7	3.6	4.5	5.0
Private Services	12.2	13.0	11.7	15.1

* Transportation, Mining, and Finance industries not included.

tastes had much to do with that. Americans heated their houses more and traveled more in closed autos; consequently they wore lighter clothes, less woolens, more rayon. New fashions not only called for trim-fitting clothes but a spare figure inside. Shortly after the turn of the century, corpulence in men and heftiness in women ceased to signify robust health and material substance. Americans ate less, turning away especially from starchy cereals. They consumed more protein, and more fruit and vegetables, many of them imported. Significantly, cattle, dairy, fruit and truck farming did not experience the recession that afflicted the grains, cotton, and wool sectors of agriculture.

After 1914 the population growth rate dropped sharply; the war, the immigration restriction acts of 1917, 1921, and 1924, and the increased use of contraceptives all played a role in this. After 1919 the domestic market no longer could absorb increases in farm production at prewar prices, and the international market had become sated by the postwar recovery of European production. Replacement of draft animals by tractors reduced demand for certain farm products, like oats. So did Prohibition. Mechanization increased productivity and worsened the condition of overproduction at desired prices. Although agricultural spokesmen wanted the government to help in dumping surpluses abroad, they resisted all efforts to include production controls in the legislative package.

Finally, the measures promoted by the Farm Bloc were designed to meet primarily the needs of the largest farmers and their merchant-banker allies. By the mid-twenties, meanwhile, the proportion of all farm operators who were tenants and sharecroppers rose above 40 percent. As of 1929, 11 percent of all farmers earned about half of all farm income. For the dominant elements in the industry, farming had become self-consciously a business. The more prosperous farmers had become employers on a large scale. Their trade association, the AFBF, had become the country's most single-minded political lobby.

The Cultural Battleground

But the discontent associated with the farm regions had larger cultural dimensions than economic. Much of that discontent found expression outside the regular political avenues, but was none the less vigorous, not to say rancorous, for it all. It was not that the nation had suddenly become "urbanized." True, the 1920 census revealed that for the first time the majority of the American people no longer lived in communities of less than 2500. But 2500 people—or 4000, or 8000—do not a city make, and there is little evidence that the mores of such small towns differed substantially from those of the old farm villages.

It was not where but *how* Americans lived that rankled. It was the failure of the melting pot to blend the millions of new immigrants into Anglo-Americans that griped. It was the inability of a whole generation of reformers and uplifters to restore confidence in the certainties of traditional moral doctrine that brought pessimism and resentment. Everywhere abounded reminders of prevailing moral decay: The 50 percent increase in the divorce rate since 1910; the spreading incidence of adultery; the new generation's immodesty of dress and speech; the bold intimacy and abandon of the new dances; the provocative scenes and themes of the cinema; the suggestive throbbing beat of jazz; the open disregard for law and lawfulness, conspicuously in defiance of Prohibition. Above all, there was the new assertiveness of Jews, Catholics, blacks, and foreigners. For a large proportion of the country's native-born white Protestants, liberalism had failed to meet the challenges of the new demographic mix, the new technology, and the new canons of good taste and behavior. It had yielded only an unseemly tolerance of things and thoughts that by their very nature ran counter to long-tested conventional standards of morality.

Reform energies persisted in the 1920s, but their most important sources no longer generated a robust optimism about the future. They expressed rather a cynicism and bitterness over the shape the future was taking. To millions of Americans who had been bred in the confidence that they were of a superior "race" destined to inherit the earth, it seemed they now looked on the passing scene as bystanders and losers.

In the early twenties the "losers" struck back with a vigor that was dismaying to those whose commitment to social causes had originated in a concern for the emancipation of the human spirit. The new insurgency was self-consciously regressive, defiantly reactionary, militantly determined to revitalize old limits on the social choices that individuals should be permitted to make.

The Fundamentalist Revolt. "Men insist vehemently upon their certainties," wrote the young Reinhold Niebuhr in 1927, "when their hold upon them has been shaken. Frantic orthodoxy is a method for obscuring doubt." The great Protestant theologian, who was then still puzzling out the proper relationship between Christian faith and social action in the working-class districts of Detroit, might have further remarked that it was also a way of coping with the inadequacy of all the solutions for contemporary moral problems offered over the previous two decades by progressive prophets and social gospelers. Skepticism and scientific rationalism had not maintained either peace or harmony; they had induced Americans to cast off moral anchors without charting a course or fixing a destination. In the backwash of the postwar disillusionment, the freedom to test new experience presented more terrors than delights. This may suggest a failure of nerve for some who mobilized for social action in the early 1920s, but probably for most it was a straightforward reassertion of faith that had been on the defensive for almost a generation.

One central salient in the attack focused on "modernism" and aimed at the return to the "fundamentals" of Christian morality. Hence the name "Fundamentalism" lovingly bestowed on it in 1920 by the Northern Baptist journal, *The Watchman-Examiner.* It made science a target, particularly Darwinism, although it struck at a broad range of forces that had assertedly undermined traditionalist standards. The "World's Christian Fundamentals Association" gave it a coalition base among a number of rival evangelical churches, especially Baptist and Methodist. Between 1920 and 1925, it enjoyed powerfully effective leadership from William Jennings Bryan, whose still-progressive political views nevertheless contrasted with the overwhelmingly conservative cast of the Fundamentalist movement as a whole.

Indeed, for the most part the new insurgency lacked generosity, goodwill, self-sacrifice, human sympathy, even fair play—all the benchmarks of the progressive movement's concern for the general welfare. In place of "Square Deal," "Social

Justice," and "New Freedom," the twenties evoke different thoughts, a different set of rubrics: Sacco and Vanzetti, the National Origins Immigration Quota Act, the Scopes Trial, the Ku Klux Klan.

Aliens and Radicals. Nicola Sacco and Bartolomeo Vanzetti were Italian immigrants, the one a shoemaker and the other a fish peddler, accused of murder during a robbery in South Braintree, Massachusetts, on April 15, 1920. Whether both were guilty, or only Sacco was, or neither, remains disputed. What is clear and indisputable is, one, that the prosecution introduced faulty evidence, probably knowingly, and, possibly in all innocence, primed alleged witnesses to fabricate testimony; two, that the judge was eager to convict the men whatever their guilt in the particular case because they were avowed anarchists, which for Judge Webster Thayer was incriminating enough; and, three, that Judge Thayer's prejudice influenced his behavior in court and compromised the case of the defendants before the jury.

The trial quickly became an international *cause célèbre.* The excessive zeal that characterized American law enforcement in the Red Scare period made it possible even for some conservatives to doubt the guilt of the two young Italians, especially in light of the judge's well-publicized indiscretions. Radicals throughout the world accepted the procedural violations as an example of the hypocrisy of the ruling classes everywhere, *even* in the U.S.A. It may have been the first time that in the eyes of the world the United States was cast in the role of an oppressor. Many of the protests took violent form, including bombings in Europe and South America that cost scores of lives. They helped those who officially reviewed the case to avoid reversing Judge Thayer's rulings. For among the many reprehensible features of the case it is clear that the appeals to higher courts and ultimately to a governor's advisory committee (headed by Harvard's A. Lawrence Lowell) failed partly on technical grounds but also—and probably in larger measure—because no one with authority cared to verify by granting a new trial the radicals' charges that the convictions were obtained through class, ethnic, and ideological prejudices rather than from the evidence.

Sacco and Vanzetti died in the electric chair on August 22, 1927, after seven long years while the world watched. Perhaps the ultimate irony resides in the statement by Justice Holmes, rejecting a plea for Supreme Court review two days before the execution, in which Holmes denied he had any jurisdiction in a state criminal case, and in which he noted: "Far stronger cases than this [concerning dubious state court procedures] have arisen with regard to the blacks when the Supreme Court has denied its power." The 1920s was not an era in which to press for a uniform application of justice throughout the states and communities of the nation. It was a time for sinking doubt beneath a bold, aggressive reassertion of the practices and pretensions of the past.

In the same spirit, the National Origins Act of 1924 reaffirmed the theory of American "racial" superiority that the intellectual history of the previous two decades had thrown into question. It directly repudiated the commitment of the nation, as inscribed in Emma Lazarus' words at the base of the Statue of Liberty, to provide sanctuary for the world's wretched and poor and persecuted. Of course it was inevitable that the United States would have to control the magnitude of immigration; the country could not continue to absorb newcomers at the accelerating pace that devel-

Ben Shahn's "The Passion of Sacco and Vanzetti" (1931-32), with A. Lawrence Lowell of Governor Fuller's Advisory Committee in the center, and a sketch of Justice Holmes on the wall behind him. From the Collection of the *Whitney Museum of American Art, New York*

oped in the prewar decade without experiencing a variety of social crises as well as protests from wage-earners who competed with immigrants for jobs. The new act placed no national quotas on immigration from western hemisphere countries, but it was designed to restrict Old World immigration to about 150,000 and total immigration to about 250,000. But it did not stop there. For five years it limited annual immigration from each identified European nation to 2 percent of Americans of the corresponding national origin, while other provisions effectively banned Asians altogether. And to make America's ethnic and racial preferences absolutely clear, the law fixed *1890,* not 1920 or 1910, as the base on which to calculate the 2 percent.* Americans of Italian, Polish, Russian, and Jewish descent, who had made up the bulk of the post-1890 immigration, were put on formal notice by the United States Congress that they were not welcome.

Monkeys and Modernists. The Scopes Trial came directly out of the Fundamentalist insurgency. It was almost deliberately contrived as a morality play, in which the

* After 1929 the immigration quota for each nation given a quota was to bear the same ratio to 150,000 as the number of Americans of the particular national origin bore to the U.S. population as of 1920.

militantly reactionary forces within the Protestant churches of the interior and southern states confronted the forces of science and secular urban sophistication. In 1925, the state of Tennessee enacted a bill prohibiting anyone from teaching in a tax-supported school any theory "that denies the story of the Divine creation of man as taught in the Bible and to teach instead that man has descended from a lower order of animals." It was neither the first nor the last of such acts; several states of the South and Southwest had or would soon have similar laws. It was a direct assault on modern rationalism, and specifically on the scientific theory of the evolution of species.

By prearrangement, in the mountain village of Dayton, Tennessee, 24-year-old biology teacher John Scopes challenged the law by reading to his class passages from a text that asserted the evolution of human beings over millions of years from simple life forms. Scopes was arrested. The defense recruited Dudley Field Malone, an eminent New York City lawyer, Arthur Garfield Hays of the American Civil Liberties Union, and Clarence Darrow, the nation's leading attorney for social upstarts and underdogs, an agnostic, a Socialist, long renowned for his defense of Eugene Debs against the contempt of court charges arising from the Pullman Strike in 1894. To meet these representatives of modernism, the state attorney general accepted the volunteered assistance of William Jennings Bryan. The big city press assembled en masse to report the drama to the world. Radio station WGN in Chicago broadcast the trial live.

The event presented one of the grotesqueries of the era. Prevented by the judge from introducing any scientific evidence, the defense called Bryan to the witness stand as an expert on the Bible. Darrow, Bible in hand, confronted him, the Great Commoner, Populist leader, three-time Democratic candidate for president of the United States, former Secretary of State. For six hours, Bryan faced Darrow's withering ridicule, sweating in galluses and shirtsleeves on a jerry-built platform outside the courtroom to accommodate the overflow crowd (it was mid-July and 100°F. in the shade). For six hours, he steadfastly asserted the literal truth of the Scriptures, denounced Hays, Malone, Darrow, and the press for having "no other purpose than ridiculing every Christian," and insisted that Scopes should suffer the penalty of the law for telling his students that the Bible errs in fixing the Creation at 4004 B.C.

Scopes was convicted, and the "antievolution" laws stood until 1968 (when the Supreme Court, deciding an Arkansas case, declared such laws an unconstitutional abridgment of the First Amendment). But the press declared Bryan the loser, and to accomodate the drama he expired of apoplexy one week later. "In this controversy," he had told reporters, "I have a larger majority on my side than in any previous controversy, and I have more intolerant opponents than I have ever had in politics." The issue was the right of each state to regulate the moral impact of the schools, especially in the light of surveys that showed how high school and college students were being led by science to reject religion. The opponents, on the other hand—in Darrow's words—were fighting "to prevent bigots and ignoramuses from controlling the educational system of the United States." The trial played a floodlight on the cultural schism in America.

The Liberal Tradition Under Attack. The same gap helps account for the sudden, spectacular growth of the Ku Klux Klan after 1920. No one knows for sure how many

Americans eventually joined the Invisible Empire, but estimates run from 1.5 million to more than 5 million. Reborn in 1915 on the wave of enthusiasm for D. W. Griffith's spectacular motion picture, *The Birth of a Nation,* which depicted the original KKK of the late 1860s as the gallant savior of southern white civilization, the organization grew only fitfully during the war and immediate postwar years. But between 1921 and 1925, the Klan took on the character of a genuine social movement. Its membership was overwhelmingly from the rural and urban lower middle class and from nonunion blue-collar employees of large businesses. At least one third of them resided in cities of over 70,000, especially cities such as Detroit, Dayton (Ohio), Memphis, Youngstown, and Houston which experienced high population growth in the 1910-30 period. The newcomers generally were the cause not the source of Klan recruitment. The potential Klansman was usually someone who had fought to get or remain above the lowest levels of social and economic status, and for whom success remained tenuous or elusive. As it appeared to him, on top of his continuing difficulties, a permissive amoral society had thrust him into competition with immigrants, Catholics, Negroes, Jews—aliens all. Didn't America reserve any advantages for true Americans? For hardworking white Protestants who still did God's work?

It would be a mistake to view the KKK as simply an organization of violence-prone sadists and bigots. Certainly it attracted more than its share of such. But recent historians, such as Kenneth Jackson in *The Ku Klux Klan in the City 1915-30* (1967) and Charles C. Alexander in *The Ku Klux Klan in the Southwest* (1965), have pointed out that many Americans joined the Klan motivated for reform by anxiety over crime rates, poor schools, lax enforcement of Prohibition laws, and corrupt politics. It was a defensive reaction to what they viewed as the intrusion of alien and hostile groups in their lives. In spite of a swaggering posture, and the publicity given to it, the Klan was not responsible for any noteworthy increase in vigilante violence, even in the South where the terrorizing of blacks had long been something of a white man's pastime. In the cities, Klansmen were often themselves targets of violence, and even police protection of meetings and parades often proved insufficient. The point is, the KKK represented something more serious in American life than could be understood if one focused entirely on the bully-boys attracted to the sheets.

The Klan presented an open and direct challenge to the nation's liberal tradition; it offered itself as an alternative to a social philosophy and technique of social organization it believed had been tried and shown to be faulty with the demise of progressivism. Imperial Wizard Hiram Wesley Evans summed it up in an article published in *The North American Review* in 1926 called "The Klan's Fight for America." America, wrote Evans, had undergone a critical reappraisal during the Progressive era. But as a result, it had lost its moorings. "In sharp contrast to the clear straightforward purposes of our earlier years," the nation currently faced "moral breakdown," and "futility in religion." "All our traditional moral standards went by the boards. . . . The sacredness of our Sabbath, of our homes, of chastity . . . even of our right to teach our own children in our own schools fundamental facts and truths." Like advanced progressive theorists Horace Kallen, John Dewey, and Randolph Bourne, Evans came to the conclusion that the Melting Pot had failed. But whereas the liberals postulated "a

Klansmen and Klan-supported candidates won governorships and Senate seats in Indiana, Colorado, Oklahoma, and Kentucky, and showed strength in Chicago, Montana, Oregon, and New Jersey in 1924. In 1925 the Klan discarded masks to stage a massive parade in the nation's capital. *UPI*

congeries of diverse peoples, living together in sweet harmony, and all working for the good of the nation," for Evans: "This solution is on a par with the optimism which foisted the melting pot on us. Diverse races never have lived together in such harmony; race antipathies are too deep and strong. . . . One race has always ruled, one always must, and there will be struggle and reprisals till the mastery is established."

The Klan's power peaked around 1924. It had already elected several U.S. senators and governors. It was a major force in the politics of Texas, Arkansas, Georgia, Ohio, Iowa, and Indiana, with pockets of great strength in states like New Jersey and Oregon, and in cities like Chicago. On the national scene, its natural ally might have been the Republican party, the party most united in support of Prohibition and immigration restriction, and which, outside the South, had a rural, traditionalist constituency. But when the Klan attempted to dictate Coolidge's running mate—Senator James Watson of Indiana—the party regulars saw the threat to their control of the GOP in time to defeat it. The Republican platform in 1924 discreetly avoided mentioning the Klan.

The Democrats, on the other hand, were as usual a badly divided party, and therefore vulnerable. KKK leaders threw their support to William G. McAdoo, Woodrow Wilson's able son-in-law who still represented the main themes of progressivism (although tainted by having had E. L. Doheny of Teapot Dome notoriety as a law client). Without Klan support, the McAdoo forces knew they hadn't a chance. Their opponents knew they could defeat him by making the Klan a central issue of the convention. They succeeded. But by a vote of 541.5 to 542.5, the McAdoo forces, aided by the aging William Jennings Bryan, defeated a motion to denounce the Klan by name in the party platform. The convention then deadlocked between McAdoo and New York's popular Irish-Catholic, anti-Prohibitionist Governor Al Smith until, on the ninth day and 103rd ballot, it named John W. Davis, a conservative Wall Street corporation lawyer, as the party's candidate to oppose Coolidge.

It was in many ways symptomatic of what had happened to American reform energies that two of the men most closely identified with progressivism, McAdoo and Bryan, found themselves associated in 1924 with the Klan. The old liberal progressive spirit was all but dead. Insofar as progressivism still endured, its crabbed and authoritarian strains prevailed. The impulse for liberal-democratic change now emanated more from sources identified with some of the very sectors of the society that progressivism had opposed—most notably the ethnic insurgency which the career and the candidacy of Al Smith so vividly symbolized.

Smith vs. Hoover, 1928. Al Smith's nomination by the Democrats in 1928 was virtually inevitable. As veteran journalist Mark Sullivan pointed out, the failure of the Democrats to nominate Smith in 1924 called for such explanation as to weaken the party drastically. He was the one big-state Democrat to win big repeatedly throughout the Republican decade. The collapse of the Klan, following recurrent financial scandals among its leadership and increasingly militant and violent hostility, especially in the cities, further strengthened the case for Smith. The risk of troubling "heartland" WASP Americans weighed less than the hazards of affronting millions of traditionally Democratic urban Catholics. The party's interest demanded Smith's nomination in 1928, and he received it with hardly any trouble.

At the same time, Smith's defeat in November by Herbert Hoover was also a foregone conclusion. And this fact had little to do with his Roman Catholicism. The country was still enjoying its rosiest prosperity. Indeed, it was in the midst of the stock market boom that would trigger the Great Crash only a year later. Pundits gleefully dubbed it "The New Era," a time of self-consciously celebrated "progressive" business leadership. Private business and the men who represented business ideals were never more favored by the American public. Even the sophisticates of social criticism expressed their contentment. "The more or less unconscious and unplanned activities of business," wrote progressive theorist Walter Lippmann, "are for once more novel, more daring and in general more revolutionary than the theories of the progressives." Muckraker-extraordinary Lincoln Steffens, author of *The Shame of the Cities* back in 1904, the man who had visited Soviet Russia in 1919, avowed himself a "Communist," and could not stop telling everyone how he had "seen the future and it works," in 1928 was telling everyone: "Big business in America is producing what the Socialists held up as their goal; food, shelter and clothing for all. You will see it during the Hoover Administration." *The New Republic,* avant garde progressive journal founded by Herbert Croly in 1914, declared fourteen years later: "American industry has itself become, after a fashion, progressive. . . . The chief task of a progressive government would be . . . to find a way of being its counsellor and friend."

No man in America fit the image of a progressive business leader more perfectly than Herbert Hoover. A self-made man whose fortune was earned by 1910 as an international engineer and mining consultant, Hoover linked the attributes of nineteenth-century entrepreneurship with twentieth-century managerial technocracy; he represented the best of the traditional and the modern business modes. As secretary of commerce (1921-29), he organized dozens of business conferences to promote industrial efficiency and the interchangeability of machine parts, successfully reducing the variety of screw bores, container sizes, plow designs, wire gauges, and the like. By sheer energy, concern, and intelligence, Hoover became the single most important administrative official in the Washington of Harding and Coolidge.

Harding had offered him his choice in the cabinet. He chose the Commerce Department because he wished to preside over business enterprise, which he regarded as the only really important activities in civilized society. For Hoover, the American business-man was not merely the agent of the highest standard of living in the world, he was civilization's paragon. Upon the soil of private business enterprise, he said, "grow those moral and intellectual forces that made our nation great." He was no laissez-faire ideologue. Like Wilson, whom he greatly admired, he favored government intervention wherever monopolistic power threatened to corrupt the competitive market system. "The Government," he said, "can and must cure abuses." But the Commerce Department offered Hoover the opportunity to demonstrate—so he believed—that with government encouragement, businessmen could regulate themselves and make superfluous the regulatory agencies spawned in the Progressive era. Self-regulation would follow almost automatically from the reorganization of business already in process. The "interdependence of all industries compels trade associations," he said, and, as he saw it, this would have to lead "toward some sort of industrial democracy." Typically, for Hoover the idea of democracy in industry had nothing to do with consumers' interests or workers' participation in business policymaking, but only with the relationships among business competitors. Trade associations would function like commercial governments. "With these private collective agencies used as the machinery for the elimination of abuses and the cultivation of high standards, I am convinced that we shall have entered a great new era of self-governing industry." The federal government's role, in his view, should be to help not control business, and toward this end the Department of Commerce published a monthly feature in *System: The Magazine of Business* called "What Washington Offers Business This Month."

Smith never challenged the narrowness and naivete of Hoover's vision. Alfred E. Smith was also a "self-made man," albeit born to second generation Irish Catholic parents in a tenement in lower Manhattan rather than a Quaker blacksmith family in a split-log cabin on the Iowa prairie. He had no rich uncle, as did Hoover, to send him on to Stanford or any other college. Nor did his ethnic and religious background open doors in the prestigious professions or businesses (though it had some advantages in New York City politics). On the other hand, like Hoover and many another self-made man, Smith became a stalwart defender of the system that he successfully ascended. "I will take off my coat and vest," he said, exhibiting the pugnacity of his background and the affluence of his achieved status, "and fight to the end against any candidate who persists in any demagogic appeal to the masses . . . by setting class against class and rich against poor."

Nor did much in Smith's political background prepare him to confront Hoover on the grounds of economic philosophy. Smith had risen in Democratic party politics with the full backing of Tammany Hall, the enduring and often corrupt Manhattan political machine. Thoroughly traditionalist in outlook, he had opposed woman suffrage, vetoed legislation to raise schoolteachers' salaries, ridiculed the idea of sending policemen to college, called the advocacy of direct primaries "only the squawk of the fellows on the outs, the squawk which, like Niagara, runs on forever," and he remained steadfastly loyal to Tammany chief Charles Murphy, a man who died with a $6 million estate without ever holding a paying job. His governorship produced some humanitarian and administrative reforms, including reorganization of penal and juvenile institutions and establishment of some conservation, recreational, and park-construction programs. But even these owed more to the genius of social worker Belle Moskowitz, who persuaded the politicos of the voter appeal such measures carried. On balance, many who worked closely with Smith, such as the pioneering parks and highway administrator Robert Moses, thought his economic outlook placed him somewhere to the right of a southern states'-rights Democrat. The opinion was confirmed by his choice of campaign manager, John J. Raskob, a member of the DuPont corporate hierarchy who had supervised the reorganization of General Motors when the auto company was taken over by the DuPonts in 1920. Raskob was not even a registered Democrat and had voted for Coolidge in 1924.

Hoover defeated Smith by a vote of 21.4 million to 15.0 million. It is improbable that any Democrat could have won. Whether Hoover's margin would have been greater or smaller if Smith were not a Roman Catholic remains a conjecture. But it is certain that Smith's Catholicism, as well as his anti-Prohibition stance and his lower-class New York City origins, had everything to do with the drastic change in voting patterns that year.

Presidential elections usually mask social divisions. But 1928 is an exception. The campaign deepened ethnic, religious, and cultural cleavages. Smith may not have been much of a reformer, but insofar as he himself personified a challenge to the American consensus, he embodied a greater radicalism than his political or economic philosophy could suggest. It is evident that by the 1920s most Americans seemed unwilling to interpret the major source of social strain in terms of the struggle between business and labor, or between business and agriculture, or between big business and small business. Especially as the glow of prosperity subdued class and commercial contention, the ethnic schisms in American life emerged loud and clear.

Smith's candidacy had some characteristics of a "politics of confrontation."

According to David Burner, a close student of Democratic politics in the 1920s, Smith made the worst of the possible case he could have brought before the electorate on behalf of an urban, wet, Catholic candidate for president, because he remained insensitive to how much he threatened the traditionalist Americans' image of their country. Smith did little to reduce the anxiety that his bid for the presidency raised among the "old stock" Americans. His Catholicism may have been among the least of the irritants. He showed no concern for Sabbatarian sensibilities: "I read in a paper somewhere," he regaled an East Side audience, "I think in Pennsylvania, somebody wouldn't let the [World] Series be announced [on the radio] on Sunday. Well, I'd like to see that place; it must be a hot one." For a decade, Prohibition had symbolized the older culture's one great holding action against the advance of the new, but Smith scarcely concealed either his drinking or his contempt for the 18th Amendment. Newsmen recorded him exclaiming, "Say, wouldn't you like to have your foot on the rail and blow the foam off some suds?" The veteran progressive publicist William Allen White wanted to know, "How does he get his liquor? He must be either violating the law or knowing that someone else does. If this is true he is not a fit man to be either Governor or President." Smith's appeal, wrote the eminent southern journalist and historian George Fort Milton, "is to the aliens, who feel that the older America, the America of the Anglo-Saxon stock, is a hateful thing which must be overturned and humiliated. . . . As great as have been my doubts about Hoover, he is sprung from American soil and stock."

Governor Al Smith, celebrating his rise from humble origins, poses with a new generation of East Side newsboy. Like many self-made men, Smith never questioned the system through which he had risen. He appealed to urban and ethnic frustrations, not working class sensibilities.

Yet it may be precisely Smith's abrasive qualities that drew the remarkable outpouring of voters in 1928 and gave him the small leverage he had for overturning Hoover's obvious advantages. For decades the "New American" and urban element in the electorate had been growing to major proportions. It was one of the developments that had activated the Klan. In 1910 a government study showed that a majority of the children in the elementary and secondary schools in the thirty-seven most populous cities had at least one foreign-born parent. In half a dozen places like New York, Chicago, and Duluth, the figure was over 67 percent. These were the children of the ten million immigrants of the 1890-1910 period, more than 80 percent of whom were non-Protestant, and they would help to make up a majority of the seventeen million persons who passed the age of twenty-one during the 1920s, in a total pool of between fifty million and sixty million eligible voters.

Traditionally, nearly all the industrial cities outside the South were reliably Republican. The indifference of the immigrant population to national politics helped keep them that way. But the education of the second generation tended to alter that circumstance. The coming of age of the new generation is reflected in the growth of urban Democratic voting strength. In the presidential elections a 1.64 million Republican plurality in 1920 in the twelve largest cities of the country dropped to 1.25 million in 1924, and with Smith's candidacy in 1928 it swung to a 38,000 Democratic plurality. Figures for lesser candidates during both the presidential and the off-year elections in a larger sample of cities show an even stronger urban Democratic trend throughout the period, while they also highlight Smith's extraordinary appeal.

Of thirty-six cities with 250,000 people or more, nineteen had "immigrant-stock" majorities. Smith carried only seven of these (up from only three carried by Democrats before), but the increase in the Democratic vote in these nineteen cities was very large —in fact in none of them was Smith's increase less than 100 percent. Smith's striking social characteristics unquestionably brought people to the polls on an unprecedented scale. Twenty-seven percent more votes were cast in 1928 than in 1924. Ironically, in view of his reservations on the subject, Smith appears to have made woman suffrage a reality for the first time; the traditionalism that had kept immigrant and lower-class women away from the polls in 1920 and 1924 appears to have given way to the appeal of Smith's candidacy.

The singular characteristics of the Democratic nominee cost him as well as favored him. Smith swung 122 previously Republican northern state counties into the Democratic column, but 200 counties in the South, including the cities of Dallas, Houston, Birmingham, and Oklahoma City, went Republican for the first time in fifty years. Four southern states broke with Democratic solidarity to give their electoral votes to Hoover. The cultural challenge Smith fronted mobilized opposition voters as well as supporters.

Altogether it is clear that, as political analyst and historian Samuel Lubell has written, "A profound social upheaval stirred beneath the Smith vote," while the campaign evoked an equally profound reaction. For once a national election gave expression to the underlying tensions of the society. The bitterness of the campaign, the vicious anti-Catholicism that emerged, sometimes from unexpected "respectable" quarters, and the head-on confrontation of "wets" and "drys," revealed more openly than before the day-to-day stresses of American life in the "Jazz Age."

The Hoover-Smith election contest symbolized the collision of two great subcultures in America, an event that had been in the making for almost two decades. In 1927 Walter Lippmann remarked: "The evil which the old-fashioned preachers ascribe to the Pope, to Babylon, to atheists, and to the devil, is simply the new urban civilization, with its irresistible science and economics and mass power." When the 18th Amendment breaks down, said Lippmann, "the fall will bring down with it the dominion of the older civilization." It would mean "the emergence of the cities as the dominant force in America, dominant politically and socially as they are already dominant economically."

There is much wisdom in the observation, although it was not perhaps quite so "simple." More was at stake than simply the dominance of "the cities." It was little less than the survival of the central image of America that had energized the progressive movement at the turn of the century.

SUGGESTED READINGS

Only Yesterday* (1931) by Frederick Lewis Allen, written when the twenties were indeed "only yesterday," is after forty-five years still the most delightful introduction to the period, in that it captures the decade's spirit—at least from the viewpoint of an urbane journalist—with a level of detail no other work has achieved though many have tried. Unfortunately the book seems responsible for having set the historiographical style of trivializing the era. There is no major work that will serve to correct this tendency, but Stanley Coben's "The First Years of Modern America, 1918-33," in W. E. Leuchtenberg, ed., *The Unfinished Century** (1973), and the first half of Donald R. McCoy's *Coming of Age: The United States During the 1920s and 1930s** (1973) offer a good beginning together with fine bibliographies. William E. Leuchtenberg's *The Perils of Prosperity, 1914-32** (1958) is a very successful original synthesis, as is the first third of Arthur M. Schlesinger, Jr. *The Crisis of the Old Order, 1919-33* (1957), though the latter especially treats the twenties primarily as an avenue into the Depression of the 1930s.

Henry F. May's "Shifting Perspectives on the 1920s," *Mississippi Valley Historical Review,* v. 43, December 1956, is a historiographical essay with a provocative thesis of its own. A. S. Link's "What Happened to the Progressive Movement in the 1920s?" *American Historical Review,* v. 65, July 1959, is a much reprinted article that has seemingly had the subject to itself, but readers may do well to glimpse at the critique of the article in R. M. Abrams and L. W. Levine, eds., *The Shaping of Twentieth-Century America: Interpretive Essays** (1971). Paul W. Glad, "Progressives and the Business Culture of the 1920s," *Journal of American History,* v. 53, June 1966, George B. Tindall, "Business Progressivism: Southern Politics in the Twenties," *South*

---

* Available in a paperback edition.

Atlantic Quarterly, v. 62, Winter 1963, and M. Heald, "Business Thought in the Twenties: Social Responsibility," *American Quarterly*, v. 13, Summer 1963, discuss the survival of progressivism, or at least of progressive rhetoric, in the postwar decade, but like Link, they all fail to note the sharp difference in the spirit of the two eras and so mistakenly equate the demands for legislation on behalf of certain special interests and some ritualized gestures of goodwill by business groups in the 1920s with the reform impulses of the Progressive era. Clarke Chambers, *Seedtime of Reform: American Social Service and Social Action, 1918-33** (1963), suggests how social workers changed their functions as they retreated from reform activism.

The postwar domestic turbulence is well covered in Robert K. Murray's *Red Scare: A Study in National Hysteria, 1919-20** (1955), William M. Tuttle, Jr. *Race Riot: Chicago in the Red Summer of 1919** (1970), Stanley Coben's *A. Mitchell Palmer* (1963), and Coben's "A Study in Nativism: The American Red Scare of 1919-20," *Political Science Quarterly*, v. 79, March 1964. Donald D. Johnson, *The Challenge to American Freedoms: World War I and the Rise of the American Civil Liberties Union* (1963), covers the first organized counterattack in defense of civil liberties. The Fitzgerald remarks in the present text come mostly from "Echoes of the Jazz Age," in *The Crack Up** (1945) Edmund Wilson, ed.

There are now three good biographies of Harding: *The Harding Era* (1969), R. K. Murray, *The Shadow of Blooming Grove* (1968), Francis Russell, and *The Available Man* (1965), Andrew Sinclair. Donald McCoy's *Calvin Coolidge: The Quiet President* (1967) is alone in its excellence. Joan Hoff Wilson's *Herbert Hoover: Forgotten Progressive** (1965) is the first good biographical summary of the man we have had, though she may make too much of the degree to which Hoover actually shared the progressive vision.

J. Leonard Bates' *The Origins of Teapot Dome: Progressives, Parties, and Petroleum, 1909-21* (1963) is indispensable for understanding the political and economic forces in contention before the scandal broke; Burl Noggle's *Teapot Dome: Oil and Politics in the 1920s** (1962), is comprehensive but curiously concerned with vindicating Albert Fall. J. W. Prothro's *The Dollar Decade: Business Ideas in the 1920s* (1954) and Alan R. Raucher's *Public Relations and Business, 1900-29* (1968) afford highly readable glimpses of business attitudes. George W. Stocking's *Workable Competition and Antitrust Policy* (1961), ch. 2, and Louis Galambos' "The Trade Association Movement in Cotton Textiles, 1900-1935," *Explorations in Entrepreneurial History*, v. 2, 1964 contain the best short accounts of the trend toward associational activities in industry, with good coverage of the literature.

George Soule's *Prosperity Decade: From War to Depression, 1917-29** (1947), Volume 8 of The Economic History of the United States series, is still valuable, but should be supplemented by some other good economic history, such as Charles H. Hession and Hyman Sardy's *Ascent to Affluence* (1969), chs. 23-25, and, for labor conditions, by Irving Bernstein's *The Lean Years: A History of the American Worker, 1920-33** (1960) cited in the present chapter. Grant McConnell, *The Decline of Agrarian Democracy** (1953) and Gilbert C. Fite, *George N. Peek and the Struggle for Farm Parity* (1954), are excellent on the subject of farm politics, although especially

Fite seems to treat the farmers as God's chosen people and neglects the transformation of "farming" into "agri-business." Theodore Saloutos and John D. Hicks, *Twentieth Century Populism: Agricultural Discontent in the Middle West, 1900-39** (1952), provide a fine survey. All three books can be used to demonstrate the sharp change in attitudes among farm interest groups over the course of the 1900-29 period.

For the social scene, Paul Carter's *The Twenties in America** (1968) is an all too brief but suggestive sketch, with much reference to contemporary commentary. The early chapters of William Chafe's *The American Woman: Her Changing Social, Economic, and Political Roles, 1920-70** (1972) contain comprehensive data. John Braeman, et al, eds., *Change and Continuity in Twentieth-Century America: The 1920s* (1968), present many excellent original essays, including the one on Prohibition by Joseph Gusfield cited earlier. Norman F. Furniss' *The Fundamentalist Controversy, 1918-31* (1954) is a fine original synthesis of the issue, but no one should overlook Lawrence W. Levine, *Defender of the Faith: William Jennings Bryan, The Last Decade 1915-25** (1965), for a keen analysis of both the fundamentalist phenomenon and the Scopes Trial; and Paul Carter's exceptional monograph, *The Decline and Revival of the Social Gospel* (1957). The most recent thorough reappraisal of the Sacco-Vanzetti affair is Francis Russell's *Tragedy at Dedham* (1962), but Louis Joughin and Edmund M. Morgan's *The Legacy of Sacco and Vanzetti** (1948), a somewhat impassioned account, much of it actually written as early as 1929, is still well worth reading for a flavor of the contemporary impact. Robert A. Divine, *American Immigration Policy, 1924-52* (1957) provides a highly readable and scholarly account of the passage of the National Origins Act of 1924, but Frank Auerbach, *Immigration Laws of the United States* (1955), spells out the more precise provisions of the act. In addition to the works by Hiram Wesley Evans, Kenneth Jackson, and Charles Alexander on the Klan, cited in the present chapter, Carl Degler's review article, "A Century of the Klans," *Journal of Southern History*, v. 31, Nov. 1965, is well worth reading.

There is no good biography of Al Smith, but Frank Friedel's *Franklin D. Roosevelt: The Ordeal* (1954), volume 2 of Friedel's projected six-volume biography, and David Burner's *The Politics of Provincialism** (1967) have much useful material; and Oscar Handlin's *Al Smith and His America** (1958) affords a friendly sketch. Jerome M. Clubb and Howard W. Allen, "The Cities and the Election of 1928: Partisan Realignment?" *American Historical Review*, v. 74, April 1969, suggests some corrections in the also excellent analyses of 1928 by Carl Degler in "American Political Parties and the Rise of the City: An Interpretation," *Journal of American History*, v. 51, June 1964, and by Samuel Lubell, *The Future of American Politics** (3rd. edition, 1965). Richard Hofstadter, "Could a Protestant Have Beaten Hoover in 1928?" *The Reporter*, March 17, 1960, addresses the perennial question with an eye on the then forthcoming Kennedy-Nixon campaign.

CHAPTER SIX

CULTURE
IN FERMENT

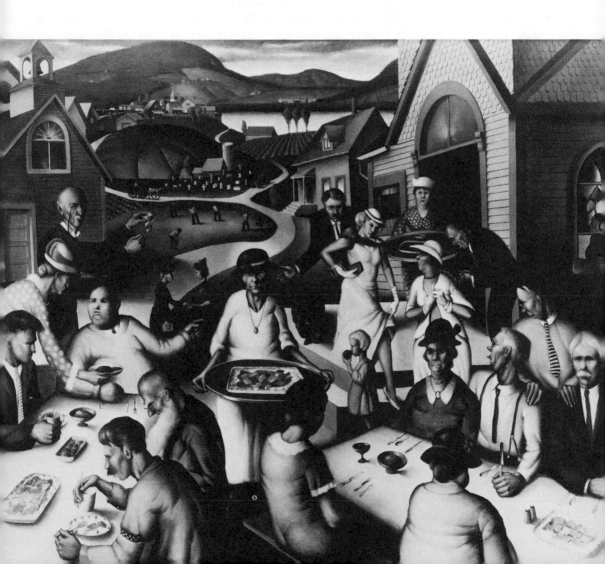

A T THE TURN of the century most Americans still lived in a deferential society. By the 1920s the traditional justifications for deference had lost their fire. It had become hard to explain, especially to young people, why one should conform, honor conventions, obey the law. And indeed, the generation that came to maturity in the early part of the twentieth century seemed strongly inclined to regard the life-style of their parents as archaic, stilted, bigoted, and irrelevant.

All the guideposts were down. Modern science, corporate and government bureaucracy, the impersonal environment of city life and mass production, the sharpening self-consciousness of ethnic subcultures, all subverted the traditional bases of authority. Before the end of the period urban intellectuals and rural traditionalists were joined in concern over the matter. In *The Modern Temper* (1929) Joseph Wood Krutch lamented the passing of a whole world of behavioral conventions that had helped provide both order and civility in social relations while satisfying the universal emotional need for meaning. "Insofar as we adhere to a code of conduct we do so largely because certain habits still persist, not because we can give any logical reason for preferring them, and insofar as we indulge ourselves in the primitive emotional satisfactions—romantic love, patriotism, zeal for justice, and so forth—our satisfaction is the result merely of the temporary suspension of our disbelief in the mythology upon which they are founded." But the myths that had sustained authority, all the symbols of social restraint that for so long had served as the very test of civilization's conquest over brute force and brute instincts, lay exposed and eroded.

It was, to be sure, a liberating experience. It freed people to think daringly without fear of hell-fire or handcuffs. It allowed them to discard inane formalisms that stifled the imagination, stunted intimacy, and perpetuated iniquities in the name of The Law, Nature, and Eternity. But there were awesome costs. The pathways of the past may have merely circled back upon themselves, but they had at least kept people from getting lost. Civilization's greater difficulties may have only begun when its members discovered they were free to do as they pleased. By the 1920s the burdens of liberation already appeared visible in the headlong hedonism of the urban nouveaux riches. In the novels of Ernest Hemingway, John Dos Passos, and F. Scott Fitzgerald, all the young protagonists seem world-weary before they turn thirty. The fifteen years before the Crash were marked by a strange mixture of elation and ennui.

The Erosion of the Canons of Order

Nineteenth-century scientific rationalism had helped to undermine the religious basis for authority. For a hundred years revelation fought a long, defensive battle against "Truth" defined by observable, reproducible, empirical evidence. In the scientific rationale a "fact" was that which could be tested and demonstrated in the laboratory or by mathematical means. The application of such truth to machines, to material production, to the development of an affluent economy, thoroughly engaged

"Church Supper." *Museum of Fine Arts, Springfield Mass. The James Philip Gray Collection*

the nineteenth-century imagination. As we have seen, the economic success of American society stimulated a powerful faith in human rationalism.

The New Science. Yet twentieth-century science would more critically wound the traditionalist ethos by throwing into question both the possibility and the efficacy of rationality itself. The work of the New Physicists—Planck, Einstein, Heisenberg, Bohr— undermined confidence that human beings could ever understand the nature of their own physical environment. Nature's most fundamental secrets lay beyond the tests of common experience. Scientists could report them only through imaginative mathematical techniques. "Relativity" began to find applications in disciplines other than physics after Eddington verified Einstein's theory empirically in 1919, and inevitably shook further the certainties that had comforted generations. Although Einstein himself refused to believe "that God plays dice with the world," and insisted that the universe contained order and harmony awaiting mathematical discovery, a growing school of Positivists proceeded from the premises that science could merely attempt to correlate the results of observing more or less arbitrarily selected natural phenomena.

Toward a New Anthropology. There was no strictly valid connection between Einstein's theory and the concept of "relativism." Yet contemporaries (such as Walter Lippmann, in *Public Opinion,* 1923) readily provided the link, especially since by the time of the Eddington experiment relativism had already crept into various branches of social thought. The environmental determinism implicit in Darwinism, for example, had suggested to sociologists like Lester Ward (*Dynamic Sociology,* 1883) and Benjamin Kidd (*Social Evolution,* 1894) that social norms derived not from eternal principles but merely embodied a society's adaptation to a particular historical and sociological environment. One might expect different societies, then, to have different value systems. And one *could* infer from this (although it would not be a common inference even among scientists till the 1920s) that no particular system of values was in itself better than some other. Oliver Wendell Holmes, Jr. applied the same idea to the law. "An evolutionist," he wrote in "The Path of the Law" (1897), "will hesitate to affirm universal validity for his social ideals. . . . He is content if he can prove them best for here and now." From his position on the bench, Holmes was sensitized to the inclination of judges to read universal "natural rights" and "natural laws" into their social and economic prejudices. His writings keyed a "Realist" movement in law led by Roscoe Pound beginning around 1906. This movement stressed the political origins of social values and sought to make law the servant of human needs rather than of logic and precedent. Benjamin N. Cardozo, appointed by Hoover to the Supreme Court in 1932, gave Realism its fullest statement in his outstanding 1920 lectures published as *The Nature of the Judicial Process* (1921). "One of the most fundamental social interests," Cardozo said, "is that law shall be uniform and impartial." On the other hand, impartiality and uniformity "may be bought at too high a price," at which point they cease to be good and become oppressive. The judge must then essentially engage in making new law; he must balance these great values "against the social interest served by equity and fairness or other elements of social welfare." The judge, no less than the legislator, "must get his knowledge . . . from experience and study and reflection; in brief from life itself." And although the judge's role is limited by the legislator's work and only "fills the open spaces in the law," he, like the legislator, is engaged in the act of making law for instrumental purposes that is, to satisfy changing social needs and perceptions of social needs.

After 1915 a new school of anthropology, inspired by the work of German-American immigrant Franz Boas, notably his *The Mind of Primitive Man* (1911), laid the basis for a theory of cultural relativism. Studies by A. L. Kroeber, Bronislaw Malinowski, Edward Sapir, Margaret Mead, and Ruth Benedict directly disputed the view that the quality, or the relative excellence, of different societies might be measured according to a scale of perfection comparable to that established in the Darwinian theory of biological evolution. They dismissed as ethnocentric arrogance the common-place assumptions of "Anglo-Saxon" cultural and racial superiority. Benedict made the relativist point explicit in her *Patterns of Culture* (1934), much of which was published in article form between 1923 and 1929: "Just as we are handicapped in dealing with ethical problems so long as we hold to an absolute definition of morality so we are handicapped in dealing with human society so long as we identify our local normalities with the inevitable necessities of existence."

The point was well made. But if morality has no "absolute" qualities, and if standards of cultural excellence can be reduced to mere "local normalities," then on what axioms of human character or universal harmony can a rational society build? Although rational science might well provide all necessary means for achieving any particular social goals, by what measure could one determine the rationality or legitimacy of the goals?

A New View of Mind and Nature. Meanwhile developments in experimental psychology further chipped at long-cherished assumptions about the fixed qualities of human character, assumptions on which had rested much of the force of traditional moral authority. William James, in his monumental *Principles of Psychology* (1890), had freed the study of the mind from premises about genetic and spiritual forces and had linked thought and emotion to physical changes and stimuli in the material environment. Edward L. Thorndike (who had studied with both James and Boas) entirely dissolved the separation of mind from organism; intelligent behavior was the consequence of a mass of neural connections forged by organic experiences. In his pioneering work, *Animal Intelligence* (1899), and in his three-volume major opus, *Educational Psychology* (1913-14), Thorndike suggested that human nature was neither inherently sinful as presented in the Bible nor essentially good as modern romanticists argued. But the mind was not altogether a blank slate, either. Thorndike reserved room for human individuality: A person begins with certain affinities that innately condition future learning. The human mind, said Thorndike, was a mass of genetic tendencies and capacities that could be shaped for good or evil, depending on how it was educated. With all the conventional tests for good and evil currently in doubt, this placed a fearsome responsibility on the educator.

It was not a responsibility either Thorndike or his elder colleague at Columbia University, John Dewey, wished to shirk. Probably no other individuals have had as much influence on education in the twentieth century as these two men. Enthusiastic for social reform, eager to break the fetters of entrenched institutions, Dewey had long argued for using the schools to improve society. He also had already advanced the idea that "virtue" and "evil" could be defined only in the context of particular social aims. He deplored the way the social aims of the past were preserved in anachronistic institutions that thwarted measures to achieve new social aims and to meet new human needs. The educational system, with its fixed curriculum that doled out the truths of the past in neat antiseptic packages, was one such institution. It had failed to meet the new facts presented by an industrial, urbanized society, bereft of the natural discipline of an agrarian upbringing.

"We cannot overlook the factors of discipline and of character-building involved in this," Dewey wrote in 1899; "we cannot overlook the importance for educational purposes of the close and intimate acquaintance got with nature at first hand, with real things and materials, with the actual processes of their manipulation, and the knowledge of their social necessities and uses." It was left to the school to provide the learning experience once provided by the family in the small-community environment. "To do this," Dewey wrote, "means to make each one of our schools an embryonic community life, active with types of occupations that reflect the life of the larger society."

It did not trouble Dewey that there were no clear or durable guides. He was intent on breaking the mindless moralistic rigidity and regimentation that characterized education in his day. The problems of formless, aimless, permissive classroom environments which trivialized education half a century later were not the problems that he confronted, nor did he anticipate them. Neither did he fully appreciate that invigorating, creative education would require invigorated, sensitive teachers who also shared an enduring enthusiasm for progressive education such as Dewey and his wife enjoyed when they founded their model Laboratory School in Chicago in 1896. Besides, the very essence of the education he championed was experimental. Since "it is impossible to tell just what civilization will be twenty years from now, . . . it is impossible to prepare the child for any precise set of conditions." He placed great faith in the scientific method "to bring about human consequences."

But science could have dehumanizing effects, too, and none the less in the area of the new psychology. In the same year Thorndike published his masterwork, John B. Watson presented his own synthesis of the recent advances in experimental psychology. It was a daring piece that purported to demonstrate the possibility of adequately explaining all human and animal behavior without using the concept of mind or consciousness. In effect, Watson reduced all thought and emotions to learned or conditioned reflexes—and all human beings to little more than complicated machines. In Watson's view, modern psychology had shown that human behavior could be understood entirely in terms of constellations of responses to various pleasurable or painful stimuli. If the psychologist could control "the internal and external environment," Watson wrote, "he can build . . . any infant along any specified line—into rich man, poor man, beggar man, thief."

Watson's preference for overstatement put him in bad standing with his professional colleagues, and eventually drove him from Johns Hopkins University into— appropriately enough for one who boasted of the ability to manipulate minds—the advertising business. After publishing *Behaviorism* in 1924, Watson gained an influence in childrearing comparable to that of Dr. Benjamin Spock in the 1960s, especially after the federal government adopted behaviorist ideas in its booklet, *Infant and Child Care* in 1925. In the Coolidge era, the government may have had a natural interest in the matter. Thorndike and Dewey worked to employ the new psychology to enlarge the human potential, to encourage the possibilities of a "creative intelligence" that might transcend existing social constraints, to force the adaptation of institutions and laws to newly perceived human needs. They saw education as a potentially powerful instrument for change. Watson, on the other hand, would encourage conformity, not challenge. He sought to prepare individuals for perfect adaptation to the prevailing institutions and social practices. The educational methods he advocated would acclimate the child to the machine age by conditioning him to exclude inefficient emotional responses. "There is a sensible way of treating children," he wrote in *Psychological Care of Infant and Child* (1928). "Treat them as though they were young adults. . . . Never hug and kiss them, never let them sit in your lap. . . . Shake hands with them in the morning."

Curiously the new psychology, for all its apparent emphasis on rational control—especially in the extreme form put forward by Watson—bore serious antirationalist implications. Behaviorism meant, as Watson explicitly argued, that human beings were infinitely malleable and that a rational intelligence could, with the appropriate psychological techniques, shape social behavior as needed to make "the perfect society." But it also implied that any two "reasonable" persons might reach exactly opposite conclusions about any specific set of facts depending on the structure of conditioned responses in their respective educations! How then know which way to perfection?

From another branch of psychology, the titillating science of psychoanalysis, came a still more potent blow to rationalism. Freud demonstrated that instinctive forces, especially sexual ones, shaped the character of one's personality, subtly but powerfully turning reason to their purposes. From earliest infancy, the imponderable interaction of instinct and environment covertly determined the adult's responses to any given stimuli. Each person, then, was unique, unpredictable, more a rationalizing than a rational creature.

Freud would be received with almost heedless enthusiasm in America, which was an oddity considering on the one hand Freud's basically pessimistic analysis of human nature and, on the other hand, Americans' traditional optimism on the subject. But Americans in the 1920s managed to turn Freud around to their preferences, which generally leaned toward liberating social behavior from conventional taboos, perhaps especially taboos having to do with sex. The Great Doctor had argued that the advance of civilization required the continual repression, or at least the sublimation, of raw sexual energies (*libido*) into behavior patterns commensurate with "culture" and a well-ordered society; at the same time, he observed, repression and sublimation created psychological tensions that often resulted in neurosis. Perhaps it was Americans' very doubts that there were any valid criteria for measuring "culture" and a "well-ordered" society that led them to prefer the benefits of libidinous release over and against society's need for repression. In any case, by the 1920s, especially among intellectuals but also in the popular culture, Freud was employed, often tiresomely, in the mounting assault upon the old canons of authority.

New Perceptions, New Doubts

Americans in the first third of the century experienced the simultaneous burgeoning of artistic, intellectual, and cultural excellence and of heavy negative appraisal of the culture by intellectuals and artists. By 1915, laments about the stifling priggishness, the vulgarity, and the mean materialism of the American ethic had become a standard of intellectual fare. Most of the historiography has affirmed the appraisal, fastening on especially the twenties the view of America as a mindlessly commercial civilization. Yet such a characterization flies in the face of another outstanding feature of the period; namely, that it would be hard to identify another span of years which produced a greater creative ferment or more evidence of advances in the things that enrich human life beyond what money alone can buy.

Perhaps the counterpoint was necessary, or at least historically inevitable. Creativity itself in that era depended heavily on a self-conscious renunciation of the accepted paradigms of truth, respectability, and legitimacy. To contemplate world politics in the light of the First World War or to imagine the physical universe after Planck and Einstein implied rejecting the received wisdom as to the existence of some Natural Harmony and the inevitability of progress. To comprehend the human mind after James and Freud or to really grasp the variety of social practices among diverse peoples spread over the globe meant surrendering ancient religious assumptions about the moral basis of human behavior, and abandoning deep-seated premises about the racial determination of social virtue. Moreover these new perceptions, in turn, threw into doubt the legitimacy of the prevailing order, an order built upon the misconceptions of the past.

In such an environment, it was not surprising that artists, whose very genius consisted in transcending the customary, found a place in the vanguard of the attack on the culture. By the turn of the century, painters began insisting on painting what they saw instead of what conventional dictates of "beauty" and "good taste" demanded. Writers chafed to produce literature that described how people really talk and behave both in public situations and when they are alone or with intimates; they rejected the convention that literature should merely inform a gentle readership of elevated social standards. Architects yearned to design buildings expressive in their form of the functions they were to serve, instead of concealing function beneath facades of Greco-Roman symmetry or prettified wedding-cake veneers. To do all these things required a deliberate snubbing of the canons of high culture.

The Visual Arts. American painters began coming into their own only after 1900, when some of them ceased attempting to imitate the Europeans, or, like James Whistler, Mary Cassatt, and John Singer Sargent, sought artistic appreciation through emigration to Europe. Among the most successful was a group who came to be called "The Eight." Putting aside landscape, seascape, portraiture, and still-life, renouncing fable and metaphor as subject matter, these painters chose instead to put on canvas

The Armory Show exhibition of European art (1913) offended many traditionalists. One wicked critic labeled Duchamp's provocative example of cubism, "An Explosion in a Shingle Factory." *Philadelphia Museum of Art: The Louise and Walter Arensberg Collection*

scenes of urban life—poverty, death, pain, and travail. Following in the line set by Thomas Eakins (1844-1916) who, in the nineteenth century, had first shook up the guardians of American aesthetic standards, "The Eight," mostly New Yorkers, produced a series of works showing people in their normal activities, not idealized bodies as aesthetic objects, but at work, at play, in sorrow or abandon. In 1908 the self-described "Realistics" gave their first exhibition at the Macbeth Galleries in New York. The critics promptly dubbed their works "The Ash-Can School" of art. McSorley's Bar on Second Avenue in Manhattan, boys swimming off East River piers, Bowery bums, clothes drying on tenement rooftops—these were the subjects of Robert Henri, George Luks, Everett Shinn, William Glacken, John Sloan, and George Bellows. As one of Henri's disciples wrote: "Life seemed somehow to flow richer and freer in the Bowery bars and flop houses than at Sherry's or the Waldorf"; and anyway, to paint such subjects "was equivalent to throwing our gauntlet in the face of the old order."

The pivotal event of the period was the New York Armory show in February 1913. For the first time, American culture critics were exposed to the work of the European Modernists, "Fauvists," and "Cubists" whose use of bawdy colors and eccentric distortion shocked sedate Victorian senses and boggled the eye. Marcel Duchamp's "Nude Descending the Staircase" was probably the most sensational of many stunning paintings exhibited. Not that there was anything salacious or even sensuous about the work; rather it was the Cubist technique of attempting to show simultaneously different perspectives of the same subject in motion that drew attention and—perhaps especially because of the title—popular ridicule. The exhibition caused an uproar. Conservatives berated the modernists; radicals rose to the defense. Especially in contrast to the European insurgents, the "Ash-Can School" gained a certain respectability among the American critics. Above all, art became newsworthy as never before. The American artist finally had a native audience that was at least willing to examine what he did. By the 1920s distinctive American art was thriving, and the Museum of Modern Art, opened in 1929, drew significantly from American works.

Sex and Sedition in the Literary Arts. Writers, like the painters, threw their challenge in the face of the old order, in both form and subject. Theodore Dreiser's *Sister Carrie* (1900), *Jennie Gerhardt* (1911), *The Financier* (1912), and *The Titan* (1914) portrayed the suffering, the cruelty, the meanness, the bestiality inspired in and imposed upon Americans caught up with the drive for success. Frank Norris, in *The Octopus* (1901), revealed the tyranny of the Southern Pacific Railroad over California farmers, and its power in state politics. In *The Pit* (1903), he reproduced the theme of the triumph of the powerful in a Chicago grain business setting. Social criticism was implicit in such novels; they fit especially well into the "muckraking" literature of the day—the nonfiction of Lincoln Steffens, *Shame of the Cities* (1904), John Spargo, *The Bitter Cry of the Children* (1906), Robert Hunter, *Poverty* (1904), and Ida Tarbell, *The History of Standard Oil* (1904). They are sometimes grouped with the more explicitly activist novels of the day, such as Upton Sinclair's assault on the working conditions of meatpacking and slaughterhouse workers, *The Jungle* (1906), and the reform-spirited political novels of the American writer, Winston Churchill, notably *Conistan* (1906) and *Mr. Crewe's Career* (1908).

Yet the naturalists, as they were called, were not specifically interested in social criticism. Norris especially preferred leaving moral judgment to inference, while he aimed more at depicting the human predicament in a realistic modern context. It is a brutish predicament in which humans no less than the lower animals are prey to irrepressible forces of Nature, both genetic and environmental. Whatever the veneer of culture that a civilization might contrive, the natural imperatives will triumph. In *McTeague* (1899), probably the grimmest of all the grim stories produced in the era, Norris foreshadows the tragedy of human degradation that unfolds relentlessly through the book by describing near the start the huge blond hero's struggle with his own dumb nature: "Below the fine fabric of all that was good in him ran the foul stream of hereditary evil, like a sewer. . . . The evil of an entire race flowed in his veins. Why should it be? He did not desire it. Was he to blame?" Near the end, after McTeague has murdered his small, miserly wife in a drunken rage and he is pursued by a posse, Norris has him wakened in the dead desert silence by "that strange sixth sense, that obscure brute instinct . . . aroused again and clamoring to be obeyed . . . and roweled him to be moving on." The passage might well have appeared in Jack

London's classic adventure-novels, *The Call of the Wild* (1903) and *White Fang* (1906), which confined the insensate struggle for existence to the realm of dogs and wolves in the Arctic wilderness.

Although they were all capable of insinuating moral statements into their stories, for writers like Norris, Dreiser, and London the triumph of superior forces had its own natural justification. The helplessness and hopelessness of the victims, while lamentable from a humane viewpoint, merely exemplified the impotence of individual will before the power of Nature which, on the whole, was viewed as beneficent. There was even a little homespun American antiintellectualism in it: "Vitality is the thing after all," wrote Norris, a year before appendicitis abruptly ended his young life. "The United States, in this year of grace 1902, does not want and need Scholars, but Men."

The Darwinistic naturalism of the new novelists struck at the old order by focusing on the sordid, unhappy, and physical qualities of life at a time when culture was supposed to emphasize the aesthetic and the uplifting, to glory in highminded achievement, to yield no margin to what was brutish, primitive, visceral, and unlovely. In rejecting Dreiser's manuscript for *Sister Carrie,* Walter Hines Page of Doubleday wrote: "This kind of people do not interest me and we find it hard to believe they will interest a great majority of readers." Even Hamlin Garland, whose own works were in the naturalist genre, said of *McTeague:* "What avail is this study of sad lives? for it does not even lead to a notion of social betterment." Such narrowness would become the target particularly of the generation of writers who came of age after 1910; their ridicule would exaggerate both the priggishness of the old culture and the ostensible radicalism of their own work.

As late as 1930, in his acceptance address for the Nobel Prize in literature, Sinclair Lewis would cite Dreiser as a "lonely pioneer" without whose work "I doubt if any of us could, unless we went to jail, seek to express life and beauty and terror." In fact, Stephen Crane (*Maggie, A Girl of the Streets,* 1896), Hamlin Garland (*Rose of Dutcher's Cooly,* 1895), Harold Frederic (*The Damnation of Theron Ware,* 1896), and Robert Herrick (*Together,* 1908), among some others, had also effectively challenged Victorian standards, as indeed had the contemporary work in educational theory and psychology. As Joseph Wood Krutch later observed: "A good deal of the talk which lingered, even during the twenties, about 'daring ideas' was no more than cant since it had long ceased to require any particular courage to question either the social or the moral code." But if Dreiser had not truly pioneered in anything remarkable, he had become a convenient symbol for a cultural cause.

A major part of that cause struck at Victorian prudery by presenting what for those timid times passed for "explicit" descriptions of sexual passion. *Sister Carrie* so troubled the custodians of morality that its publication was withdrawn for more than a decade, thus contributing to Dreiser's literary martyrdom. William Dean Howells, the reputed spokesman for literary "Realism," and generally regarded in the Progressive era as the elder statesman of modern American literature, was still complaining in 1913 that too many popular authors "have not conceived of decently leaving the reader to suppose the clasping and kissing which perhaps [*sic!*] goes on in life." Such evidence may reveal how sensitive the older generation was to sexual matters; how important it was to keep references to the subject subdued and indirect; how threatening to the fragile order of things so many self-assigned spokesmen for the culture viewed any formal break with the inherited ethic.

The sexual ethic became a major battleground for the old and new generations. In the first place, a growing number of the urban educated classes were less encumbered than their elders by the guilt prescribed by the traditional religious wisdom. But moreover sexual insurgency had what may be considered ideological dimensions. That is, it served younger people, and older rebels, too, as a way of striking a blow against the crabbed life-style of the old order. "The anti-Puritan revolt," wrote the anthropologist Edward Sapir, "is much more than a revolt against sex repression alone. It is a generalized revolt against everything that is hard, narrow, and intolerant in the old American life, and which sees in sex repression its most potent symbol of attack."

Sexual repression had long played a subtly significant role in the development of modern industrial society. It was a major element in the more generalized ethic of self-discipline and postponed rewards that was so essential to the success of the factory system and capital formation. It had much to do with the emphasis placed on the nuclear family as a basic unit of social education and control in a society that since at least the early eighteenth century was increasingly given to voluntaristic personal and economic arrangements outside the authority of both church and state. It had become an integral part of the general tendency to identify behavioral restraint with superior culture.

But Americans who came of age in the new century enjoyed a society that for the first time in history saw as its chief economic problem not the scarcity but the uses and distribution of material goods. Quite naturally they found it hard to understand the inhibitions, the discipline, the self-denial which were grafted onto the culture in more meager times. Excessive pressures for conformity struck them as a far greater problem than the dangers of license or profligacy. A superior culture, by their definition, enjoyed freedom of expression and of choice in life-styles.

Among especially the painters and writers, the old ethic was assaulted first by those who championed freedom of expression for art's sake. Characteristic of the Progressive era, there was initially much optimism about breaking through native priggishness and provincialism to uplift Americans' appreciation of high-minded cultural achievement and of liberal humanism generally. Even the complaint by the critic Van Wyck Brooks that the American mind had become stultified by the stand-off between the "high-brow" and the "low-brow," between formalistic cultural pendantry at one end and day-to-day commercial practicality at the other (*America's Coming-of-Age*, 1915), still allowed for expectations that the artist might yet stimulate a middle ground of popular intellectual growth.

There was reason for hope, after all, in the remarkable development of public schools and higher education in America, unmatched anywhere in the Western World. Between 1900 and 1930 the number of persons who remained in public school past ninth grade increased nine times, from half a million to 4.4 million. Moreover the average number of days attended by each pupil rose from 99 in 1900 to 143 in 1930.

At the turn of the century barely 10 percent of children of high school age were in school; by 1930, 50 percent were. In all, 29 percent of the seventeen-year-old population finished high school in 1930, while only 6.4 percent did in 1900. And 15 percent of the age group 18-24 was in college in 1930, up from 3 percent in 1900.

The advent of good roads and the motor bus sent the one-room school house into the category of the horse and buggy. Consolidated school districts afforded students specialized classes, a choice among electives, and often a rich extracurricular program that turned many schools into something approaching the miniature communities envisioned by John Dewey. In the environment of the necessarily mass-oriented school system, progressive education never had a chance, even with the scores of new teachers' colleges straining to provide the teaching skills that Dewey's model for creative learning required. (Total instructional staff in the public schools doubled, but just barely kept pace with enrollment increases during the 1900-1930 period.) But there is no doubt of the vastly improved literacy of the American people and of the much enlarged part of the population willing and able to cope with an idea, perhaps even a novel one.

Whether or not for these reasons, the period witnessed the emergence of numerous new literary journals, amidst an atmosphere of "renascence." *Poetry*, founded in Chicago in 1912 by Harriet Monroe, gave its pages to dozens of new writers, including Vachel Lindsay and Carl Sandburg; Ezra Pound, the Idaho-born eccentric genius who was already in "exile" in Europe, served the magazine as its foreign editor. Max Eastman, Floyd Dell, and some other socialist writers turned radical criticism into a high-art form after they took over a pedestrian Marxist journal, *The Masses,* in 1913. The following year, *The Little Review,* founded by Margaret Anderson in Chicago, began publishing avant-garde European works and giving some American writers such as Sherwood Anderson their first chance. James Oppenheim and Waldo Frank launched *The Seven Arts* in New York in 1916 with a burst of enthusiasm for the coming age of "that national self-consciousness which is the beginning of greatness."

Demise of the Dream. The war—accompanied as it was by ugly zealotry, a vengeful nationalist populism, alongside vulgar piety and business-as-usual profiteering—had the effect on art that it did on politics: It brought disenchantment with the prospect of democratic liberation. For the intellectual, patriotism and Prohibition joined prudery in the ranks of low-brow American absurdities, and progressivism itself soon followed. D. W. Griffith, the pioneer moviemaker, pursued his triumph in *The Birth of a Nation* with a second extravaganza called *Intolerance* (1916) in which reformers appeared as bigots seeking to impose their narrow life-style on everyone else. Essayists, especially H. L. Mencken, editor of *The Smart Set* (1916-23) and later *The American Mercury,* labeled the problem "Puritanism" and belabored it to the point of exaggerating both the substance of their own rebelliousness and the public's resistance to their challenge. Mencken, chief pundit for a willfully sophomoric generation of negativists, described "Puritanism" as "the haunting fear that someone, somewhere may be having a good time," and like most of the new generation, he chucked social causes out the door. "If I'm convinced of anything, it is that Doing Good is in bad taste"—a sentiment echoed by one of Ernest Hemingway's characters in the war novel, *A*

Farewell to Arms (1929): "I was always embarrassed by the words sacred, glorious, and sacrifice. . . . There were so many words that you could not stand to hear and finally only the names of places had dignity."

Rural America, and in particular the American small town, became a principal focus of the literature of alienation. Once the nation's very showcase of its enterprising, liberty-inspired tradition, it became the special target of social criticism. "The civilization of America," wrote Louis Reid in Harold Stearns's anthology of American literary alienation, *Civilization in the United States* (1922), "is predominantly the civilization of the small town . . . of secret societies, of chambers of commerce, of boosters' clubs, of the Ford motor car, of moving pictures, of talking machines, of evangelists, of nerve tonics, of the Saturday Evening Post . . . of church socials, of parades and pageants . . . county fairs, firemen's conventions." All these "unmistakable provincial signs and symbols" offer "a true perspective of America," Reid claimed.

Edgar Lee Masters's *Spoon River Anthology* (1915) marked the outbreak of the literary war between the traditionalist and modernist cultures in America. A collection of short poems inspired by the tombstones in a village graveyard, it undertook to expose the raw despair and sordidness of life in the supposed heartland of progressive America. Sherwood Anderson's *Winesburg, Ohio* (1919), using Freudian insights, followed in the same vein. In *Main Street* (1920), Sinclair Lewis emerged as a major novelist with his "definitive" work on the subject. "This is America," he led off in a brief forward opposite Chapter I; "a town of a few thousand, in a region of wheat and corn and dairies and little groves. . . . Main Street is the climax of civilization. That this Ford car might stand in front of the Bon Ton Store, Hannibal invaded Rome and Erasmus wrote in Oxford cloisters." In *Babbitt* (1922), a novel about a crude, consummate real-estate salesman, Lewis continued the assault on the low-brow Rotarian culture that so evidently dominated American society and politics. Unlike Dreiser and Norris, Lewis portrayed American businessmen not as truculent titans but as inane, bombastic, and cliché-ridden human beings, more than a little ridiculous in their aggressive banality—and yet all the more powerful because they pervaded the society and possessed relentless energy.

While writers such as Lewis and Mencken used satire and ridicule to deflate American pretensions to high civilization, Ernest Hemingway chose a kind of low-key disdain for idealism in general. His clipped, straightforward writing set a popular new style for fiction. The technique fitted his view of life, hardened by five weeks as an ambulance driver during the war and confirmed by the fruitless peace. It also suited well one of the developing themes of twentieth-century attitudes. Inspiration for living could come no longer from the labored striving after ideals but only from the visceral experience of living itself. For the unthinking and the young this usually took on various forms of hedonism, for which the popular culture of the twenties has been well known. For Hemingway, it was never more powerfully expressed than when Life brushed with Death or fell before it with stoic dignity. Hemingway's heroes are non-heroes, at least in the traditional view of the heroic. That is, they do not triumph over adversity or against evil. They take defeat and futility as among the constants in human existence, yet in the face of the knowledge of the inevitability of human failure, they persevere. Hemingway does not even offer to the reader Norris' exhortation—"Vitality is the thing after all"—for by the twenties there were few who still saw in Nature a transcending beneficence.

It is in the fiction of F. Scott Fitzgerald—especially *This Side of Paradise* (1920), *The Beautiful and Damned* (1922), and *Tales of the Jazz Age* (1922)—that the unfulfilling hedonism of the postwar era found its best-known portrayal. His stories focused on the very rich, not at work but at their leisure. The achievers of affluent America appear empty, banal, discontented, often anguished in their aimlessness. *The Great Gatsby* (1925), Fitzgerald's masterpiece, contains elements of allegory in which the promise of American life turns into ashes at the moment of its apparent consummation. Americans had once imagined that their country had some special liberating meaning in the history of humanity. But this meaning resided mainly in the opportunities it afforded for gaining wealth, with only an accompanying presumption that abundance would itself bring on the millenium. As long as affluence was still something to be pursued, it sustained ambition, even idealism. But, as in the novel, the instant Gatsby achieves the object of his dreams—Daisy, whose voice was "like money"—"and forever wed his unutterable visions to her perishable breath, his mind would never romp again like the mind of God." The book concludes with a touching reflection on the end of the American dream, indeed perhaps the end of humanity's dream that America might have provided a leavening example for the rest of the world: "For a transitory enchanted moment man must have held his breath in the presence of this continent, compelled into an aesthetic contemplation he neither understood nor desired, face to face for the last time in history with something commensurate to his capacity for wonder. . . . It eluded us then, but that's no matter—tomorrow we will run faster, stretch out our arms further. . . . So we beat on, boats against the current, borne back ceaselessly into the past."

In Praise of Folly The dissipation of the dream and "the end of innocence" are recurrent themes in the historiography of American progress in the period. But while intellectuals lamented America's submersion in stultifying commercialism, heedless hedonism, and provincial prudery, most Americans appear to have preferred contemplating other problems. Urban America was busy taking care of the important things first, namely, getting rich and enjoying life without the somberly crusading hangups of the previous generation; village America continued its rearguard action against the onslaught of modernism; and commercial America confronted the critics head on. "Dare to be a Babbitt!" exclaimed *The Nation's Business*, organ of the United States Chamber of Commerce. "What the world needs is more Babbitts who live orderly lives, save money, go to church, play golf, and send their children to school." Two years after Sinclair Lewis' searing portrayal of the American salesman, Bruce Barton saw nothing incongruous in his pseudo-biography, *The Man Nobody Knows* (1924), in describing Jesus as an "A-1 Salesman" who "picked up twelve men from the bottom ranks of business and forged them into an organization that conquered the world." Polly Adler, New York's most famous madam, summed it up in her autobiography, *A House Is Not A Home* (1948): "Viewed in retrospect, after the sobering years which have intervened . . . the senseless cavortings of 'flaming youth,' the determined squandering and guzzling and wenching of the newly rich, combine to form a lurid picture of a race of monsters outrageously at play. . . . But *I* didn't know there was anything unusual about the times any more than I realized that conditions then were peculiarly suited to promoting a career like mine. In fact, if I had had all history to choose from, I could hardly have picked a better age in which to be a madam. In the world of the twenties, as I saw it, the only unforgivable sin was to be poor."

The tastelessness of mainstream America did much to justify the contempt social critics then and now have cast upon the post-1915 American ethos. But to focus entirely on it may be to miss features of life of equal and perhaps redeeming importance. One must keep in mind that the very ethic and the very institutions under attack had nurtured and sustained the insurgents who sharpened their art in criticism and nonconformity; such elements of American culture must have had strengths as well as crudities.

Indeed the word "tastelessness" begs the very question about the character of "The Good Society" that the intellectuals and the defenders of the old order answered in their own distinctly different way. The traditionalists recoiled at the decline of restraint in social behavior. They accurately saw in it the end of the world they knew. The intellectuals rebelled at the self-satisfying materialism promoted so crassly by the commercial ethos of the day. They saw in it a sorry outcome of all that America had promised and something of a masquerade of the old order as well. The traditionalists conceded nothing worthwhile in the fresh challenges of the new order. The intellectuals had little that was kind to say about the conventions from which they were sprung.

Jazz became one of the symbols of the age, not merely for the intellectuals, such as Fitzgerald for whom it symbolized the moral irresponsibility and abandon he half-celebrated and half-pitied, but for the traditionalists who saw in the rhythms and the dances the full evidence of civilization's regression toward animal dissipation. The critics left nothing to symbolic inference. Baptist minister, Dr. John R. Straton, who became the leading spokesman for Fundamentalism after Bryan's death, saw the nature of the threat plainly: "This modern jazz tendency . . . is part of the lawless spirit which is being manifested in many departments of life, endangering our civilization in its general revolt against authority and established order." Another complained of "this Bolshevistic smashing of the rules and tenets of decorus music, this excessive freedom of interpretation . . . disregard for the self-contained and self-restrained attitude that has been prescribed by the makers of the rules of dignified social intercourse."

The African lineage of jazz got special attention. For many conservatives, it was sufficiently condemning to point out that jazz was "coon music," and therefore nothing a sensitive, civilized people could properly enjoy without being contaminated. "The consensus of opinion [*sic*] of leading medical and other scientific authorities," wrote the medical director of a Philadelphia high school, "is that its influence is harmful and degrading to civilized races as it always has been among savages from whom we borrowed it." (Philadelphia was one of more than a dozen cities that prohibited jazz in public dance halls.) Another critic saw the prospect of civilization

King Oliver's Band in Chicago, with the young Louis Armstrong in the center, Joe Oliver to his left, and Lil Hardin at the piano. The very fact that jazz grew from the music of the southern black subculture made it especially popular among rebellious young white Americans. *Culver Pictures*

"reduced to the low state of inferior races now on this planet." "Unspeakable Jazz Must Go," headed an article in the December 1921 *Ladies Home Journal*. "Anyone who says the youth of both sexes can mingle in close embrace with limbs intertwined and torso in contact without suffering harm lies. Add to this position the wriggling movement and sensuous stimulation of the abominable jazz orchestra with its voodoo-born minors and its direct appeal to the sensory center and if you can believe that youth is the same after this experience as before, then God help your child."

The connection with black people of course made jazz even more delectably attractive to the culture rebels. Among the smart set there developed a special "vogue in things Negro," as one black journalist wryly commented. In the 1920s, Gilbert Osofsky has pointed out in his recent study of Harlem, "Negroes were still thought to be alienated from traditional American virtues and values, as they had been since colonial times, but this was now considered a great asset." Social insurgents of white America came to prize blacks as "expressive," "primitive," "exotic," an invigorating contrast to a society burdened with "unnatural inhibitions." (The quoted words are those of Osofsky found repeatedly in the swollen contemporary literature on "the New Negro.")

Harlem became a Mecca for intellectuals, black and white. For a while in the twenties, the northeastern corner of upper Manhattan seethed with literary, theatrical, and artistic activity, and until the Crash in 1929 black writers and artists enjoyed a public acceptance such as would not be equaled again till the 1960s. In Harlem black leaders found for the first time a base for an urbane intellectual community. But whereas black intellectuals self-consciously strove for a niche in the dominant American culture, white intellectuals looked upon the black subculture of the American scene mostly as a useful counterpoint for their assault on what they regarded as the prevailing philistinism. Harlem came to be viewed as the antithesis of Main Street and Gopher Prairie. As one black writer remarked, for white America "the Negro was not a person but a concept." A trip to Harlem to listen to jazz, watch risqué revues, hobnob with "sensuous" and "rhythmic" Africans, converse with black literati, became a "must." As the black newspaper, *The New York Age,* quipped in 1926, it was a place for white bourgeois Americans "to go on a moral vacation," to gain relief from "the asperities of a Puritan conscience."

Meanwhile jazz (or what was loosely called that) made up 80 percent of the music broadcast by radio during the twenties, and radio sets were selling as fast as light bulbs. America's most distinctively original music quickly conquered Europe, evolving from ragtime and New Orleans and Memphis blues through the genius of Duke Ellington, Louis Armstrong, Fats Waller, and Don Redman. Composers like George Gershwin, Igor Stravinsky, and Darius Milhaud took its theme into the symphony halls as well. It was raucous, frankly sensual, even bawdy and countercultural. It was daring, creative, liberating, and artistic. It was all these things, like the age in which it thrived.

It was also an age of "Ballyhoo"—the contemporary word for the blowing up of events and persons to larger-than-life dimensions. Against the old order's model of studied restraint, the new order reacted with exaggeration. With the advent of motion pictures, radio, and motor highways, the changes in life-styles Americans were witnessing would appear shockingly sharp and sudden anyway, for those inventions brought to nearly every provincial enclave whatever was novel in clothes, comedy, courting, music, dance, drama, and sport. The rise to power of the advertising and public relations industries made it additionally certain that for at least a generation, extravagance would become common form.

It was inevitable that for the critics, some of the very achievements of the era characterized America's failure. "The movies, radio, cheap reading matter and motor car with all they stand for," complained John Dewey in 1927, ". . . did not originate in deliberate desire to divert attention from political interest [but it] does not lessen their effectiveness in that direction." Yet perhaps it was not a mistake to hope that a nonpolitical culture might still be a humane one. Was it such a loss that the heroes and heroines of the twenties came not as usual from politics and the military, but from sports and entertainment? That millions of Americans experienced deep empathy with the exploits of baseball's Ty Cobb and Babe Ruth, football's Red Grange, Hollywood's Rudolph Valentino, Clara Bow, Douglas Fairbanks, and Mary Pickford? Was it deplorable that 100,000 spectators paid more than $1 million to watch Jack Dempsey box Georges Carpentier instead of attending political rallies in Madison Square Garden? Or that millions hung by the radio to listen for news of Charles Lindbergh's lonely progress across the Atlantic rather than aggravate over imperialism and class struggles and racial iniquities?

Perhaps so. One feels compelled to recall that Dempsey might never have been so exalted if racial prejudice had not kept Harry Wills from a chance to fight for the heavyweight title (especially because so many thought Wills would win). Marion Anderson had to find in Europe the singing experience and acclaim that American concert halls denied her in the twenties because of her color. Poverty as well as racism was still with us; there were an estimated twenty million Americans living below decent living standards in the 1920s. In the South more than a million sharecropper families lived scarcely better than peons, virtual subjects of autocratic landlords. Unemployment in the United States was rarely less than ten percent of the work force. And many of those who worked in mines, boiler rooms, textile mills, hop fields, and orchards were sometimes engaged in deadly industrial warfare during the "prosperity decade." But no one was watching.

There were, then, causes to fight and faiths to inspire, while most Americans turned their head. All the same, there is room for understanding that a generation weaned on the Roosevelts, the Wilsons, the Bryans, the Kaisers, and the Lenins—and was already hearing from the Mussolinis—might have wished for something different.

SUGGESTED READINGS

The subtitle of Morton White's *Social Thought in America: The Revolt Against Formalism* + (1947; revised 1957) has provided the commonly used phrase for describing the erosion of the traditional bases for authority in the early twentieth century. White closely analyzes the assault on the absolutism of nineteenth century thought by Oliver Wendell Holmes, Jr. and Roscoe Pound (law), Charles Beard, Carl Becker, and James Harvey Robinson (history), Thorstein Veblen (economics), and William James and John Dewey (psychology, education, and philosophy). The revised edition has an epilogue that deals with the theologian Reinhold Niebuhr and the popular social theorist Walter Lippmann. Chapters 4-10 in Eric Goldman's *Rendezvous with Destiny* * (1953) treat in a very readable form many of the same issues, but with more direct attention to political events. David A. Noble's *The Paradox of Progressive Thought* (1958) is often unjustly overlooked. Paul K. Conkin's chapters on William James and John Dewey in his *Puritans and Pragmatists* * (1968) are rather technical but afford valuable coverage and interesting interpretations. For a relatively painless introduction to the difficult ideas in these books, *Paths of American Thought* (1963), Arthur M. Schlesinger, Jr. and Morton White, eds., contains many short but useful essays on the transformation of thought in a number of areas: notably, Eugene V. Rostow on "Realism" in law; Alfred Kazin on the roots of "Realism" in literature, and Irving Howe on the early "Moderns"; Richard Hofstadter on "The Revolution in Higher Education"; William Lee Miller on the emergence of "Neo-Orthodoxy" in Protestant thought; and Morton White on pragmatism and the problem of the relationship between experimental science and what we call "knowledge."

The most useful analysis of the revolution in the thinking about race appears in a book by George W. Stocking, Jr., *Race, Culture, and Evolution: Essays on the History*

* Available in a paperback edition.

of *Anthropology** (1968), esp. chs. 8-11. The anthropologists mentioned in the present chapter typically reported their innovative findings in the form of papers and articles years before they were fleshed out in book form. Some of the relevant books published in the 1920s include A. L. Kroeber's *Anthropology* (First Edition, 1923) and Bronislaw Malinowski's *Crime and Custom in Savage Society** (1926) and *Sex and Repression in Savage Society** (1927). See also Franz Boas' *Race, Language, and Culture** (1940), which reprints some of his early papers, including a key originative address on ethnology delivered in 1911.

The history of the other social sciences is not so well covered as anthropology is in Stocking's work. Readers may find A. A. Roback's *A History of American Psychology** (1952; revised 1964) useful. *Freud and the Americans* (1971), Nathan G. Hale, Jr., is probably the most important book on Freud in the last ten years. J. C. Burnham, "Psychiatry, Psychology and the Progressive Movement," *American Quarterly*, v. 12, Winter 1960, capsules one significant part of the new study of the mind. J. B. Watson's article, "Psychology as the Behaviorist Views It," first appeared in *The Psychological Review*, v. 20, 1913.

Frederick Hoffman's *The Twenties: American Writing in the Postwar Decade** (1949; revised 1962), Alfred Kazin's *On Native Grounds** (1942; revised 1957), and Malcolm Cowley's *Exiles Return: A Literary Saga of the 1920s** (1934) are some of the most often cited studies of the period. In *The Literary Fallacy* (1944), reflecting the new affirmatism about America inspired by the war against Hitler and Tojo, Bernard DeVoto assailed the adolescent nihilism of the social critics of the 1920s, but in a way that appeared to align him with "reactionaries" concerned only with restoring the Victorian ethic. Whether or not that assessment of DeVoto is accurate—or relevant —in the newly disenchanting aftermath of the Second World War his argument found relatively few friends among intellectuals and consequently less exposure than those portrayals belaboring American culture in the 1920s. More recently, Ernest Earnest, *The Single Vision: The Alienation of American Intellectuals* (1970) presents a new attack (though without any particular references to DeVoto) arguing persuasively that American literature in the 1910-30 period was "intellectually shallow" and constituted a gross misreading of both the contemporary scene and the American past. For an introduction to the whole subject and a sampling of contemporary writings with sharp commentary alongside them, readers should use Henry F. May's *The Discontent of the Intellectuals: A Problem of the Twenties** (1963).

Lawrence Cremin's *The Transformation of the School: Progressivism in American Education, 1876-1956** (1961) is the major work in the field, but readers should not overlook the relevant chapters in Rush Welter's *Popular Education and Democratic Thought in America** (1962). Raymond Callahan's *Education and the Cult of Efficiency** (1962) highlights the failure of the progressive education theorists to anticipate how the flexible curricula advocated by Dewey and others would play into the hands of the dominant social forces of each community, especially the business interests.

Nathan I. Huggins' *Harlem Renaissance** (1971), a judicious and thorough account of the artistic ferment among black intellectuals centering in upper Manhattan during the 1920s, should be read along with G. Osofsky's *Harlem: The Making of a Ghetto**